Cloud Security Handbook

Find out how to effectively secure cloud
environments using AWS, Azure, and GCP

Eyal Estrin

BIRMINGHAM—MUMBAI

Cloud Security Handbook

Copyright © 2022 Packt Publishing

Group Product Manager: Rahul Nair

Publishing Product Manager: Rahul Nair

Senior Editor: Arun Nadar

Content Development Editor: Sulagna Mohanty

Technical Editor: Arjun Varma

Copy Editor: Safis Editing

Project Coordinator: Shagun Saini

Proofreader: Safis Editing

Indexer: Pratik Shirodkar

Production Designer: Joshua Misquitta

Marketing Coordinator: Hemangi Lotlikar

First published: March 2022
Production reference: 1100322

Published by Packt Publishing Ltd.
Livery Place
35 Livery Street
Birmingham
B3 2PB, UK.

ISBN 978-1-80056-919-5
www.packt.com

I wish to dedicate this book to my loving wife for all the support she provided me with during the long hours spent writing this book.

– Eyal Estrin

Contributors

About the author

Eyal Estrin is a cloud security architect who has been working with cloud services since 2015. He has been involved in the design and implementation of cloud environments from both the IT and security aspects.

He has worked with AWS, Azure, and Google Cloud in a number of different organizations (in the banking, academia, and healthcare sectors).

He has attained several top cloud security certifications – CCSP, CCSK, and AWS.

He shares his knowledge through social media (LinkedIn, Twitter, Medium, and more) for the benefit of cloud experts around the world.

About the reviewers

Randy M. Black is a 25-year veteran in the IT industry and an ea
Randy has spent the last decade working in some form or other of cloud technology and
security. He abhors the silos that traditional IT creates and the detriment they pose to
organizations. Randy is a strong advocate of transferring knowledge without fear of being
transparent, misunderstood, or seemingly odd.

> *To Jesus, my rock and salvation, for His grace and peace in accompanying*
> *me through this crazy, upside-down world. And to my wife, Jill, who*
> *has supported and stood by me in everything that I do, and who is the*
> *cornerstone of my success. And finally, to my four children, who don't*
> *always understand what I do, but appreciate the fact that I am doing it.*

Timothy Orr (@easttim0r on Twitter) designs, builds, and operates secure systems in
complex cloud environments. He supports customers with cloud security automation,
serverless architecture, threat detection and response, security analysis, and multi-tenant
cloud brokering and governance. Tim holds a master's degree in InfoSec, CISSP, AWS
Security Specialty, AWS Solutions Architect Professional, and AWS SysOps Administrator
Associate certifications.

Table of Contents

3

Securing Storage Services

4

Securing Networking Services

Section 2: Deep Dive into IAM, Auditing, and Encryption

5

Effective Strategies to Implement IAM Solutions

6

Monitoring and Auditing Your Cloud Environments

7

Applying Encryption in Cloud Services

Section 3: Threats and Compliance Management

8

Understanding Common Security Threats to Cloud Services

9

Handling Compliance and Regulation

10
Engaging with Cloud Providers

Section 4: Advanced Use of Cloud Services

11
Managing Hybrid Clouds

12
Managing Multi-Cloud Environments

13

Security in Large-Scale Environments

Preface

Cloud Security Handbook provides complete coverage of security aspects when designing, building, and maintaining environments in the cloud. This book is filled with best practices to help you smoothly transition to the public cloud, while keeping your environments secure. You do not have to read everything - simply find out which cloud provider is common at your workplace, or which cloud provider you wish to focus on, and feel free to skip the rest.

Who this book is for

This book is for IT or information security personnel taking their first steps in the public cloud or migrating existing environments to the cloud. DevOps professionals, cloud engineers, or cloud architects maintaining production environments in the cloud will also benefit from this book.

What this book covers

Chapter 1, *Introduction to Cloud Security*, in order to give you a solid understanding of cloud security, helps you to understand concepts such as **Infrastructure as a Service (IaaS)**, **Platform as a Service (PaaS)**, **Software as a Service (SaaS)**, private cloud, public cloud, hybrid cloud, multi-cloud, and the Shared Responsibility Model. This and the rest of the chapters in this book will allow you to understand how to implement security in various cloud environments.

Chapter 2, *Securing Compute Services*, covers how **Amazon Web Services (AWS)**, Microsoft Azure, and **Google Cloud Platform (GCP)** implement virtual machines, managed databases, containers, Kubernetes, and serverless architectures, and what the best practices for securing those services are.

Chapter 3, *Securing Storage Services*, covers how AWS, Microsoft Azure, and GCP implement object storage, block storage, and managed file storage, and what the best practices for securing those services are.

Chapter 4, Securing Network Services, covers how AWS, Microsoft Azure, and GCP implement virtual networks, security groups, DNS services, CDN, VPN services, DDoS protection services, and web application firewalls, and what the best practices for securing those services are.

Chapter 5, Effective Strategies to Implement IAM Solutions, covers how AWS, Microsoft Azure, and GCP implement directory services, how these cloud providers implement identity and access management for modern cloud applications, how to implement multi-factor authentication, and how to secure all these services.

Chapter 6, Monitoring and Auditing of Your Cloud Environment, covers how AWS, Microsoft Azure, and GCP implement audit mechanisms, how to detect threats in automated and large-scale environments, and how to capture network traffic for troubleshooting and security incident detection (digital forensics).

Chapter 7, Applying Encryption in Cloud Services, covers when to use symmetric and asymmetric encryption in a cloud environment, what the various alternatives for key management services in AWS, Azure, and GCP are, what the alternatives and best practices for storing secrets in code are, and how to implement encryption in traffic and encryption at rest on the AWS, Azure, and GCP cloud services.

Chapter 8, Understanding Common Security Threats to Cloud Computing, covers what the common security threats in public cloud environments are, how to detect those threats, and what the countermeasures to mitigate such threats using built-in services in AWS, Azure, and GCP are.

Chapter 9, Handling Compliance and Regulation, covers what the common security standards related to cloud environments are, what the different levels of **Security Operations Center** (**SOC**) are, and how to use cloud services to comply with the European data privacy regulation, GDPR.

Chapter 10, Engaging with Cloud Providers, covers how to conduct a risk assessment in a public cloud environment, what the important questions to ask a cloud provider prior to the engagement phase are, and what important topics to embed inside a contractual agreement with the cloud provider.

Chapter 11, Managing Hybrid Clouds, covers how to implement common features such as identity and access management, patch management, vulnerability management, configuration management, monitoring, and network security aspects in hybrid cloud environments.

Chapter 12, Managing Multi-Cloud Environments, covers how to implement common topics such as identity and access management, patch management, vulnerability management, configuration management, monitoring, and network security aspects in multi-cloud environments.

Chapter 13, Security in Large-Scale Environments, covers what the common **Infrastructure as a Code (IaC)** alternatives are, how to implement patch management in a centralized manner, how to control configuration and compliance management, and how to detect vulnerabilities in cloud environments (managed services and sample tools) in a large production environment.

To get the most out of this book

The following are some of the requirements to get the most out of the book:

Software/hardware covered in the book	OS requirements
An up-to-date web browser	Windows, macOS, or Linux (any)
Credentials to access the AWS, Azure, or GCP web console	

Download the color images

We also provide a PDF file that has color images of the screenshots/diagrams used in this book. You can download it here: `https://static.packt-cdn.com/downloads/9781800569195_ColorImages.pdf`.

Conventions used

There are a number of text conventions used throughout this book.

`Code in text`: Indicates code words in text, database table names, folder names, filenames, file extensions, pathnames, dummy URLs, user input, and Twitter handles. Here is an example: "If a resource node has set `inheritFromParent = true`, then the effective policy of the parent resource is inherited."

Bold: Indicates a new term, an important word, or words that you see onscreen. For example, words in menus or dialog boxes appear in the text like this. Here is an example: "**Azure Event Hubs**: This is for sending audit logs to an external SIEM system for further analysis."

> **Tips or Important Notes**
> Appear like this.

Get in touch

Feedback from our readers is always welcome.

General feedback: If you have questions about any aspect of this book, mention the book title in the subject of your message and email us at customercare@packtpub.com.

Errata: Although we have taken every care to ensure the accuracy of our content, mistakes do happen. If you have found a mistake in this book, we would be grateful if you would report this to us. Please visit www.packtpub.com/support/errata, selecting your book, clicking on the Errata Submission Form link, and entering the details.

Piracy: If you come across any illegal copies of our works in any form on the Internet, we would be grateful if you would provide us with the location address or website name. Please contact us at copyright@packt.com with a link to the material.

If you are interested in becoming an author: If there is a topic that you have expertise in and you are interested in either writing or contributing to a book, please visit authors.packtpub.com.

Share your thoughts

Once you've read *Cloud Security Handbook*, we'd love to hear your thoughts! Scan the QR code below to go straight to the Amazon review page for this book and share your feedback.

https://packt.link/r/180056919X

Your review is important to us and the tech community and will help us make sure we're delivering excellent quality content.

Section 1: Securing Infrastructure Cloud Services

On completion of this part, you will have a solid understanding of how to secure the basic building blocks of cloud services (cloud deployment and service models, compute, storage, and network)

This part of the book comprises the following chapters:

- *Chapter 1, Introduction to Cloud Security*
- *Chapter 2, Securing Compute Services*
- *Chapter 3, Securing Storage Services*
- *Chapter 4, Securing Network Services*

1
Introduction to Cloud Security

This book, *Cloud Security Techniques and Best Practices*, is meant for various audiences. You could be taking your first steps working with cloud services, or you could be coming from an IT perspective and want to know about various compute and storage services and how to configure them securely. Or, you might be working in information security and want to know the various authentication, encryption, and audit services and how to configure them securely, or you might be working with architecture and want to know how to design large-scale environments in the cloud in a secure way.

Reading this book will allow you to make the most of cloud services while focusing on security aspects. Before discussing cloud services in more detail, let me share my opinion regarding cloud services.

The world of IT is changing. For decades, organizations used to purchase physical hardware, install operating systems, and deploy software. This routine required a lot of ongoing maintenance (for patch deployment, backup, monitoring, and so on).

The cloud introduced a new paradigm – that is, the ability to consume managed services to achieve the same goal of running software (from file servers to **Enterprise Resource Planning (ERP)** or **Customer Relationship Management (CRM)** products), while using the expertise of the hyper-scale cloud providers.

Some well-known use cases of cloud computing are as follows:

- **Netflix** – one of the largest video streaming services world-wide. It uses AWS to run its media streaming services:

  `https://aws.amazon.com/solutions/case-studies/netflix-case-study`

- **Mercedes-Benz** – one of the most famous automotive brands. It uses Azure to run its research and development:

  `https://customers.microsoft.com/en-us/story/784791-mercedes-benz-r-and-d-creates-container-driven-cars-powered-by-microsoft-azure`

- **Home Depot** – the largest home improvement retailer in the United States. It uses Google Cloud to run its online stores:

  `https://cloud.google.com/customers/featured/the-home-depot`

In this book, we will compare various aspects of cloud computing (from fundamental services such as compute, storage, and networking, to compliance management and best practices for building and maintaining large-scale environments in a secure way), while reviewing the different alternatives offered by **Amazon Web Services** (**AWS**), **Microsoft Azure**, and **Google Cloud Platform** (**GCP**).

It does not matter which organization you are coming from – this book will allow you to have a better understanding of how to achieve security in any of the large hyper-scale cloud providers.

You do not have to read everything – simply find out which cloud provider is common at your workplace or which cloud provider you wish to focus on, and feel free to skip the rest.

In this chapter, we will cover the following topics:

- Why we need security
- Cloud service models
- Cloud deployment models
- The shared responsibility model

Technical requirements

This chapter is an introduction to cloud security, so there are no technical requirements.

What is a cloud service?

As part of this introduction, let's define the terminology to make sure we are all on the same page.

The **National Institute of Standards and Technology** (**NIST**) defines *cloud* as a technology that has the following five characteristics:

- **On-demand self-service**: Imagine you wish to open a blog and you need compute resources. Instead of purchasing hardware and waiting for the vendor to ship it to your office and having to deploy software, the easier alternative can be a self-service portal, where you can select a pre-installed operating system and content management system that you can deploy within a few minutes by yourself.

- **Broad network access**: Consider having enough network access (the type that large **Internet Service Providers** (**ISPs**) have) to serve millions of end users with your application.

- **Resource pooling**: Consider having thousands of computers, running in a large server farm, and being able to maximize their use (from CPU, memory, and storage capacity), instead of having a single server running 10% of its CPU utilization.

- **Rapid elasticity**: Consider having the ability to increase and decrease the amount of compute resources (from a single server to thousands of servers, and then back to a single server), all according to your application or service needs.

- **Measured service**: Consider having the ability to pay for only the resources you consumed and being able to generate a billing report that shows which resources have been used and how much you must pay for the resources.

Further details relating to the NIST definition can be found at the following link:

```
https://nvlpubs.nist.gov/nistpubs/Legacy/SP/
nistspecialpublication800-145.pdf
```

What are the cloud deployment models?

Now that we understand what the cloud characteristics are, let's talk about cloud deployment models:

- **Private cloud**: An infrastructure deployed and maintained by a single organization. Let's say we are a large financial organization (such as a bank or insurance organization), we would like to serve various departments in our organization (from HR, IT, sales, and so on), and we might have regulatory requirements to keep customers' data on-premises – a private cloud can be a suitable solution.

- **Public cloud**: An infrastructure deployed and maintained by a service provider for serving multiple customers and organizations, mostly accessible over the internet. Naturally, this book will focus on the public cloud model, with reference to various services offered by AWS, Azure, and GCP.

- **Hybrid cloud**: A combination of a private cloud (or on-premises cloud) and at least one public cloud infrastructure. I like to consider the hybrid cloud as an extension of the local data center. We should not consider this extension as something separate, and we should protect it the same way we protect our local data center.

- **Multi-cloud**: A scenario where our organization is either using multiple managed services (see the definition of **SaaS** in the next section) or using multiple public cloud infrastructure (see the definitions of **IaaS** and **PaaS** in the next section).

What are the cloud service models?

An essential part of understanding clouds is understanding the three cloud service models:

- **Infrastructure as a Service (IaaS)**: This is the most fundamental service model, where a customer can select the virtual machine size (in terms of the amount of CPU and memory), select a pre-configured operating system, and deploy software inside the virtual machine instance according to business needs (services such as **Amazon EC2**, **Azure Virtual Machines**, and **Google Compute Engine**).

- **Platform as a Service (PaaS)**: This type of service model varies from managed database services to managed application services (where a customer can import code and run it inside a managed environment) and more (services such as **AWS Elastic Beanstalk**, **Azure Web Apps**, and **Google App Engine**).

- **Software as a Service (SaaS)**: This is the most widely used service model – a fully managed software environment where, as a customer, you usually open a web browser, log in to an application, and consume services. These could be messaging services, ERP, CRM, business analytics, and more (services such as **Microsoft Office 365**, **Google Workspaces**, **Salesforce CRM**, **SAP SuccessFactors**, and **Oracle Cloud HCM**).

Understanding the cloud service models will allow you to understand your role as a customer, explained later in the *What is the shared responsibility model?* section.

Why we need security

As mentioned previously, we can see clear benefits of using cloud services that enable our business to focus on what brings us value (from conducting research in a pharmaceutical lab, to selling products on a retail site, and so on).

But what about security? And, specifically, cloud security?

Why should our organization focus on the overhead called *information security* (and, in the context of this book, *cloud security*)?

The cloud has changed the paradigm of organizations controlling their data on-premises (from HR data to customers' data) and investing money in maintaining data centers, servers, storage, network equipment, and the application tier.

Using public clouds has changed the way organizations look at information security (in the context of this book, cloud security).

The following are a few common examples of the difference between on-premises data solutions and the cloud:

	Traditional data center	Cloud environment
Who is responsible for physical security?	The organization	The cloud service provider
Where is the data located?	On-premises data center	Cloud provider's data center
Who controls access to the data?	The organization	Both the organization and the cloud service provider
Who is responsible for vulnerability management and patch management?	The organization	IaaS – The organization PaaS – The cloud provider SaaS – The cloud provider
Who is in charge of incident response?	The organization	Both the organization and the cloud service provider
Who is responsible for law, privacy, and regulation?	The organization	Both the organization and the cloud service provider

Table 1.1 – Differences between on-premises data solutions and the cloud

Organizations are often unwilling to migrate to a public cloud for security reasons because the physical servers are located outside of the organization's direct control, and sometimes even outside their physical geography.

Here are a few questions often asked by organizations' management:

- Are my servers going to behave the same as if they were on-premises?
- How do I protect my servers outside my data center from a data breach?
- How do I know the cloud provider will not have access to my data?
- Do my employees have enough knowledge to work in new environments such as the public cloud?

Perhaps the most obvious question asked is – *is the public cloud secure enough to store my data?*

From my personal experience, the answer is *yes*.

By design, the hyper-scale cloud providers invest billions of dollars protecting their data centers, building secure services, investing in employee training, and locating security incidents and remediating them fast. This is all with much higher investment, attention, and expertise than most organizations can dedicate to protecting their local data centers.

The reason for this is simple – if a security breach happens to one of the hyper-scale cloud providers, their customers' trust will be breached, and the cloud providers will run out of business.

At the end of the day, cloud security enables our organization to achieve (among other things) the following:

- **Decreased attack surface**: Using central authentication, data encryption, DDoS protection services, and more
- **Compliance with regulation**: Deploying environments according to best practices
- **Standardization and best practices**: Enforcing security using automated tools and services

Reading this book will allow you to have a better understanding of various methods to secure your cloud environments – most of them using the cloud vendor's built-in services and capabilities.

What is the shared responsibility model?

When speaking about cloud security and cloud service models (IaaS/PaaS/SaaS), the thing that we all hear about is the **shared responsibility model**, which tries to draw a line between the cloud provider and the customer's responsibilities regarding security.

As you can see in the following diagram, the cloud provider is always responsible for the lower layers – from the physical security of their data centers, through networking, storage, host servers, and the virtualization layers:

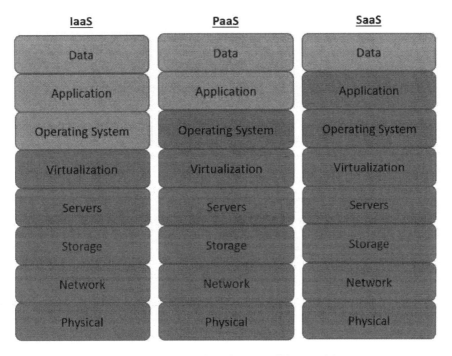

Figure 1.1 – The shared responsibility model

Above the virtualization layer is where the responsibility begins to change.

When working with IaaS, we, as the customers, can select a pre-installed image of an operating system (with or without additional software installed inside the image), deploy our applications, and manage permissions to access our data.

When working with PaaS, we, as the customers, may have the ability to control code in a managed environment (services such as AWS Elastic Beanstalk, Azure Web Apps, and Google App Engine) and manage permissions to access our data.

When working with SaaS, we, as the customers, received a fully managed service, and all we can do is manage permissions to access our data.

In the next sections, we will look at how the various cloud providers (AWS, Azure, and GCP) look at the shared responsibility model from their own perspective.

For more information on the shared responsibility model, you can check the following link: https://tutorials4sharepoint.wordpress.com/2020/04/24/shared-responsibility-model/.

AWS and the shared responsibility model

Looking at the shared responsibility model from AWS's point of view, we can see the clear distinction between AWS's responsibility for the security *of* the cloud (physical hardware and the lower layers such as host servers, storage, database, and network) and the customer's responsibility for security *in* the cloud (everything the customer controls – operating system, data encryption, network firewall rules, and customer data). The following diagram depicts AWS and the shared responsibility model:

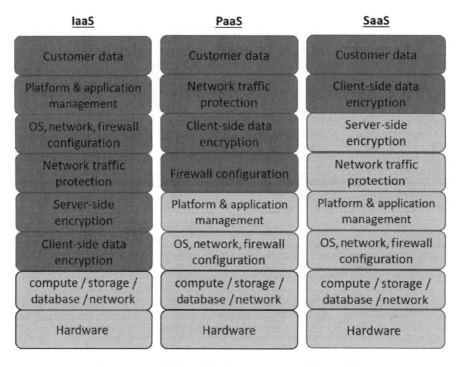

Figure 1.2 – AWS and the shared responsibility model

As a customer of AWS, reading this book will allow you to gain the essential knowledge and best practices for using common AWS services (including compute, storage, networking, authentication, and so on) in a secure way.

More information on the AWS shared responsibility model can be found at the following link: `https://aws.amazon.com/blogs/industries/applying-the-aws-shared-responsibility-model-to-your-gxp-solution/`.

Azure and the shared responsibility model

Looking at the shared responsibility model from Azure's point of view, we can see the distinction between Azure's responsibility for its data centers (physical layers) and the customer's responsibility at the top layers (identities, devices, and customers' data). In the middle layers (operating system, network controls, and applications) the responsibility changes between Azure and the customers, according to various service types. The following diagram depicts Azure and the shared responsibility model:

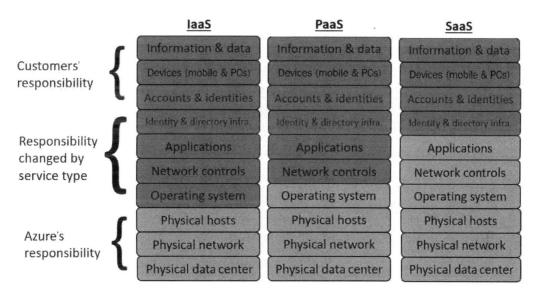

Figure 1.3 – Azure and the shared responsibility model

As a customer of Azure, reading this book will allow you to gain the essential knowledge and best practices for using common Azure services (including compute, storage, networking, authentication, and others) in a secure way.

More information on the Azure shared responsibility model can be found at the following link: `https://docs.microsoft.com/en-us/azure/security/fundamentals/shared-responsibility`.

GCP and the shared responsibility model

Looking at the shared responsibility model from GCP's point of view, we can see that Google would like to emphasize that it builds its own hardware, which enables the company to control the hardware, boot, and kernel of its platform, including the storage layer encryption, network equipment, and logging of everything that Google is responsible for.

When looking at things that the customer is responsible for we can see a lot more layers, including everything from the guest operating system, network security rules, authentication, identity, and web application security, to things such as deployment, usage, access policies, and content (customers' data). The following diagram depicts GCP and the shared responsibility model:

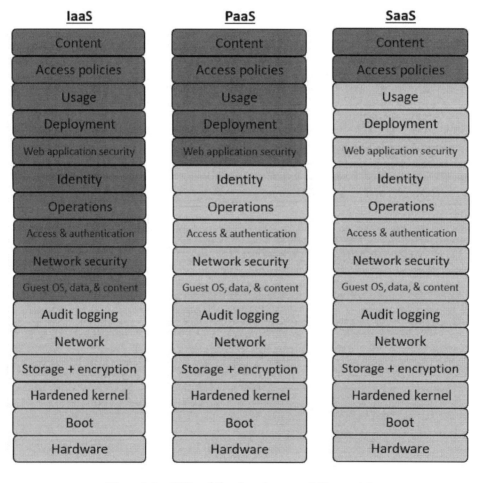

Figure 1.4 – GCP and the shared responsibility model

As a customer of GCP, reading this book will allow you to gain the essential knowledge and best practices for using common GCP services (including compute, storage, networking, authentication, and more) in a secure way.

More information about the GCP shared responsibility model can be found at the following link: `https://services.google.com/fh/files/misc/google-cloud-security-foundations-guide.pdf`.

As a customer, understanding the shared responsibility model allows you, at any given time, to understand which layers are under the cloud vendor's responsibility and which layers are under the customer's responsibility.

Command-line tools

One of the things that makes cloud environments so robust is the ability to control almost anything using the **Application Programming Interface** (**API**) or using the command line.

Most mature cloud providers have already published and maintain their own **Command-Line Interface** (**CLI**) to allow customers to perform actions in an easy and standard way.

An alternative to using the command line to interact with the cloud provider's API is using a **Software Developer Kit** (**SDK**) – a method to control actions (from deploying a virtual machine to encrypting storage), query information from a service (checking whether auditing is enabled for my customers logging into my web application), and more.

Since this book doesn't require previous development experience, I will provide examples for performing actions using the command-line tools.

During various chapters of this book, I will provide you with examples of commands that will allow you to easily implement the various security controls over AWS, Azure, and GCP.

I highly recommend that you become familiar with those tools.

AWS CLI

AWS CLI can be installed on **Windows** (64 bit), **Linux** (both x86 and ARM processors), **macOS**, and even inside a **Docker** container.

The AWS CLI documentation explains how to install the tool and provides a detailed explanation of how to use it.

The documentation can be found at `https://aws.amazon.com/cli`.

Azure CLI

Azure CLI can be installed on Windows, Linux (**Ubuntu**, **Debian**, **RHEL**, **CentOS**, **Fedora**, **openSUSE**), and macOS.

The Azure CLI documentation explains how to install the tool and provides a detailed explanation of how to use it.

The documentation can be found at `https://docs.microsoft.com/en-us/cli/azure`.

Google Cloud SDK

The Google command-line tool (**gcloud CLI**) can be installed on Windows, Linux (Ubuntu, Debian, RHEL, CentOS, Fedora), and macOS.

The Google Cloud SDK documentation explains how to install the tool and provides a detailed explanation of how to use it.

The documentation can be found at `https://cloud.google.com/sdk`.

Summary

In the first chapter of this book, we learned the definition of a *cloud*, the different cloud deployment models, and the different cloud service models.

We also learned what the shared cloud responsibility model is, and how AWS, Azure, and GCP look at this concept from their own point of view.

Lastly, we had a short introduction to the AWS, Azure, and GCP built-in command-line tools, and, during the next chapters, I will provide you with examples of how to implement various tasks using the command-line tools.

This introduction will be referred to in the following chapters, where we will dive deeper into the best practices for securing cloud services using (in most cases) the cloud providers' built-in capabilities.

Securing cloud environments can be challenging, depending on your previous knowledge in IT or information security or cloud services in general.

Reading this book will assist you in gaining the necessary knowledge of how to secure cloud environments, regardless of your role in the organization or your previous experience.

In the next chapter, we will review the various compute services in the cloud (including virtual machines, managed databases, container services, and finally serverless services).

2
Securing Compute Services

Speaking about cloud services, specifically **Infrastructure as a Service (IaaS)**, the most common resource everyone talks about is compute – from the traditional **virtual machines (VMs)**, through managed databases (run on VMs on the backend), to modern compute architecture such as containers and eventually serverless.

This chapter will cover all types of compute services and provide you with best practices on how to securely deploy and manage each of them.

In this chapter, we will cover the following topics:

- Securing VMs (authentication, network access control, metadata, serial console access, patch management, and backups)

- Securing Managed Database Services (identity management, network access control, data protection, and auditing and monitoring)

- Securing Containers (identity management, network access control, auditing and monitoring, and compliance)

- Securing serverless/function as a service (identity management, network access control, auditing and monitoring, compliance, and configuration change)

Technical requirements

For this chapter, you need to have an understanding of VMs, what managed databases are, and what containers (and Kubernetes) are, as well as a fundamental understanding of serverless.

Securing VMs

Each cloud provider has its own implementation of VMs (or virtual servers), but at the end of the day, the basic idea is the same:

1. Select a machine type (or size) – a ratio between the amount of **virtual CPU (vCPU)** and memory, according to their requirements (general-purpose, compute-optimized, memory-optimized, and so on).

2. Select a preinstalled image of an operating system (from Windows to Linux flavors).

3. Configure storage (adding additional volumes, connecting to file sharing services, and others).

4. Configure network settings (from network access controls to micro-segmentation, and others).

5. Configure permissions to access cloud resources.

6. Deploy an application.

7. Begin using the service.

8. Carry out ongoing maintenance of the operating system.

According to the shared responsibility model, when using IaaS, we (as the customers) are responsible for the deployment and maintenance of virtual servers, as explained in the coming section.

Next, we are going to see what the best practices are for securing common VM services in AWS, Azure, and GCP.

Securing Amazon Elastic Compute Cloud (EC2)

Amazon EC2 is the Amazon VM service.

General best practices for EC2 instances

Following are some of the best practices to keep in mind:

- Use only trusted AMI when deploying EC2 instances.

- Use a minimal number of packages inside an AMI, to lower the attack surface.

- Use Amazon built-in agents for EC2 instances (backup, patch management, hardening, monitoring, and others).

- Use the new generation of EC2 instances, based on the AWS Nitro System, which offloads virtualization functions (such as network, storage, and security) to dedicated software and hardware chips. This allows the customer to get much better performance, with much better security and isolation of customers' data.

For more information, please refer the following resources:

Best practices for building AMIs:

`https://docs.aws.amazon.com/marketplace/latest/userguide/best-practices-for-building-your-amis.html`

Amazon Linux AMI:

`https://aws.amazon.com/amazon-linux-2/`

AWS Nitro System:

`https://aws.amazon.com/ec2/nitro/`

Best practices for authenticating to an instance

AWS does not have access to customers' VMs.

It doesn't matter whether you choose to deploy a Windows or a Linux machine, by running the EC2 launch deployment wizard, you must choose either an existing key pair or create a new key. This set of private/public keys is generated at the client browser – AWS does not have any access to these keys, and therefore cannot log in to your EC2 instance.

For Linux instances, the key pair is used for logging in to the machine via the SSH protocol.

Refer to the following link: `https://docs.aws.amazon.com/AWSEC2/latest/UserGuide/ec2-key-pairs.html`.

For Windows instances, the key pair is used to retrieve the built-in administrator's password.

Refer to the following link: `https://docs.amazonaws.cn/en_us/AWSEC2/latest/WindowsGuide/ec2-windows-passwords.html`.

The best practices are as follows:

- Keep your private keys in a secured location. A good alternative for storing and retrieving SSH keys is to use AWS Secrets Manager.

- Avoid storing private keys on a bastion host or any instance directly exposed to the internet. A good alternative to logging in using SSH, without an SSH key, is to use AWS Systems Manager, through Session Manager.

- Join Windows or Linux instances to an **Active Directory** (**AD**) domain and use your AD credentials to log in to the EC2 instances (and avoid using local credentials or SSH keys completely).

For more information, please refer the following resources:

How to use AWS Secrets Manager to securely store and rotate SSH key pairs:

```
https://aws.amazon.com/blogs/security/how-to-use-aws-secrets-
manager-securely-store-rotate-ssh-key-pairs/
```

Allow SSH connections through Session Manager:

```
https://docs.aws.amazon.com/systems-manager/latest/userguide/
session-manager-getting-started-enable-ssh-connections.html
```

Seamlessly join a Windows EC2 instance:

```
https://docs.aws.amazon.com/directoryservice/latest/admin-
guide/launching_instance.html
```

Seamlessly join a Linux EC2 instance to your AWS-managed Microsoft AD directory:

```
https://docs.aws.amazon.com/directoryservice/latest/admin-
guide/seamlessly_join_linux_instance.html
```

Best practices for securing network access to an instance

Access to AWS resources and services such as EC2 instances is controlled via *security groups* (at the EC2 instance level) or a **network access control list** (**NACL**) (at the subnet level), which are equivalent to the on-premises layer 4 network firewall or access control mechanism.

As a customer, you configure parameters such as source IP (or CIDR), destination IP (or CIDR), destination port (or predefined protocol), and whether the port is TCP or UDP.

You may also use another security group as either the source or destination in a security group.

For remote access and management of Linux machines, limit inbound network access to TCP port 22.

For remote access and management of Windows machines, limit inbound network access to TCP port 3389.

The best practices are as follows:

- For remote access protocols (SSH/RDP), limit the source IP (or CIDR) to well-known addresses. Good alternatives for allowing remote access protocols to an EC2 instance are to use a VPN tunnel, use a bastion host, or use AWS Systems Manager Session Manager.

- For file sharing protocols (CIFS/SMB/FTP), limit the source IP (or CIDR) to well-known addresses.

- Set names and descriptions for security groups to allow a better understanding of the security group's purpose.

- Use tagging (that is, *labeling*) for security groups to allow a better understanding of which security group belongs to which AWS resources.

- Limit the number of ports allowed in a security group to the minimum required ports for allowing your service or application to function.

For more information, please refer the following resources:

Amazon EC2 security groups for Linux instances: `https://docs.aws.amazon.com/AWSEC2/latest/UserGuide/ec2-security-groups.html`

Security groups for your **virtual private cloud** (**VPC**): `https://docs.aws.amazon.com/vpc/latest/userguide/VPC_SecurityGroups.html`

AWS Systems Manager Session Manager:

`https://docs.aws.amazon.com/systems-manager/latest/userguide/session-manager.html`

Compare security groups and network ACLs:

`https://docs.aws.amazon.com/vpc/latest/userguide/VPC_Security.html#VPC_Security_Comparison`

Best practices for securing instance metadata

Instance metadata is a method to retrieve information about a running instance, such as the hostname and internal IP address.

An example of metadata about a running instance can be retrieved from within an instance, by either opening a browser from within the operating system or using the command line, to a URL such as http://169.254.169.254/latest/meta-data/.

Even though the IP address is an internal IP (meaning it cannot be accessed from outside the instance), the information, by default, can be retrieved locally without authentication.

AWS allows you to enforce authenticated or session-oriented requests to the instance metadata, also known as **Instance Metadata Service Version 2 (IMDSv2)**.

The following command uses the AWS CLI tool to enforce IMDSv2 on an existing instance:

```
aws ec2 modify-instance-metadata-options \
    --instance-id <INSTANCE-ID> \
    --http-endpoint enabled --http-tokens required
```

For more information, please refer the following resource:

Configure the instance metadata service:

https://docs.aws.amazon.com/AWSEC2/latest/UserGuide/
configuring-instance-metadata-service.html

Best practices for securing a serial console connection

For troubleshooting purposes, AWS allows you to connect using a *serial console* (a similar concept to what we used to have in the physical world with network equipment) to resolve network or operating system problems when SSH or RDP connections are not available.

The following command uses the AWS CLI tool to allow serial access at the AWS account level to a specific AWS Region:

```
aws ec2 enable-serial-console-access --region <Region_Code>
```

Since this type of remote connectivity exposes your EC2 instance, it is recommended to follow the following best practices:

- Access to the EC2 serial console should be limited to the group of individuals using **identity and access management (IAM)** roles.
- Only allow access to EC2 serial console when required.
- Always set a user password on an instance before allowing the EC2 serial console.

For more information, please refer the following resource:

Configure access to the EC2 serial console:

```
https://docs.aws.amazon.com/AWSEC2/latest/UserGuide/configure-
access-to-serial-console.html
```

Best practices for conducting patch management

Patch management is a crucial part of every instance of ongoing maintenance.

To deploy security patches for either Windows or Linux-based instances in a standard manner, it is recommended to use AWS Systems Manager Patch Manager, following this method:

1. Configure the patch baseline.
2. Scan your EC2 instances for deviation from the patch baseline at a scheduled interval.
3. Install missing security patches on your EC2 instances.
4. Review the Patch Manager reports.

The best practices are as follows:

- Use AWS Systems Manager Compliance to make sure all your EC2 instances are up to date.

- Create a group with minimal IAM privileges to allow only relevant team members to conduct patch deployment.

- Use tagging (that is, *labeling*) for your EC2 instances to allow patch deployment groups per tag (for example, *prod* versus *dev* environments).

- For stateless EC2 instances (where no user session data is stored inside an EC2 instance), replace an existing EC2 instance with a new instance, created from an up-to-date operating system image.

For more information, please refer the following resource:

Software patching with AWS Systems Manager:

```
https://aws.amazon.com/blogs/mt/software-patching-with-aws-
systems-manager/
```

Best practices for securing backups

Backing up is crucial for EC2 instance recovery.

The AWS Backup service encrypts your backups in transit and at rest using AWS encryption keys, stored in AWS **Key Management Service** (**KMS**) (as explained in *Chapter 7, Applying Encryption in Cloud Services*), as an extra layer of security, independent of your **Elastic Block Store** (**EBS**) volume or snapshot encryption keys.

The best practices are as follows:

- Configure the AWS Backup service with an IAM role to allow access to the encryption keys stored inside AWS KMS.
- Configure the AWS Backup service with an IAM role to allow access to your backup vault.
- Use tagging (that is, *labeling*) for backups to allow a better understanding of which backup belongs to which EC2 instance.
- Consider replicating your backups to another region.

For more information, please refer the following resources:

Protecting your data with AWS Backup:

```
https://aws.amazon.com/blogs/storage/protecting-your-data-
with-aws-backup/
```

Creating backup copies across AWS Regions:

```
https://docs.aws.amazon.com/aws-backup/latest/devguide/cross-
region-backup.html
```

Summary

In this section, we have learned how to securely maintain a VM, based on AWS infrastructure – from logging in to securing network access, troubleshooting using a serial console, patch management, and backup.

Securing Azure Virtual Machines

Azure Virtual Machines is the Azure VM service.

General best practices for Azure Virtual Machines

Following are some of the best practices to keep in mind:

- Use only trusted images when deploying Azure Virtual Machines.
- Use a minimal number of packages inside an image, to lower the attack surface.
- Use Azure built-in agents for Azure Virtual Machines (backup, patch management, hardening, monitoring, and others).
- For highly sensitive environments, use Azure confidential computing images, to ensure security and isolation of customers' data.

For more information, please refer the following resources:

Azure Image Builder overview:

```
https://docs.microsoft.com/en-us/azure/virtual-machines/image-
builder-overview
```

Using Azure for cloud-based confidential computing:

```
https://docs.microsoft.com/en-us/azure/confidential-computing/
overview#using-azure-for-cloud-based-confidential-computing-
```

Best practices for authenticating to a VM

Microsoft does not have access to customers' VMs.

It doesn't matter whether you choose to deploy a Windows or a Linux machine, by running the **create a virtual machine** wizard, to deploy a new Linux machine, by default, you must choose either an existing key pair or create a new key pair.

This set of private/public keys is generated at the client side – Azure does not have any access to these keys, and therefore cannot log in to your Linux VM.

For Linux instances, the key pair is used for logging in to the machine via the SSH protocol.

For more information, please refer the following resource:

Generate and store SSH keys in the Azure portal:

```
https://docs.microsoft.com/en-us/azure/virtual-machines/
ssh-keys-portal
```

For Windows machines, when running the **create a new virtual machine** wizard, you are asked to specify your own administrator account and password to log in to the machine via the RDP protocol.

For more information, please refer the following resource:

Create a Windows VM:

```
https://docs.microsoft.com/en-us/azure/virtual-machines/
windows/quick-create-portal#create-virtual-machine
```

The best practices are as follows:

- Keep your credentials in a secured location.
- Avoid storing private keys on a bastion host (VMs directly exposed to the internet).
- Join Windows or Linux instances to an AD domain and use your AD credentials to log in to the VMs (and avoid using local credentials or SSH keys completely).

For more information, please refer the following resources:

Azure Bastion:

```
https://azure.microsoft.com/en-us/services/azure-bastion
```

Join a Windows Server VM to an Azure AD Domain Services-managed domain using a Resource Manager template:

```
https://docs.microsoft.com/en-us/azure/active-directory-
domain-services/join-windows-vm-template
```

Join a Red Hat Enterprise Linux VM to an Azure AD Domain Services-managed domain:

```
https://docs.microsoft.com/en-us/azure/active-directory-
domain-services/join-rhel-linux-vm
```

Best practices for securing network access to a VM

Access to Azure resources and services such as VMs is controlled via **network security groups,** which are equivalent to the on-premises layer 4 network firewall or access control mechanism.

As a customer, you configure parameters such as source IP (or CIDR), destination IP (or CIDR), source port (or a predefined protocol), destination port (or a predefined protocol), whether the port is TCP or UDP, and the action to take (either allow or deny).

For remote access and management of Linux machines, limit inbound network access to TCP port 22.

For remote access and management of Windows machines, limit inbound network access to TCP port 3389.

The best practices are as follows:

- For remote access protocols (SSH/RDP), limit the source IP (or CIDR) to well-known addresses. Good alternatives for allowing remote access protocols to an Azure VM is to use a VPN tunnel, use Azure Bastion, or use Azure **Privileged Identity Management** (**PIM**) to allow just-in-time access to a remote VM.

- For file sharing protocols (CIFS/SMB/FTP), limit the source IP (or CIDR) to well-known addresses.

- Set names for network security groups to allow a better understanding of the security group's purpose.

- Use tagging (that is, *labeling*) for network security groups to allow a better understanding of which network security group belongs to which Azure resources.

- Limit the number of ports allowed in a network security group to the minimum required ports for allowing your service or application to function.

For more information, please refer the following resources:

Network security groups:

```
https://docs.microsoft.com/en-us/azure/virtual-network/
network-security-groups-overview
```

How to open ports to a VM with the Azure portal:

```
https://docs.microsoft.com/en-us/azure/virtual-machines/
windows/nsg-quickstart-portal
```

Azure Bastion:

```
https://azure.microsoft.com/en-us/services/azure-bastion
```

What is Azure AD PIM?

```
https://docs.microsoft.com/en-us/azure/active-directory/
privileged-identity-management/pim-configure
```

Best practices for securing a serial console connection

For troubleshooting purposes, Azure allows you to connect using a *serial console* (a similar concept to what we used to have in the physical world with network equipment) to resolve network or operating system problems when SSH or RDP connections are not available.

The following commands use the Azure CLI tool to allow serial access for the entire Azure subscription level:

```
subscriptionId=$(az account show --output=json | jq -r .id)
```

```
az resource invoke-action --action enableConsole \
    --ids "/subscriptions/$subscriptionId/providers/
Microsoft.SerialConsole/consoleServices/default" --api-
version="2018-05-01"
```

Since this type of remote connectivity exposes your VMs, it is recommended to follow the following best practices:

- Access to the serial console should be limited to the group of individuals with the *Virtual Machine Contributor* role for the VM and the *Boot diagnostics* storage account.
- Always set a user password on the target VM before allowing access to the serial console.

For more information, please refer the following resources:

Azure serial console for Linux:

https://docs.microsoft.com/en-us/troubleshoot/azure/virtual-machines/serial-console-linux

Azure serial console for Windows:

https://docs.microsoft.com/en-us/troubleshoot/azure/virtual-machines/serial-console-windows

Best practices for conducting patch management

Patch management is a crucial part of every instance of ongoing maintenance.

To deploy security patches for either Windows or Linux-based instances in a standard manner, it is recommended to use **Azure Automation Update Management**, using the following method:

1. Create an automation account.

2. Enable Update Management for all Windows and Linux machines.

3. Configure the schedule settings and reboot options.

4. Install missing security patches on your VMs.

5. Review the deployment status.

The best practices are as follows:

- Use minimal privileges for the account using Update Management to deploy security patches.

- Use update classifications to define which security patches to deploy.

- When using an Azure Automation account, encrypt sensitive data (such as variable assets).

- When using an Azure Automation account, use private endpoints to disable public network access.

- Use tagging (that is, *labeling*) for your VMs to allow defining dynamic groups of VMs (for example, *prod* versus *dev* environments).

- For stateless VMs (where no user session data is stored inside an Azure VM), replace an existing Azure VM with a new instance, created from an up-to-date operating system image.

For more information, please refer the following resources:

Azure Automation Update Management:

`https://docs.microsoft.com/en-us/azure/architecture/hybrid/azure-update-mgmt`

Manage updates and patches for your VMs:

`https://docs.microsoft.com/en-us/azure/automation/update-management/manage-updates-for-vm`

Update management permissions:

`https://docs.microsoft.com/en-us/azure/automation/automation-role-based-access-control#update-management-permissions`

Best practices for securing backups

Backing up is crucial for VM recovery.

The Azure Backup service encrypts your backups in transit and at rest using Azure Key Vault (as explained in *Chapter 7, Applying Encryption in Cloud Services*).

The best practices are as follows:

- Use Azure **role-based access control** (**RBAC**) to configure Azure Backup to have minimal access to your backups.
- For sensitive environments, encrypt data at rest using customer-managed keys.
- Use private endpoints to secure access between your data and the recovery service vault.
- If you need your backups to be compliant with a regulatory standard, use *Regulatory Compliance in Azure Policy*.
- Use Azure security baselines for Azure Backup (*Azure Security Benchmark*).
- Enable the *soft delete* feature to protect your backups from accidental deletion.
- Consider replicating your backups to another region.

For more information, please refer the following resources:

Security features to help protect hybrid backups that use Azure Backup:

```
https://docs.microsoft.com/en-us/azure/backup/backup-azure-
security-feature
```

Use Azure RBAC to manage Azure backup recovery points:

```
https://docs.microsoft.com/en-us/azure/backup/backup-rbac-rs-
vault
```

Azure Policy Regulatory Compliance controls for Azure Backup:

```
https://docs.microsoft.com/en-us/azure/backup/security-
controls-policy
```

Soft delete for Azure Backup:

```
https://docs.microsoft.com/en-us/azure/backup/backup-azure-
security-feature-cloud
```

Cross Region Restore (CRR) for Azure Virtual Machines using Azure Backup:

```
https://azure.microsoft.com/en-us/blog/cross-region-restore-
crr-for-azure-virtual-machines-using-azure-backup/
```

Summary

In this section, we have learned how to securely maintain a VM, based on Azure infrastructure – from logging in to securing network access, troubleshooting using a serial console, patch management, and backup.

Securing Google Compute Engine (GCE) and VM instances

GCE is Google's VM service.

General best practices for Google VMs

Following are some of the best practices to keep in mind:

- Use only trusted images when deploying Google VMs.

- Use a minimal number of packages inside an image, to lower the attack surface.

- Use GCP built-in agents for Google VMs (patch management, hardening, monitoring, and so on).

- For highly sensitive environments, use Google Confidential Computing images, to ensure security and isolation of customers' data.

For more information, please refer the following resources:

List of public images available on GCE:

```
https://cloud.google.com/compute/docs/images
```

Confidential Computing:

```
https://cloud.google.com/confidential-computing
```

Best practices for authenticating to a VM instance

Google does not have access to customers' VM instances.

When you run the **create instance** wizard, no credentials are generated.

For Linux instances, you need to manually create a key pair and add the public key to either the instance metadata or the entire GCP project metadata to log in to the machine instance via the SSH protocol.

For more information, please refer the following resource:

Managing SSH keys in metadata:

```
https://cloud.google.com/compute/docs/instances/adding-
removing-ssh-keys
```

For Windows machine instances, you need to manually reset the built-in administrator's password to log in to the machine instance via the RDP protocol.

For more information, please refer the following resource:

Creating passwords for Windows VMs:

```
https://cloud.google.com/compute/docs/instances/windows/
creating-passwords-for-windows-instances
```

The best practices are as follows:

- Keep your private keys in a secured location.
- Avoid storing private keys on a bastion host (machine instances directly exposed to the internet).
- Periodically rotate SSH keys used to access compute instances.
- Periodically review public keys inside the compute instance or GCP project-level SSH key metadata and remove unneeded public keys.
- Join Windows or Linux instances to an AD domain and use your AD credentials to log in to the VMs (and avoid using local credentials or SSH keys completely).

For more information, please refer the following resources:

Quickstart: Joining a Windows VM to a domain:

```
https://cloud.google.com/managed-microsoft-ad/docs/quickstart-
domain-join-windows
```

Quickstart: Joining a Linux VM to a domain:

```
https://cloud.google.com/managed-microsoft-ad/docs/quickstart-
domain-join-linux
```

Best practices for securing network access to a VM instance

Access to GCP resources and services such as VM instances is controlled via **VPC firewall rules**, which are equivalent to the on-premises layer 4 network firewall or access control mechanism.

As a customer, you configure parameters such as the source IP (or CIDR), source service, source tags, destination port (or a predefined protocol), whether the port is TCP or UDP, whether the traffic direction is ingress or egress, and the action to take (either allow or deny).

For remote access and management of Linux machines, limit inbound network access to TCP port 22.

For remote access and management of Windows machines, limit inbound network access to TCP port 3389.

The best practices are as follows:

- For remote access protocols (SSH/RDP), limit the source IP (or CIDR) to well-known addresses.

- For file sharing protocols (CIFS/SMB/FTP), limit the source IP (or CIDR) to well-known addresses.

- Set names and descriptions for firewall rules to allow a better understanding of the security group's purpose.

- Use tagging (that is, *labeling*) for firewall rules to allow a better understanding of which firewall rule belongs to which GCP resources.

- Limit the number of ports allowed in a firewall rule to the minimum required ports for allowing your service or application to function.

For more information, please refer the following resource:

Use fewer, broader firewall rule sets when possible:

```
https://cloud.google.com/architecture/best-practices-vpc-
design#fewer-firewall-rules
```

Best practices for securing a serial console connection

For troubleshooting purposes, GCP allows you to connect using a *serial console* (a similar concept to what we used to have in the physical world with network equipment) to resolve network or operating system problems when SSH or RDP connections are not available.

The following command uses the Google Cloud SDK to allow serial access on the entire GCP project:

```
gcloud compute project-info add-metadata \
    --metadata serial-port-enable=TRUE
```

Since this type of remote connectivity exposes your VMs, it is recommended to follow these best practices:

- Configure password-based login to allow users access to the serial console.
- Disable interactive serial console login per compute instance when not required.
- Enable disconnection when the serial console connection is idle.
- Access to the serial console should be limited to the required group of individuals using Google Cloud IAM roles.
- Always set a user password on the target VM instance before allowing access to the serial console.

For more information, please refer the following resource:

Troubleshooting using the serial console:

```
https://cloud.google.com/compute/docs/troubleshooting/
troubleshooting-using-serial-console
```

Best practices for conducting patch management

Patch management is a crucial part of every instance of ongoing maintenance.

To deploy security patches for either Windows- or Linux-based instances, in a standard manner, it is recommended to use Google operating system patch management, using the following method:

1. Deploy the operating system config agent on the target instances.
2. Create a patch job.
3. Run patch deployment.
4. Schedule patch deployment.
5. Review the deployment status inside the operating system patch management dashboard.

The best practices are as follows:

- Use minimal privileges for the accounts using operating system patch management to deploy security patches, according to Google Cloud IAM roles.

- Gradually deploy security patches zone by zone and region by region.

- Use tagging (that is, *labeling*) for your VM instances to allow defining groups of VM instances (for example, *prod* versus *dev* environments).

- For stateless VMs (where no user session data is stored inside a Google VM), replace an existing Google VM with a new instance, created from an up-to-date operating system image.

For more information, please refer the following resources:

Operating system patch management:

`https://cloud.google.com/compute/docs/os-patch-management`

Creating patch jobs:

`https://cloud.google.com/compute/docs/os-patch-management/create-patch-job`

Best practices for operating system updates at scale:

`https://cloud.google.com/blog/products/management-tools/best-practices-for-os-patch-management-on-compute-engine`

Summary

In this section, we have learned how to securely maintain a VM, based on GCP infrastructure – from logging in to securing network access, troubleshooting using the serial console, and patch management.

Securing managed database services

Each cloud provider has its own implementation of managed databases.

According to the shared responsibility model, if we choose to use a managed database, the cloud provider is responsible for the operating system and database layers of the managed database (including patch management, backups, and auditing).

If we have the requirement to deploy a specific build of a database, we can always deploy it inside a VM, but according to the shared responsibility model, we will oversee the entire operating system and database maintenance (including hardening, backup, patch management, and monitoring).

A managed solution for running the database engine – either a common database engine such as MySQL, PostgreSQL, Microsoft SQL Server, an Oracle Database server, or proprietary databases such as Amazon DynamoDB, Azure Cosmos DB, or Google Cloud Spanner, but at the end of the day, the basic idea is the same:

1. Select the database type according to its purpose or use case (relational database, NoSQL database, graph database, in-memory database, and others).

2. Select a database engine (for example, MySQL, PostgreSQL, Microsoft SQL Server, or Oracle Database server).

3. For relational databases, select a machine type (or size) – a ratio between the amount of vCPU and memory, according to their requirements (general-purpose, memory-optimized, and so on).

4. Choose whether high availability is required.

5. Deploy a managed database instance (or cluster).

6. Configure network access control from your cloud environment to your managed database.

7. Enable logging for any access attempt or configuration changes in your managed database.

8. Configure backups on your managed database for recovery purposes.

9. Connect your application to the managed database and begin using the service.

There are various reasons for choosing a managed database solution:

- Maintenance of the database is under the responsibility of the cloud provider.
- Security patch deployment is under the responsibility of the cloud provider.
- Availability of the database is under the responsibility of the cloud provider.
- Backups are included as part of the service (up to a certain amount of storage and amount of backup history).
- Encryption in transit and at rest are embedded as part of a managed solution.
- Auditing is embedded as part of a managed solution.

Since there is a variety of database types and several database engines, in this chapter, we will focus on a single, popular relational database engine – MySQL.

This chapter will not be focusing on non-relational databases.

Next, we are going to see what the best practices are for securing common managed MySQL database services from AWS, Azure, and GCP.

Securing Amazon RDS for MySQL

Amazon **Relational Database Service (RDS)** for MySQL is the Amazon-managed MySQL service.

Best practices for configuring IAM for a managed MySQL database service

MySQL supports the following types of authentication methods:

- Local username/password authentication against MySQL's built-in authentication mechanism.

- AWS IAM database authentication.

- AWS Directory Service for Microsoft AD authentication.

The best practices are as follows:

- For the local MySQL master user, create a strong and complex password (at least 15 characters, made up of lowercase and uppercase letters, numbers, and special characters), and keep the password in a secured location.

- For end users who need direct access to the managed database, the preferred method is to use the AWS IAM service, since it allows you to centrally manage all user identities, control their password policy, conduct an audit on their actions (that is, *API calls*), and, in the case of a suspicious security incident, disable the user identity.

- If you manage your user identities using AWS Directory Service for Microsoft AD (AWS-managed Microsoft AD), use this service to authenticate your end users using the Kerberos protocol.

For more information, please refer the following resources:

IAM database authentication for MySQL:

```
https://docs.aws.amazon.com/AmazonRDS/latest/UserGuide/
UsingWithRDS.IAMDBAuth.html
```

Using Kerberos authentication for MySQL:

```
https://docs.aws.amazon.com/AmazonRDS/latest/UserGuide/mysql-
kerberos.html
```

Best practices for securing network access to a managed MySQL database service

Access to a managed MySQL database service is controlled via *database security groups*, which are equivalent to *security groups* and the on-premises layer 4 network firewall or access control mechanism.

As a customer, you configure parameters such as the source IP (or CIDR) of your web or application servers and the destination IP (or CIDR) of your managed MySQL database service, and AWS configures the port automatically.

The best practices are as follows:

- Managed databases must never be accessible from the internet or a publicly accessible subnet – always use private subnets to deploy your databases.
- Configure security groups for your web or application servers and set the security group as target CIDR when creating a database security group.
- If you need to manage the MySQL database service, either use an EC2 instance (or bastion host) to manage the MySQL database remotely or create a VPN tunnel from your remote machine to the managed MySQL database.
- Since Amazon RDS is a managed service, it is located outside the customer's VPC. An alternative to secure access from your VPC to the managed RDS environment is to use AWS PrivateLink, which avoids sending network traffic outside your VPC, through a secure channel, using an interface VPC endpoint.
- Set names and descriptions for the database security groups to allow a better understanding of the database security group's purpose.
- Use tagging (that is, *labeling*) for database security groups to allow a better understanding of which database security group belongs to which AWS resources.

For more information, please refer the following resources:

Controlling access to RDS with security groups:

```
https://docs.aws.amazon.com/AmazonRDS/latest/UserGuide/
Overview.RDSSecurityGroups.html
```

Amazon RDS API and interface VPC endpoints (AWS PrivateLink):

```
https://docs.aws.amazon.com/AmazonRDS/latest/UserGuide/
vpc-interface-endpoints.html
```

Best practices for protecting data stored in a managed MySQL database service

A database is meant to store data.

In many cases, a database (and, in this case, a managed MySQL database) may contain sensitive customer data (from a retail store containing customers' data to an organization's sensitive HR data).

To protect customers' data, it is recommended to encrypt data both in transport (when data passes through the network), to avoid detection by an external party, and at rest (data stored inside a database), to avoid data being revealed, even by an internal database administrator.

Encryption allows you to maintain data confidentiality and data integrity (make sure your data is not changed by an untrusted party).

The best practices are as follows:

- Enable SSL/ TLS 1.2 transport layer encryption to your database.

- For non-sensitive environments, encrypt data at rest using AWS KMS (as explained in *Chapter 7, Applying Encryption in Cloud Services*).

- For sensitive environments, encrypt data at rest using **customer master key (CMK)** management (as explained in *Chapter 7, Applying Encryption in Cloud Services*).

For more information, please refer the following resources:

Using SSL with a MySQL database instance:

```
https://docs.aws.amazon.com/AmazonRDS/latest/UserGuide/CHAP_
MySQL.html#MySQL.Concepts.SSLSupport
```

Updating applications to connect to MySQL database instances using new SSL/TLS certificates:

```
https://docs.aws.amazon.com/AmazonRDS/latest/UserGuide/
ssl-certificate-rotation-mysql.html
```

Select the right encryption options for Amazon RDS database engines:

```
https://aws.amazon.com/blogs/database/selecting-the-right-
encryption-options-for-amazon-rds-and-amazon-aurora-database-
engines/
```

CMK management:

```
https://docs.aws.amazon.com/AmazonRDS/latest/UserGuide/
Overview.Encryption.Keys.html
```

Best practices for conducting auditing and monitoring for a managed MySQL database service

Auditing is a crucial part of data protection.

As with any other managed service, AWS allows you to enable logging and auditing using two built-in services:

- **Amazon CloudWatch**: A service that allows you to log database activities and raise an alarm according to predefined thresholds (for example, a high number of failed logins)
- **AWS CloudTrail**: A service that allows you to monitor API activities (basically, any action performed as part of the AWS RDS API)

The best practices are as follows:

- Enable Amazon CloudWatch alarms for high-performance usage (which may indicate anomalies in the database behavior).
- Enable AWS CloudTrail for any database, to log any activity performed on the database by any user, role, or AWS service.
- Limit access to the CloudTrail logs to the minimum number of employees – preferably in an AWS management account, outside the scope of your end users (including outside the scope of your database administrators), to avoid possible deletion or changes to the audit logs.

For more information, please refer the following resources:

Using Amazon RDS event notifications:

```
https://docs.aws.amazon.com/AmazonRDS/latest/UserGuide/USER_
Events.html
```

Working with AWS CloudTrail and Amazon RDS:

```
https://docs.aws.amazon.com/AmazonRDS/latest/UserGuide/
logging-using-cloudtrail.html
```

Summary

In this section, we have learned how to securely maintain a managed MySQL database, based on AWS infrastructure – from logging in, to securing network access, to data encryption (in transit and at rest), and logging and auditing.

Securing Azure Database for MySQL

Azure Database for MySQL is the Azure-managed MySQL service.

Best practices for configuring IAM for a managed MySQL database service

MySQL supports the following types of authentication methods:

- Local username/password authentication against the MySQL built-in authentication mechanism
- Azure AD authentication

The best practices are as follows:

- For the local MySQL master user, create a strong and complex password (at least 15 characters, made up of lowercase and uppercase letters, numbers, and special characters), and keep the password in a secured location.
- For end users who need direct access to the managed database, the preferred method is to use Azure AD authentication, since it allows you to centrally manage all user identities, control their password policy, conduct an audit on their actions (that is, *API calls*), and, in the case of a suspicious security incident, disable the user identity.

For more information, please refer the following resources:

Use Azure AD for authenticating with MySQL:

```
https://docs.microsoft.com/en-us/azure/mysql/concepts-azure-
ad-authentication
```

Use Azure AD for authentication with MySQL:

```
https://docs.microsoft.com/en-us/azure/mysql/howto-configure-
sign-in-azure-ad-authentication
```

Best practices for securing network access to a managed MySQL database service

Access to a managed MySQL database service is controlled via *firewall rules*, which allows you to configure which IP addresses (or CIDR) are allowed to access your managed MySQL database.

The best practices are as follows:

- Managed databases must never be accessible from the internet or a publicly accessible subnet – always use private subnets to deploy your databases.
- Configure the start IP and end IP of your web or application servers, to limit access to your managed database.
- If you need to manage the MySQL database service, either use an Azure VM (or bastion host) to manage the MySQL database remotely or create a VPN tunnel from your remote machine to the managed MySQL database.
- Since Azure Database for MySQL is a managed service, it is located outside the customer's **virtual network** (**VNet**). An alternative to secure access from your VNet to Azure Database for MySQL is to use a VNet service endpoint, which avoids sending network traffic outside your VNet, through a secure channel.

For more information, please refer the following resources:

Azure Database for MySQL server firewall rules:

```
https://docs.microsoft.com/en-us/azure/mysql/concepts-
firewall-rules
```

Use VNet service endpoints and rules for Azure Database for MySQL:

```
https://docs.microsoft.com/en-us/azure/mysql/concepts-data-
access-and-security-vnet
```

Best practices for protecting data stored in a managed MySQL database service

A database is meant to store data.

In many cases, a database (and, in this case, a managed MySQL database) may contain sensitive customer data (from a retail store containing customers' data to an organization's sensitive HR data).

To protect customers' data, it is recommended to encrypt data both in transport (when the data passes through the network), to avoid detection by an external party, and at rest (data stored inside a database), to avoid data being revealed, even by an internal database administrator.

Encryption allows you to maintain data confidentiality and data integrity (make sure your data is not changed by an untrusted party).

The best practices are as follows:

- Enable TLS 1.2 transport layer encryption to your database.

- For sensitive environments, encrypt data at rest using customer-managed keys stored inside the Azure Key Vault service (as explained in *Chapter 7, Applying Encryption in Cloud Services*).

- Keep your customer-managed keys in a secured location for backup purposes.

- Enable the *soft delete* and *purge protection* features on Azure Key Vault to avoid accidental key deletion (which will harm your ability to access your encrypted data).

- Enable auditing on all activities related to encryption keys.

For more information, please refer the following resources:

Azure Database for MySQL data encryption with a customer-managed key:

```
https://docs.microsoft.com/en-us/azure/mysql/concepts-data-
encryption-mysql
```

Azure security baseline for Azure Database for MySQL:

```
https://docs.microsoft.com/en-us/security/benchmark/azure/
baselines/mysql-security-baseline
```

Best practices for conducting auditing and monitoring for a managed MySQL database service

Auditing is a crucial part of data protection.

As with any other managed service, Azure allows you to enable logging and auditing using two built-in services:

- Built-in Azure Database for MySQL audit logs
- Azure Monitor logs

The best practices are as follows:

- Enable audit logs for MySQL.
- Use the Azure Monitor service to detect failed connections.
- Limit access to the Azure Monitor service data to the minimum number of employees to avoid possible deletion or changes to the audit logs.
- Use Advanced Threat Protection for Azure Database for MySQL to detect anomalies or unusual activity in the MySQL database.

For more information, please refer the following resources:

Audit logs in Azure Database for MySQL:

```
https://docs.microsoft.com/en-us/azure/mysql/concepts-audit-
logs
```

Configure and access audit logs for Azure Database for MySQL in the Azure portal:

```
https://docs.microsoft.com/en-us/azure/mysql/howto-configure-
audit-logs-portal
```

Best practices for alerting on metrics with Azure Database for MySQL monitoring:

```
https://azure.microsoft.com/en-us/blog/best-practices-for-
alerting-on-metrics-with-azure-database-for-mysql-monitoring/
```

Security considerations for monitoring data:

```
https://docs.microsoft.com/en-us/azure/azure-monitor/roles-
permissions-security#security-considerations-for-monitoring-
data
```

Summary

In this section, we have learned how to securely maintain a managed MySQL database, based on Azure infrastructure – from logging in, to securing network access, to data encryption (in transit and at rest), and logging and auditing.

Securing Google Cloud SQL for MySQL

Google Cloud SQL for MySQL is the Google-managed MySQL service.

Best practices for configuring IAM for a managed MySQL database service

MySQL supports the following types of authentication methods:

- Local username/password authentication against the MySQL built-in authentication mechanism
- Google Cloud IAM authentication

The best practices are as follows:

- For the local MySQL master user, create a strong and complex password (at least 15 characters, made up of lowercase and uppercase letters, numbers, and special characters), and keep the password in a secured location.
- For end users who need direct access to the managed database, the preferred method is to use Google Cloud IAM authentication, since it allows you to centrally manage all user identities, control their password policy, conduct an audit on their actions (that is, *API calls*), and, in the case of a suspicious security incident, disable the user identity.

For more information, please refer the following resources:

Creating and managing MySQL users:

`https://cloud.google.com/sql/docs/mysql/create-manage-users`

MySQL users:

`https://cloud.google.com/sql/docs/mysql/users`

Roles and permissions in Cloud SQL:

`https://cloud.google.com/sql/docs/mysql/roles-and-permissions`

Best practices for securing network access to a managed MySQL database service

Access to a managed MySQL database service is controlled via one of the following options:

- Authorized networks: Allows you to configure which IP addresses (or CIDR) are allowed to access your managed MySQL database
- Cloud SQL Auth proxy: Client installed on your application side, which handles authentication to the Cloud SQL for MySQL database in a secure and encrypted tunnel

The best practices are as follows:

- Managed databases must never be accessible from the internet or a publicly accessible subnet – always use private subnets to deploy your databases.
- If possible, the preferred option is to use the Cloud SQL Auth proxy.
- Configure authorized networks for your web or application servers to allow them access to your Cloud SQL for MySQL.
- If you need to manage the MySQL database service, use either a GCE VM instance to manage the MySQL database remotely or a Cloud VPN (configures an IPSec tunnel to a VPN gateway device).

For more information, please refer the following resources:

Authorizing with authorized networks:

`https://cloud.google.com/sql/docs/mysql/authorize-networks`

Connecting using the Cloud SQL Auth proxy:

`https://cloud.google.com/sql/docs/mysql/connect-admin-proxy`

Cloud VPN overview:

`https://cloud.google.com/network-connectivity/docs/vpn/concepts/overview`

Best practices for protecting data stored in a managed MySQL database service

A database is meant to store data.

In many cases, a database (and, in this case, a managed MySQL database) may contain sensitive customer data (from a retail store containing customer data to an organization's sensitive HR data).

To protect customers' data, it is recommended to encrypt data both in transport (when the data passes through the network), to avoid detection by an external party, and at rest (data stored inside a database), to avoid data being revealed, even by an internal database administrator.

Encryption allows you to maintain data confidentiality and data integrity (make sure your data is not changed by an untrusted party).

The best practices are as follows:

- Enforce TLS 1.2 transport layer encryption on your database.

- For sensitive environments, encrypt data at rest using **customer-managed encryption keys** (**CMEKs**) stored inside the Google Cloud KMS service (as explained in *Chapter 7, Applying Encryption in Cloud Services*).

- When using CMEKs, create a dedicated service account, and grant permission to the customers to access the encryption keys inside Google Cloud KMS.

- Enable auditing on all activities related to encryption keys.

For more information, please refer the following resources:

Configuring SSL/TLS certificates:

```
https://cloud.google.com/sql/docs/mysql/configure-ssl-
instance#enforce-ssl
```

Client-side encryption:

```
https://cloud.google.com/sql/docs/mysql/client-side-encryption
```

Overview of CMEKs:

```
https://cloud.google.com/sql/docs/mysql/cmek
```

Using CMEKs:

```
https://cloud.google.com/sql/docs/mysql/configure-cmek
```

Best practices for conducting auditing and monitoring for a managed MySQL database service

Auditing is a crucial part of data protection.

As with any other managed service, GCP allows you to enable logging and auditing using Google Cloud Audit Logs.

The best practices are as follows:

- Admin activity audit logs are enabled by default and cannot be disabled.
- Explicitly enable **data access audit logs** to log activities performed on the database.
- Limit the access to audit logs to the minimum number of employees to avoid possible deletion or changes to the audit logs.

For more information, please refer the following resources:

Audit logs:

`https://cloud.google.com/sql/docs/mysql/audit-logging`

Cloud Audit Logs:

`https://cloud.google.com/logging/docs/audit`

Configuring data access audit logs:

`https://cloud.google.com/logging/docs/audit/configure-data-access`

Permissions and roles:

`https://cloud.google.com/logging/docs/access-control#permissions_and_roles`

Summary

In this section, we have learned how to securely maintain a managed MySQL database, based on GCP infrastructure – from logging in, to securing network access, to data encryption (in transit and at rest), and logging and auditing.

Securing containers

Following VMs, the next evolution in the compute era is containers.

Containers behave like VMs, but with a much smaller footprint.

Instead of having to deploy an application above an entire operating system, you could use containers to deploy your required application, with only the minimum required operating system libraries and binaries.

Containers have the following benefits over VMs:

- **Small footprint**: Only required libraries and binaries are stored inside a container.

- **Portability**: You can develop an application inside a container on your laptop and run it at a large scale in a production environment with hundreds or thousands of container instances.

- Fast deployment and updates compared to VMs.

The following diagram presents the architectural differences between VMs and containers:

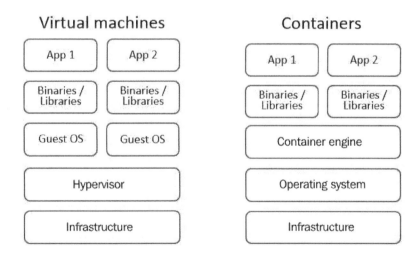

Figure 2.1 – VMs versus containers

If you are still in the development phase, you can install a container engine on your laptop and create a new container (or download an existing container) locally, until you complete the development phase.

When you move to production and have a requirement to run hundreds of container instances, you need an orchestrator – a mechanism (or a managed service) for managing container deployment, health check monitoring, container recycling, and more.

Docker was adopted by the industry as a de facto standard for wrapping containers, and in the past couple of years, more and more cloud vendors have begun to support a new initiative for wrapping containers called the **Open Container Initiative (OCI)**.

Kubernetes is an open source project (developed initially by Google) and is now considered the industry de facto standard for orchestrating, deploying, scaling, and managing containers.

In this section, I will present the most common container orchestrators available as managed services.

For more information, please refer the following resources:

What is a container?

```
https://www.docker.com/resources/what-container
```

Open Container Initiative:

```
https://opencontainers.org/
```

OCI artifact support in Amazon ECR:

```
https://aws.amazon.com/blogs/containers/oci-artifact-support-
in-amazon-ecr/
```

Azure and OCI images:

```
https://docs.microsoft.com/en-us/azure/container-registry/
container-registry-image-formats#oci-images
```

GCP and OCI image format:

```
https://cloud.google.com/artifact-registry/docs/supported-
formats#oci
```

The Kubernetes project:

```
https://kubernetes.io/
```

Next, we are going to see what the best practices are for securing common container and Kubernetes services from AWS, Azure, and GCP.

Securing Amazon Elastic Container Service (ECS)

ECS is the Amazon-managed container orchestration service.

It can integrate with other AWS services such as Amazon **Elastic Container Registry (ECR)** for storing containers, AWS IAM for managing permissions to ECS, and Amazon CloudWatch for monitoring ECS.

Best practices for configuring IAM for Amazon ECS

AWS IAM is the supported service for managing permissions to access and run containers through Amazon ECS.

The best practices are as follows:

- Grant minimal IAM permissions for the Amazon ECS service (for running tasks, accessing S3 buckets, monitoring using CloudWatch Events, and so on).

- If you are managing multiple AWS accounts, use temporary credentials (using AWS Security Token Service or the *AssumeRole* capability) to manage ECS on the target AWS account with credentials from a source AWS account.

- Use service roles to allow the ECS service to assume your role and access resources such as S3 buckets, RDS databases, and so on.

- Use IAM roles to control access to Amazon **Elastic File System** (**EFS**) from ECS.

- Enforce **multi-factor authentication** (**MFA**) for end users who have access to the AWS console and perform privileged actions such as managing the ECS service.

- Enforce policy conditions such as requiring end users to connect to the ECS service using a secured channel (SSL/TLS), connecting using MFA, log in at specific hours of the day, and so on.

- Store your container images inside Amazon ECR and grant minimal IAM permissions for accessing and managing Amazon ECR.

For more information, please refer the following resources:

Amazon ECS container instance IAM role:

```
https://docs.aws.amazon.com/AmazonECS/latest/developerguide/
instance_IAM_role.html
```

IAM roles for tasks:

```
https://docs.aws.amazon.com/AmazonECS/latest/developerguide/
task-iam-roles.html
```

Authorization based on Amazon ECS tags:

```
https://docs.aws.amazon.com/AmazonECS/latest/userguide/
security_iam_service-with-iam.html#security_iam_service-with-
iam-tags
```

Using IAM to control filesystem data access:

```
https://docs.aws.amazon.com/efs/latest/ug/iam-access-control-
nfs-efs.html
```

Amazon ECS task and container security:

```
https://docs.aws.amazon.com/AmazonECS/latest/
bestpracticesguide/security-tasks-containers.html
```

Best practices for securing network access to Amazon ECS

Since Amazon ECS is a managed service, it is located outside the customer's VPC. An alternative to secure access from your VPC to the managed ECS environment is to use AWS PrivateLink, which avoids sending network traffic outside your VPC, through a secure channel, using an interface VPC endpoint.

The best practices are as follows:

- Use a secured channel (TLS 1.2) to control Amazon ECS using API calls.
- Use VPC security groups to allow access from your VPC to the Amazon ECS VPC endpoint.
- If you use AWS Secrets Manager to store sensitive data (such as credentials) from Amazon ECS, use a Secrets Manager VPC endpoint when configuring security groups.
- If you use AWS Systems Manager to remotely execute commands on Amazon ECS, use Systems Manager VPC endpoints when configuring security groups.
- Store your container images inside Amazon ECR and for non-sensitive environments, encrypt your container images inside Amazon ECR using AWS KMS (as explained in *Chapter 7, Applying Encryption in Cloud Services*).
- For sensitive environments, encrypt your container images inside Amazon ECR using CMK management (as explained in *Chapter 7, Applying Encryption in Cloud Services*).
- If you use Amazon ECR to store your container images, use VPC security groups to allow access from your VPC to the Amazon ECR interface's VPC endpoint.

For more information, please refer the following resource:

Amazon ECS interface VPC endpoints (AWS PrivateLink):

```
https://docs.aws.amazon.com/AmazonECS/latest/developerguide/
vpc-endpoints.html
```

Best practices for conducting auditing and monitoring in Amazon ECS

Auditing is a crucial part of data protection.

As with any other managed service, AWS allows you to enable logging and auditing using two built-in services:

- **Amazon CloudWatch**: A service that allows you to log containers' activities and raise an alarm according to predefined thresholds (for example, low memory resources or high CPU, which requires up-scaling your ECS cluster)
- **AWS CloudTrail**: A service that allows you to monitor API activities (basically, any action performed on the ECS cluster)

The best practices are as follows:

- Enable Amazon CloudWatch alarms for high-performance usage (which may indicate an anomaly in the ECS cluster behavior).
- Enable AWS CloudTrail for any action performed on the ECS cluster.
- Limit the access to the CloudTrail logs to the minimum number of employees – preferably in an AWS management account, outside the scope of your end users (including outside the scope of your ECS cluster administrators), to avoid possible deletion or changes to the audit logs.

For more information, please refer the following resources:

Logging and monitoring in Amazon ECS:

```
https://docs.aws.amazon.com/AmazonECS/latest/developerguide/
ecs-logging-monitoring.html
```

Logging Amazon ECS API calls with AWS CloudTrail:

```
https://docs.aws.amazon.com/AmazonECS/latest/developerguide/
logging-using-cloudtrail.html
```

Best practices for enabling compliance on Amazon ECS

Security configuration is a crucial part of your infrastructure.

Amazon allows you to conduct ongoing compliance checks against well-known security standards (such as the Center for Internet Security Benchmarks).

The best practices are as follows:

- Use only trusted image containers and store them inside Amazon ECR – a private repository for storing your organizational images.
- Run the *Docker Bench for Security* tool on a regular basis to check for compliance with CIS Benchmarks for Docker containers.
- Build your container images from scratch (to avoid malicious code in preconfigured third-party images).
- Scan your container images for vulnerabilities in libraries and binaries and update your images on a regular basis.
- Configure your images with a read-only root filesystem to avoid unintended upload of malicious code into your images.

For more information, please refer the following resources:

Docker Bench for Security:

```
https://github.com/docker/docker-bench-security
```

Amazon ECR private repositories:

```
https://docs.aws.amazon.com/AmazonECR/latest/userguide/
Repositories.html
```

Summary

In this section, we have learned how to securely maintain Amazon ECS, based on AWS infrastructure – from logging in, to securing network access, to logging and auditing, and security compliance.

Securing Amazon Elastic Kubernetes Service (EKS)

EKS is the Amazon-managed Kubernetes orchestration service.

It can integrate with other AWS services, such as Amazon ECR for storing containers, AWS IAM for managing permissions to EKS, and Amazon CloudWatch for monitoring EKS.

Best practices for configuring IAM for Amazon EKS

AWS IAM is the supported service for managing permissions to access and run containers through Amazon EKS.

The best practices are as follows:

- Grant minimal IAM permissions for accessing and managing Amazon EKS.

- If you are managing multiple AWS accounts, use temporary credentials (using AWS Security Token Service or the *AssumeRole* capability) to manage EKS on the target AWS account with credentials from a source AWS account.

- Use service roles to allow the EKS service to assume your role and access resources such as S3 buckets and RDS databases.

- For authentication purposes, avoid using service account tokens.

- Create an IAM role for each newly created EKS cluster.

- Create a service account for each newly created application.

- Always run applications using a non-root user.

- Use IAM roles to control access to storage services (such as Amazon EBS, Amazon EFS, and Amazon FSx for Lustre) from EKS.

- Enforce MFA for end users who have access to the AWS console and perform privileged actions such as managing the EKS service.

- Store your container images inside Amazon ECR and grant minimal IAM permissions for accessing and managing Amazon ECR.

For more information, please refer the following resources:

How Amazon EKS works with IAM:

```
https://docs.aws.amazon.com/eks/latest/userguide/security_iam_
service-with-iam.html
```

IAM roles for service accounts:

```
https://docs.aws.amazon.com/eks/latest/userguide/iam-roles-
for-service-accounts.html
```

IAM:

```
https://aws.github.io/aws-eks-best-practices/security/docs/
iam/
```

Best practices for securing network access to Amazon EKS

Since Amazon EKS is a managed service, it is located outside the customer's VPC. An alternative to secure access from your VPC to the managed EKS environment is to use AWS PrivateLink, which avoids sending network traffic outside your VPC, through a secure channel, using an interface VPC endpoint.

The best practices are as follows:

- Use TLS 1.2 to control Amazon EKS using API calls.
- Use TLS 1.2 when configuring Amazon EKS behind AWS Application Load Balancer or AWS Network Load Balancer.
- Use TLS 1.2 between your EKS control plane and the EKS cluster's worker nodes.
- Use VPC security groups to allow access from your VPC to the Amazon EKS VPC endpoint.
- Use VPC security groups between your EKS control plane and the EKS cluster's worker nodes.
- Use VPC security groups to protect access to your EKS Pods.
- Disable public access to your EKS API server – either use an EC2 instance (or bastion host) to manage the EKS cluster remotely or create a VPN tunnel from your remote machine to your EKS cluster.
- If you use AWS Secrets Manager to store sensitive data (such as credentials) from Amazon EKS, use a Secrets Manager VPC endpoint when configuring security groups.
- Store your container images inside Amazon ECR, and for non-sensitive environments, encrypt your container images inside Amazon ECR using AWS KMS (as explained in *Chapter 7, Applying Encryption in Cloud Services*).
- For sensitive environments, encrypt your container images inside Amazon ECR using CMK management (as explained in *Chapter 7, Applying Encryption in Cloud Services*).
- If you use Amazon ECR to store your container images, use VPC security groups to allow access from your VPC to the Amazon ECR interface VPC endpoint.

For more information, please refer the following resources:

Network security:

```
https://aws.github.io/aws-eks-best-practices/security/docs/
network
```

Amazon EKS networking:

```
https://docs.aws.amazon.com/eks/latest/userguide/
eks-networking.html
```

Introducing security groups for Pods:

```
https://aws.amazon.com/blogs/containers/introducing-security-
groups-for-pods/
```

EKS best practice guides:

```
https://aws.github.io/aws-eks-best-practices/
```

Best practices for conducting auditing and monitoring in Amazon EKS

Auditing is a crucial part of data protection.

As with any other managed service, AWS allows you to enable logging and auditing using two built-in services:

- **Amazon CloudWatch**: A service that allows you to log EKS cluster activities and raise an alarm according to predefined thresholds (for example, low memory resources or high CPU, which requires up-scaling your EKS cluster).

- **AWS CloudTrail**: A service that allows you to monitor API activities (basically, any action performed on the EKS cluster).

The best practices are as follows:

- Enable the Amazon EKS control plane when logging in to Amazon CloudWatch – this allows you to log API calls, audit, and authentication information from your EKS cluster.

- Enable AWS CloudTrail for any action performed on the EKS cluster.

- Limit the access to the CloudTrail logs to the minimum number of employees – preferably in an AWS management account, outside the scope of your end users (including outside the scope of your EKS cluster administrators), to avoid possible deletion or changes to the audit logs.

For more information, please refer the following resources:

Amazon EKS control plane logging:

```
https://docs.aws.amazon.com/eks/latest/userguide/control-
plane-logs.html
```

Auditing and logging:

```
https://aws.github.io/aws-eks-best-practices/security/docs/
detective/
```

Best practices for enabling compliance on Amazon EKS

Security configuration is a crucial part of your infrastructure.

Amazon allows you to conduct ongoing compliance checks against well-known security standards (such as CIS Benchmarks).

The best practices are as follows:

- Use only trusted image containers and store them inside Amazon ECR – a private repository for storing your organizational images.
- Run the `kube-bench` tool on a regular basis to check for compliance with CIS Benchmarks for Kubernetes.
- Run the *Docker Bench for Security* tool on a regular basis to check for compliance with CIS Benchmarks for Docker containers.
- Build your container images from scratch (to avoid malicious code in preconfigured third-party images).
- Scan your container images for vulnerabilities in libraries and binaries and update your images on a regular basis.
- Configure your images with a read-only root filesystem to avoid unintended upload of malicious code into your images.

For more information, please refer the following resources:

Configuration and vulnerability analysis in Amazon EKS:

```
https://docs.aws.amazon.com/eks/latest/userguide/
configuration-vulnerability-analysis.html
```

Introducing the CIS Amazon EKS Benchmark:

```
https://aws.amazon.com/blogs/containers/introducing-cis-
amazon-eks-benchmark/
```

Compliance:

```
https://aws.github.io/aws-eks-best-practices/security/docs/
compliance/
```

Image security:

```
https://aws.github.io/aws-eks-best-practices/security/docs/
image/
```

Pod security:

```
https://aws.github.io/aws-eks-best-practices/security/docs/
pods/
```

```
kube-bench:
```

```
https://github.com/aquasecurity/kube-bench
```

Docker Bench for Security:

```
https://github.com/docker/docker-bench-security
```

Amazon ECR private repositories:

```
https://docs.aws.amazon.com/AmazonECR/latest/userguide/
Repositories.html
```

Summary

In this section, we have learned how to securely maintain Amazon EKS, based on AWS infrastructure – from logging in, to securing network access, to logging and auditing, and security compliance.

Securing Azure Container Instances (ACI)

ACI is the Azure-managed container orchestration service.

It can integrate with other Azure services, such as **Azure Container Registry** (**ACR**) for storing containers, Azure AD for managing permissions to ACI, Azure Files for persistent storage, and Azure Monitor.

Best practices for configuring IAM for ACI

Although ACI does not have its own authentication mechanism, it is recommended to use ACR to store your container images in a private registry.

ACR supports the following authentication methods:

- **Managed identity**: A user or system account from Azure AD
- **Service principal**: An application, service, or platform that needs access to ACR

The best practices are as follows:

- Grant minimal permissions for accessing and managing ACR, using Azure RBAC.
- When passing sensitive information (such as credential secrets), make sure the traffic is encrypted in transit through a secure channel (TLS).
- If you need to store sensitive information (such as credentials), store it inside the Azure Key Vault service.
- For sensitive environments, encrypt information (such as credentials) using *customer-managed keys*, stored inside the Azure Key Vault service.
- Disable the ACR built-in admin user.

For more information, please refer the following resources:

Authenticate with ACR:

```
https://docs.microsoft.com/en-us/azure/container-registry/
container-registry-authentication
```

ACR roles and permissions:

```
https://docs.microsoft.com/en-us/azure/container-registry/
container-registry-roles
```

Encrypt a registry using a customer-managed key:

```
https://docs.microsoft.com/en-us/azure/container-registry/
container-registry-customer-managed-keys
```

Best practices for conducting auditing and monitoring in ACI

Auditing is a crucial part of data protection.

As with any other managed service, Azure allows you to enable logging and auditing using Azure Monitor for containers – a service that allows you to log container-related activities and raise an alarm according to predefined thresholds (for example, low memory resources or high CPU, which requires up-scaling your container environment).

The best practices are as follows:

- Enable audit logging for Azure resources, using Azure Monitor, to log authentication-related activities of your ACR.

- Limit the access to the Azure Monitor logs to the minimum number of employees to avoid possible deletion or changes to the audit logs.

For more information, please refer the following resources:

Container insights overview:

```
https://docs.microsoft.com/en-us/azure/azure-monitor/
containers/container-insights-overview
```

Container monitoring solution in Azure Monitor:

```
https://docs.microsoft.com/en-us/azure/azure-monitor/
containers/containers
```

Best practices for enabling compliance on ACI

Security configuration is a crucial part of your infrastructure.

Azure allows you to conduct ongoing compliance checks against well-known security standards (such as CIS Benchmarks).

The best practices are as follows:

- Use only trusted image containers and store them inside ACR – a private repository for storing your organizational images.

- Integrate ACR with Azure Security Center, to detect non-compliant images (from the CIS standard).

- Build your container images from scratch (to avoid malicious code in preconfigured third-party images).

- Scan your container images for vulnerabilities in libraries and binaries and update your images on a regular basis.

For more information, please refer the following resources:

Azure security baseline for ACI:

```
https://docs.microsoft.com/en-us/security/benchmark/azure/
baselines/container-instances-security-baseline
```

Azure security baseline for ACR:

```
https://docs.microsoft.com/en-us/security/benchmark/azure/
baselines/container-registry-security-baseline
```

Security considerations for ACI:

```
https://docs.microsoft.com/en-us/azure/container-instances/
container-instances-image-security
```

Introduction to private Docker container registries in Azure:

```
https://docs.microsoft.com/en-us/azure/container-registry/
container-registry-intro
```

Summary

In this section, we have learned how to securely maintain ACI, based on Azure infrastructure – from logging in to auditing and monitoring and security compliance.

Securing Azure Kubernetes Service (AKS)

AKS is the Azure-managed Kubernetes orchestration service.

It can integrate with other Azure services, such as ACR for storing containers, Azure AD for managing permissions to AKS, Azure Files for persistent storage, and Azure Monitor.

Best practices for configuring IAM for Azure AKS

Azure AD is the supported service for managing permissions to access and run containers through Azure AKS.

The best practices are as follows:

- Enable Azure AD integration for any newly created AKS cluster.
- Grant minimal permissions for accessing and managing AKS, using Azure RBAC.
- Grant minimal permissions for accessing and managing ACR, using Azure RBAC.
- Create a unique service principal for each newly created AKS cluster.

- When passing sensitive information (such as credential secrets), make sure the traffic is encrypted in transit through a secure channel (TLS).

- If you need to store sensitive information (such as credentials), store it inside the Azure Key Vault service.

- For sensitive environments, encrypt information (such as credentials) using *customer-managed keys*, stored inside the Azure Key Vault service.

For more information, please refer the following resources:

AKS-managed Azure AD integration:

`https://docs.microsoft.com/en-us/azure/aks/managed-aad`

Best practices for authentication and authorization in AKS:

`https://docs.microsoft.com/en-us/azure/aks/operator-best-practices-identity`

Best practices for securing network access to Azure AKS

Azure AKS exposes services to the internet – for that reason, it is important to plan before deploying each Azure AKS cluster.

The best practices are as follows:

- Avoid exposing the AKS cluster control plane (API server) to the public internet – create a private cluster with an internal IP address and use authorized IP ranges to define which IPs can access your API server.

- Use the Azure Firewall service to restrict outbound traffic from AKS cluster nodes to external DNS addresses (for example, software updates from external sources).

- Use TLS 1.2 to control Azure AKS using API calls.

- Use TLS 1.2 when configuring Azure AKS behind Azure Load Balancer.

- Use TLS 1.2 between your AKS control plane and the AKS cluster's nodes.

- For small AKS deployments, use the `kubenet` plugin to implement network policies and protect the AKS cluster.

- For large production deployments, use the Azure CNI Kubernetes plugin to implement network policies and protect the AKS cluster.

- Use Azure network security groups to block SSH traffic to the AKS cluster nodes, from the AKS subnets only.

- Use network policies to protect the access between the Kubernetes Pods.

- Disable public access to your AKS API server – either use an Azure VM (or Azure Bastion) to manage the AKS cluster remotely or create a VPN tunnel from your remote machine to your AKS cluster.

- Disable or remove the HTTP application routing add-on.

- If you need to store sensitive information (such as credentials), store it inside the Azure Key Vault service.

- For sensitive environments, encrypt information (such as credentials) using *customer-managed keys*, stored inside the Azure Key Vault service.

For more information, please refer the following resources:

Best practices for network connectivity and security in AKS:

```
https://docs.microsoft.com/en-us/azure/aks/operator-best-
practices-network
```

Best practices for cluster isolation in AKS:

```
https://docs.microsoft.com/en-us/azure/aks/operator-best-
practices-cluster-isolation
```

Create a private AKS cluster:

```
https://docs.microsoft.com/en-us/azure/aks/private-clusters
```

Best practices for conducting auditing and monitoring in Azure AKS

Auditing is a crucial part of data protection.

As with any other managed service, Azure allows you to enable logging and auditing using Azure Monitor for containers – a service that allows you to log container-related activities and raise an alarm according to predefined thresholds (for example, low memory resources or high CPU, which requires up-scaling your container environment).

The best practices are as follows:

- Enable audit logging for Azure resources, using Azure Monitor, to log authentication-related activities of your ACR.

- Limit the access to the Azure Monitor logs to the minimum number of employees to avoid possible deletion or changes to the audit logs.

For more information, please refer the following resources:

ACI overview:

```
https://docs.microsoft.com/en-us/azure/azure-monitor/
containers/container-insights-overview
```

Container monitoring solution in Azure Monitor:

```
https://docs.microsoft.com/en-us/azure/azure-monitor/
containers/containers
```

Best practices for enabling compliance on Azure AKS

Security configuration is a crucial part of your infrastructure.

Azure allows you to conduct ongoing compliance checks against well-known security standards (such as CIS Benchmarks).

The best practices are as follows:

- Use only trusted image containers and store them inside ACR – a private repository for storing your organizational images.
- Use Azure Defender for Kubernetes to protect Kubernetes clusters from vulnerabilities.
- Use Azure Defender for container registries to detect and remediate vulnerabilities in container images.
- Integrated Azure Container Registry with Azure Security Center to detect non-compliant images (from the CIS standard).
- Build your container images from scratch (to avoid malicious code in preconfigured third-party images).
- Scan your container images for vulnerabilities in libraries and binaries and update your images on a regular basis.

For more information, please refer the following resources:

Introduction to Azure Defender for Kubernetes:

```
https://docs.microsoft.com/en-us/azure/security-center/
defender-for-kubernetes-introduction
```

Use Azure Defender for container registries to scan your images for vulnerabilities:

`https://docs.microsoft.com/en-us/azure/security-center/`
`defender-for-container-registries-usage`

Azure security baseline for ACI:

`https://docs.microsoft.com/en-us/security/benchmark/azure/`
`baselines/container-instances-security-baseline`

Azure security baseline for ACR:

`https://docs.microsoft.com/en-us/security/benchmark/azure/`
`baselines/container-registry-security-baseline`

Security considerations for ACI:

`https://docs.microsoft.com/en-us/azure/container-instances/`
`container-instances-image-security`

Introduction to private Docker container registries in Azure:

`https://docs.microsoft.com/en-us/azure/container-registry/`
`container-registry-intro`

Summary

In this section, we have learned how to securely maintain AKS, based on Azure infrastructure – from logging in, to network access, to auditing and monitoring, and security compliance.

Securing Google Kubernetes Engine (GKE)

GKE is the Google-managed Kubernetes orchestration service.

It can integrate with other GCP services, such as Google Container Registry for storing containers, Google Cloud IAM for managing permissions to GKE, Google Filestore for persistent storage, and Google Cloud operations for monitoring.

Best practices for configuring IAM for GKE

Google Cloud IAM is the supported service for managing permissions to access and run containers through GKE.

The best practices are as follows:

- Grant minimal permissions for accessing and managing the Google Cloud IAM service, using Kubernetes RBAC.
- Use Google Groups to manage permissions to your GKE cluster.
- Use the Google IAM recommender to set the minimal permissions for your GKE cluster.
- Create a unique service account with minimal permissions for any newly created GKE cluster.
- Enforce the use of MFA for any user who needs access to manage your GKE cluster.
- If you need to store sensitive information (such as credentials), store it inside the Google Cloud KMS service.
- For sensitive environments, encrypt information (such as credentials) using CMEKs stored inside the Google Cloud KMS service.

For more information, please refer the following resources:

Creating IAM policies:

`https://cloud.google.com/kubernetes-engine/docs/how-to/iam`

Configuring RBAC:

`https://cloud.google.com/kubernetes-engine/docs/how-to/role-based-access-control`

Enforce least privilege with recommendations:

`https://cloud.google.com/iam/docs/recommender-overview`

Use least privilege Google service accounts:

`https://cloud.google.com/kubernetes-engine/docs/how-to/hardening-your-cluster#permissions`

Secret management:

`https://cloud.google.com/kubernetes-engine/docs/how-to/hardening-your-cluster#secret_management`

Best practices for securing network access to GKE

GKE exposes services to the internet – for that reason, it is important to plan before deploying each GKE cluster.

The best practices are as follows:

- Create private GKE clusters to avoid exposing the GKE cluster control plane (API server) to the public internet – use alias IP ranges to configure which IPs can access your GKE cluster.

- Use authorized networks to configure who can access your GKE cluster control plane.

- Use VPC-native networking to protect the access between the Kubernetes Pods.

- Use network policies for Kubernetes to protect the access between the Kubernetes Pods.

- Use shielded GKE nodes as an additional layer of protection to your GKE cluster nodes.

- Create separate namespaces for your applications, according to RBAC requirements.

- Enable a GKE sandbox to achieve better isolation of your GKE cluster Pods.

- Use TLS 1.2 to control your GKE cluster using API calls.

- Use TLS 1.2 between your GKE control plane and the GKE cluster's nodes.

- Use TLS 1.2 when configuring the GKE cluster behind Google Load Balancer.

- Disable public access to your GKE cluster API server – use a Google VM (or a Bastion host) to manage the GKE cluster remotely.

For more information, please refer the following resources:

Creating a private cluster:

```
https://cloud.google.com/kubernetes-engine/docs/how-to/
private-clusters
```

Restrict network access to the control plane and nodes:

```
https://cloud.google.com/kubernetes-engine/docs/how-to/
hardening-your-cluster#restrict_network_access_to_the_control_
plane_and_nodes
```

Restrict traffic among Pods with a network policy:

```
https://cloud.google.com/kubernetes-engine/docs/how-to/
hardening-your-cluster#restrict_with_network_policy
```

Network security:

```
https://cloud.google.com/kubernetes-engine/docs/concepts/
security-overview#network_security
```

Harden workload isolation with a GKE sandbox:

```
https://cloud.google.com/kubernetes-engine/docs/how-to/
sandbox-pods
```

Best practices for conducting auditing and monitoring in GKE

Auditing is a crucial part of data protection.

As with any other managed service, Google allows you to enable logging and auditing using the Google Cloud Logging service – a service that allows you to audit container-related activities.

The best practices are as follows:

- Enable logging for any newly created GKE cluster and integrate the item with the Google Cloud Logging service, to log all audit activities related to your GKE cluster.

- When using a *container-optimized operating system* image, make sure you send its Linux audit logs to the Google Cloud Logging service.

- Limit the access to the Google Cloud Logging service logs to the minimum number of employees to avoid possible deletion or changes to the audit logs.

For more information, please refer the following resources:

Audit policy:

```
https://cloud.google.com/kubernetes-engine/docs/concepts/
audit-policy
```

Overview of Google Cloud's operations suite for GKE:

```
https://cloud.google.com/stackdriver/docs/solutions/gke
```

Remediating security health analytics findings:

```
https://cloud.google.com/security-command-center/docs/how-to-
remediate-security-health-analytics-findings#container_
vulnerability_findings
```

Best practices for enabling compliance in GKE

Security configuration is a crucial part of your infrastructure.

Google allows you to conduct ongoing compliance checks against well-known security standards (such as CIS Benchmarks).

The best practices are as follows:

- Use only trusted image containers and store them inside Google Container Registry – a private repository for storing your organizational images.

- Always use the latest build of Kubernetes on both your GKE cluster and cluster nodes.

- Use the GKE auditor to detect GKE misconfigurations.

- Use container-optimized operating systems when creating new container images, for better security.

- Build your container images from scratch (to avoid malicious code in preconfigured third-party images).

- Scan your container images for vulnerabilities in libraries and binaries and update your images on a regular basis.

- Use Google Binary Authorization to make sure you use only signed container images from trusted authorities.

- Use container threat detection to detect attacks against your container images in real time.

For more information, please refer the following resources:

Container threat detection conceptual overview:

`https://cloud.google.com/security-command-center/docs/concepts-container-threat-detection-overview`

GKE CIS 1.1.0 Benchmark Inspec Profile:

`https://github.com/GoogleCloudPlatform/inspec-gke-cis-benchmark`

GKE auditor:

`https://github.com/google/gke-auditor`

Node images:

`https://cloud.google.com/kubernetes-engine/docs/concepts/node-images#containerd_node_images`

Binary authorization:

`https://cloud.google.com/binary-authorization`

Container Registry:

`https://cloud.google.com/container-registry`

Summary

In this section, we have learned how to securely maintain the Google Kubernetes service, based on GCP infrastructure – from logging in, to network access, to auditing and monitoring, and security compliance.

Securing serverless/function as a service

Although the name implies that there are no servers, the term *serverless* or *function as a service* means that you, as a customer of the service, are not in charge of the underlying compute infrastructure (operating system maintenance, scale, runtime management, and so on) – you simply import your code (according to the supported language by each cloud provider), select your preferred runtime, select the amount of required memory per function (which affects the amount of CPU), and set the trigger to invoke the function.

The following diagram presents the architectural differences between VMs, containers, and serverless:

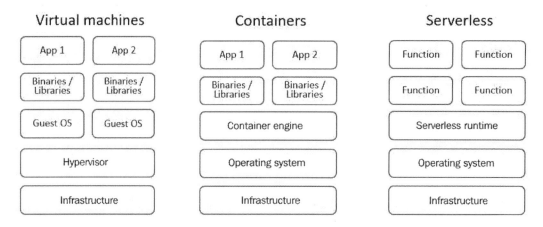

Figure 2.2 – VMs versus containers versus serverless

In this section, I will present the most common serverless/function as a service platforms.

Then, we are going to see what the best practices are for securing common serverless services from AWS, Azure, and GCP.

Securing AWS Lambda

AWS Lambda is the Amazon serverless service.

It can integrate with other AWS services, such as AWS IAM for managing permissions to AWS Lambda, Amazon CloudWatch for monitoring AWS Lambda, and Amazon S3 and Amazon EFS for persistent storage.

Best practices for configuring IAM for AWS Lambda

AWS IAM is the supported service for managing permissions to AWS Lambda.

The best practices are as follows:

- Grant minimal IAM permissions for any newly created AWS Lambda function (for running tasks, accessing S3 buckets, monitoring using CloudWatch Events, and so on) – match a specific IAM role to any newly created AWS Lambda function.

- Use open source tools such as `serverless-puresec-cli` to generate IAM roles for your function.

- Avoid storing credentials inside AWS Lambda code.

- If you need to store sensitive data (such as credentials), use AWS Secrets Manager.

- For better protection of your Lamba functions, configure AWS Lambda behind Amazon API Gateway.

- For sensitive environments, encrypt Lambda environment variables using CMK management (as explained in *Chapter 7, Applying Encryption in Cloud Services*).

- Use TLS 1.2 to encrypt sensitive data over the network.

- Enforce MFA for end users who have access to the AWS API (console, CLI, and SDK) and perform privileged actions such as managing the Lambda service.

For more information, please refer the following resources:

Identity-based IAM policies for Lambda:

```
https://docs.aws.amazon.com/lambda/latest/dg/access-control-
identity-based.html
```

Security best practices:

```
https://docs.aws.amazon.com/whitepapers/latest/serverless-
architectures-lambda/security-best-practices.html
```

Encrypting Lambda environment variables:

```
https://docs.aws.amazon.com/whitepapers/latest/kms-best-
practices/encrypting-lambda-environment-variables.html
```

```
serverless-puresec-cli:
```

```
https://github.com/puresec/serverless-puresec-cli
```

Best practices for securing network access to AWS Lambda

AWS Lambda can be deployed either as an external resource outside your VPC or inside your VPC – for that reason, it is important to plan before deploying each Lambda function.

The best practices are as follows:

- Use Amazon API Gateway to restrict access to your Lambda function, from a specific IP address or CIDR.

- If your Lambda function is located outside a VPC, and the Lambda function needs access to resources inside your VPC, use AWS PrivateLink, which avoids sending network traffic outside your VPC, through a secure channel, using an interface VPC endpoint.

- If your Lambda function is located inside your VPC, and the Lambda function needs access to external resources on the internet, use the NAT gateway to give your Lambda function the required access, without exposing Lambda to the internet directly.

- Use TLS 1.2 to encrypt traffic to and from your Lambda functions.

For more information, please refer the following resources:

Data protection in AWS Lambda:

```
https://docs.aws.amazon.com/lambda/latest/dg/security-
dataprotection.html
```

AWS Lambda now supports AWS PrivateLink:

```
https://aws.amazon.com/about-aws/whats-new/2020/10/aws-lambda-
now-supports-aws-privatelink/
```

Configuring a Lambda function to access resources in a VPC:

```
https://docs.aws.amazon.com/lambda/latest/dg/configuration-
vpc.html
```

How do I give internet access to a Lambda function that's connected to an Amazon VPC?

```
https://aws.amazon.com/premiumsupport/knowledge-center/
internet-access-lambda-function/
```

Best practices for conducting auditing and monitoring in AWS Lambda

Auditing is a crucial part of data protection.

As with any other managed service, AWS allows you to enable auditing using the AWS CloudTrail service – a service that allows you to audit API-related activities.

The best practices are as follows:

- Enable enhanced monitoring of your Lambda functions.
- Use Amazon CloudWatch to detect spikes in Lambda usage.
- Use AWS CloudTrail to monitor API activities related to your Lambda function.

For more information, please refer the following resources:

Using AWS Lambda with AWS CloudTrail:

```
https://docs.aws.amazon.com/lambda/latest/dg/with-cloudtrail.
html
```

Using AWS Lambda with Amazon CloudWatch Events:

```
https://docs.aws.amazon.com/lambda/latest/dg/services-
cloudwatchevents.html
```

Best practices for conducting compliance, configuration change, and secure coding in AWS Lambda

Serverless, or function as a service, is mainly code running inside a closed managed environment.

As a customer, you cannot control the underlying infrastructure – as a result, you must invest in secure coding to avoid attackers breaking into your application and causing harm that AWS cannot protect.

The best practices are as follows:

- Follow the *OWASP Serverless Top 10* project documentation when writing your Lambda function code.
- Enable versions in your Lambda functions, to be able to roll back to previous code.
- Use AWS Signer to sign your Lambda function code and make sure you only run signed code.
- If you use Amazon API Gateway in front of your Lambda functions, use the API Gateway Lambda authorizer as an extra layer of protection for authorizing access to your Lambda functions.
- Use AWS Config to check for changes in your Lambda functions.
- Use Amazon Inspector assessment templates to detect non-compliance or the use of old versions of a runtime in your Lambda functions.

For more information, please refer the following resources:

Using AWS Lambda with AWS Config:

`https://docs.aws.amazon.com/lambda/latest/dg/services-config.html`

Lambda function versions:

`https://docs.aws.amazon.com/lambda/latest/dg/configuration-versions.html`

Use API Gateway Lambda authorizers:

`https://docs.aws.amazon.com/apigateway/latest/developerguide/apigateway-use-lambda-authorizer.html`

Setting up automatic assessment runs through a Lambda function:

`https://docs.aws.amazon.com/inspector/latest/userguide/inspector_assessments.html#assessment_runs-schedule`

Configuring code signing for AWS Lambda:

`https://docs.aws.amazon.com/lambda/latest/dg/configuration-codesigning.html`

OWASP Serverless Top 10:

`https://owasp.org/www-project-serverless-top-10/`

Summary

In this section, we have learned how to securely maintain the AWS Lambda service, based on AWS infrastructure – from logging in, to network access, to auditing and monitoring, and security compliance.

Securing Azure Functions

Azure Functions is the Azure function as a service.

It can integrate with other Azure services, such as Azure AD for managing permissions to Azure Functions, Azure Monitor Application Insights for monitoring Azure Functions, and Azure Blob storage for persistent storage.

Best practices for configuring IAM for Azure Functions

Azure AD is the supported service for managing permissions to your Azure Functions.

The best practices are as follows:

- Enable Azure AD authentication for any newly created Azure function by turning on Azure App Service authentication.

- Avoid allowing anonymous access to your Azure function – require clients to authenticate before using Azure Functions.

- Grant minimal permissions for any newly created Azure function using Azure RBAC.

- Prefer to use temporary credentials to your Azure function – use **Shared Access Signature (SAS)** tokens to achieve this task.

- Where possible, prefer to use client certificates to authenticate clients to your Azure functions.

- To allow your Azure functions access to Azure resources, use a system-assigned managed identity from Azure AD.

- If you need to store sensitive data (such as credentials), use Azure Key Vault.

- For sensitive environments, encrypt the Azure Functions application settings using customer-managed key management inside Azure Key Vault (as explained in *Chapter 7, Applying Encryption in Cloud Services*).

For more information, please refer the following resources:

How to use managed identities for App Service and Azure Functions:

```
https://docs.microsoft.com/en-us/azure/app-service/overview-
managed-identity?toc=/azure/azure-functions/toc.json
```

Azure Functions authorizations:

```
https://docs.microsoft.com/en-us/azure/api-management/import-
function-app-as-api#authorization
```

Use Key Vault references for App Service and Azure Functions:

```
https://docs.microsoft.com/en-us/azure/app-service/
app-service-key-vault-references
```

Best practices for securing data and network access to Azure Functions

Azure Functions can access resources in your Azure subscription – for that reason, it is important to plan before deploying each Azure function.

The best practices are as follows:

- For better protection of your Azure functions, configure the Azure function behind Azure API Gateway.
- Use TLS 1.2 to encrypt sensitive data over the network.
- Create a separate Azure storage account for any newly created Azure function.
- Use Azure network security groups to block outbound traffic from your Azure functions (when internet access is not required).
- Use the Azure VNet service endpoint to control access to your Azure functions.
- Use Azure App Service static IP restrictions to control access to your Azure functions.
- Use either an Azure App Service Standard plan or an Azure App Service Premium plan to configure network isolations of your Azure functions.
- Use Azure Defender for App Service as an extra layer of protection for your Azure functions that have inbound access from the internet.
- Use Azure Web Application Firewall as an extra layer of protection for your Azure functions that have inbound access from the internet.
- Disable and block the use of the FTP protocol with your Azure functions.

For more information, please refer the following resources:

Azure Functions networking options:

```
https://docs.microsoft.com/en-us/azure/azure-functions/
functions-networking-options
```

Secure an HTTP endpoint in production:

```
https://docs.microsoft.com/en-us/azure/azure-functions/
functions-bindings-http-webhook-trigger?tabs=csharp#secure-an-
http-endpoint-in-production
```

IP address restrictions:

```
https://docs.microsoft.com/en-us/azure/azure-functions/
ip-addresses#ip-address-restrictions
```

Azure Functions and FTP:

```
https://docs.microsoft.com/en-us/azure/azure-functions/
functions-deployment-technologies#ftp
```

Protect your web apps and APIs:

```
https://docs.microsoft.com/en-us/azure/security-center/
defender-for-app-service-introduction
```

Best practices for conducting auditing and monitoring in Azure Functions

Auditing is a crucial part of data protection.

As with any other managed service, Azure allows you to enable logging and auditing using the Azure Monitor service.

The best practices are as follows:

- Use the Azure Monitor service to log authentication-related activities of your Azure functions.
- Use the Security Center threat detection capability (Azure Defender).

For more information, please refer the following resources:

Logging and threat detection:

```
https://docs.microsoft.com/en-us/security/benchmark/azure/
baselines/functions-security-baseline#logging-and-threat-
detection
```

Azure security baseline for Azure Functions:

```
https://docs.microsoft.com/en-us/azure/azure-functions/
security-baseline#logging-and-monitoring
```

Best practices for conducting compliance, configuration change, and secure coding in Azure Functions

Serverless, or function as a service, is mainly code running inside a closed, managed environment.

As a customer, you cannot control the underlying infrastructure – as a result, you must invest in secure coding to avoid attackers breaking into your application and causing harm that Azure cannot protect against.

The best practices are as follows:

- Follow the *OWASP Serverless Top 10* project documentation when writing your Azure Functions code.
- Use the Azure security baseline for Azure Functions (Azure Security Benchmark).
- Use the Security Center threat detection capability (Azure Defender).

For more information, please refer the following resources:

Azure security baseline for Azure Functions:

```
https://docs.microsoft.com/en-us/security/benchmark/azure/
baselines/functions-security-baseline
```

Posture and vulnerability management:

```
https://docs.microsoft.com/en-us/security/benchmark/
azure/baselines/functions-security-baseline#posture-and-
vulnerability-management
```

OWASP Serverless Top 10:

```
https://owasp.org/www-project-serverless-top-10/
```

Summary

In this section, we have learned how to securely maintain the Azure Functions service, based on Azure infrastructure – from logging in, to network access, to auditing and monitoring, and security compliance.

Securing Google Cloud Functions

Google Cloud Functions is the GCP function as a service.

It can integrate with other GCP services, such as Google Cloud IAM for managing permissions to Google Cloud Functions, Google Cloud Audit Logs for monitoring Google Cloud Functions, and Google Cloud Storage for persistent storage.

Best practices for configuring IAM for Google Cloud Functions

Google Cloud IAM is the supported service for managing permissions on your Google Cloud Functions.

The best practices are as follows:

- Use Google Cloud IAM to manage permissions to your Google Cloud functions.
- Grant minimal permissions for accessing and managing the Google Cloud IAM service.
- Create a unique service account for each newly created Google Cloud function with minimal permissions using the Google Cloud IAM service.

For more information, please refer the following resources:

Authorizing access via IAM:

```
https://cloud.google.com/functions/docs/securing/managing-
access-iam
```

Authenticating for invocation:

```
https://cloud.google.com/functions/docs/securing/
authenticating
```

Securing access with identity:

```
https://cloud.google.com/functions/docs/securing#identity
```

Best practices for securing data and network access to Google Cloud Functions

Google Cloud Functions can access resources in your GCP project – for that reason, it is important to plan before deploying each Google Cloud function.

The best practices are as follows:

- Use Google Cloud Functions ingress settings to control which IP address (or CIDR) can access your Google Cloud function.

- If you need your Google Cloud function to have access to resources inside your VPC, use serverless VPC access to restrict access to your VPC.

- If your Google Cloud function is connected to your VPC and needs access to external resources, use Google Cloud Functions egress settings to control outbound destinations.

- If your Google Cloud function needs to have direct inbound access from the internet, use VPC service controls as an extra layer of protection to secure your perimeter from data leakage.

- For sensitive environments, encrypt Google Cloud Functions environment variables using CMEK management (as explained in *Chapter 7, Applying Encryption in Cloud Services*).

- Use TLS 1.2 to encrypt sensitive data over the network.

For more information, please refer the following resources:

Configuring network settings:

```
https://cloud.google.com/functions/docs/networking/network-settings
```

Connecting to a VPC network:

```
https://cloud.google.com/functions/docs/networking/connecting-vpc
```

Configuring serverless VPC access:

```
https://cloud.google.com/vpc/docs/configure-serverless-vpc-access
```

Using VPC service controls:

```
https://cloud.google.com/functions/docs/securing/using-vpc-
service-controls
```

Managing secrets:

```
https://cloud.google.com/functions/docs/env-var#managing_
secrets
```

Best practices for conducting auditing and monitoring in Google Cloud Functions

Auditing is a crucial part of data protection.

As with any other managed service, Google allows you to enable logging and auditing using the Google Cloud Audit Logs service.

The best practices are as follows:

- Admin activity audit logs are enabled by default and cannot be disabled.
- Explicitly enable **data access audit logs** to log activities performed on the database.
- Limit the access to audit logs to the minimum number of employees to avoid possible deletion or changes to the audit logs.

For more information, please refer the following resources:

Using Cloud audit logging with Cloud Functions:

```
https://cloud.google.com/functions/docs/monitoring/audit-
logging
```

Summary

In this section, we have learned how to securely maintain the Google Cloud Functions service, based on GCP infrastructure – from logging in, to network access, to auditing and monitoring.

Summary

In this chapter, we have focused on the various compute services in AWS, Azure, and GCP, from VMs, through managed MySQL databases, containers, and finally serverless (or functions as a service).

In each section, we have reviewed how to manage identity (for authentication and authorization), how to control network access (from access controls to network encryption), how to configure auditing and logging, and finally, how to configure compliance or security standards (for services that support those capabilities).

In the next chapter, we will review the various storage services in the cloud (from object storage to block storage and finally, file storage).

3
Securing Storage Services

In the previous chapter, we covered compute services. After compute services, the second most common resource everyone talks about is storage – from object storage to block storage (which is also known as *instance attached storage*), to file storage.

We are using storage services to store our data.

The following is a list of common threats that might impact our data when it is stored in the cloud:

- Unauthorized access
- Data leakage
- Data exfiltration
- Data loss

As a best practice, we should always use the following countermeasures when storing data in the cloud:

- **Access-control lists** (**ACLs**; note that each cloud provider has its own implementation) and **Identity and Access Management** (**IAM**), to restrict access from our cloud environment to the storage service

- Encryption at both transit and rest to ensure data confidentiality
- Auditing to have a log of who has access to our data and what actions were performed on our data (for instance, uploads, downloads, updates, deletions, and more)
- Backups or taking snapshots to allow us to restore deleted data or return to the previous version of our data (for example, in the event of ransomware encrypting our data)

This chapter will cover all types of storage services and provide you with best practices on how to securely connect and use each of them.

In this chapter, we will cover the following topics:

- Securing object storage
- Securing block storage
- Securing file storage
- Securing the **Container Storage Interface** (**CSI**)

Technical requirements

For this chapter, you are required to have a fundamental understanding of object storage, block storage, and file storage.

Securing object storage

Each cloud provider has its own implementation of object storage, but at the end of the day, the basic idea is the same:

- Object storage is a special type of storage that is meant to store data.
- Files (or objects) are stored inside buckets (these are logical concepts such as directories or logical containers).
- Access to files on object storage is either done through the HTTP(S) protocol API via web command-line tools or programmatically using SDK tools.
- Object storage is not meant to store operating systems or databases (please refer to the *Securing block storage* section).

Next, we are going to examine what the best practices are for securing object storage services from AWS, Azure, and GCP.

For more information, please refer to the following resource:

Object storage: `https://en.wikipedia.org/wiki/Object_storage`

Securing Amazon Simple Storage Service

Amazon Simple Storage Service (**Amazon S3**) is the Amazon object storage service.

Best practices for conducting authentication and authorization for Amazon S3

AWS controls access to S3 buckets using ACLs.

Access can be controlled at the entire bucket level (along with all objects inside this bucket) and on a specific object level (for example, let's suppose you would like to share a specific file with several of your colleagues).

AWS supports the following methods to access S3 bucket permissions:

- **IAM policies**: This allows you to set permissions for what actions are allowed or denied from an identity (for instance, a user, a group, or a role).

- **Bucket policies**: This allows you to set permissions at the S3 bucket level – it applies to all objects inside a bucket.

- **S3 access points**: This gives you the ability to grant access to S3 buckets to a specific group of users or applications.

    Additionally, AWS controls permissions for identities (regardless of resources such as S3) on an AWS organizational basis (these are also called **service control policies** or **SCPs**).

    The effective permissions of an S3 bucket are the sum of SCPs with identity permissions (IAM policies), total resource permissions (bucket policies), and an AWS KMS policy (such as allowing access to an encrypted object), assuming the user was not denied in any of the previous criteria.

Here is a list of best practices to follow:

- Create an IAM group, add users to the IAM group, and grant the required permissions on the target S3 bucket to the target IAM group.

- Use IAM roles for services (such as applications or non-human identities) that require access to S3 buckets.

- Restrict access for IAM users/groups to a specific S3 bucket, rather than using wildcard permissions for all S3 buckets in the AWS account.

- Remove default bucket owner access permissions to S3 buckets.

- Use IAM policies for applications (or non-human identities)/service-linked roles that need access to S3 buckets.

- Enable **MFA delete** for S3 buckets to avoid the accidental deletion of objects from a bucket.

- Grant minimal permissions to S3 buckets (that is, a specific identity on a specific resource with specific conditions).

- Use the bucket ACL's **write** permissions for the Amazon S3 log delivery group to allow this group the ability to write access logs (for further analysis).

- For data that you need to retain for long periods (due to regulatory requirements), use the S3 object lock to protect the data from accidental deletion.

- Encrypt data at rest using **Amazon S3-Managed Encryption Keys (SSE-S3)**. This is explained in more detail in *Chapter 7, Applying Encryption in Cloud Services*.

- For sensitive environments, encrypt data at rest using **Customer-Provided Encryption Keys (SSE-C)**. This is explained, in more detail, in *Chapter 7, Applying Encryption in Cloud Services*.

For more information, please refer to the following resources:

Identity and access management in Amazon S3:

```
https://docs.aws.amazon.com/AmazonS3/latest/userguide/
s3-access-control.html
```

IAM policies, bucket policies, and ACLs:

```
https://aws.amazon.com/blogs/security/iam-policies-and-bucket-
policies-and-acls-oh-my-controlling-access-to-s3-resources/
```

How IAM roles differ from resource-based policies:

```
https://docs.aws.amazon.com/IAM/latest/UserGuide/id_roles_
compare-resource-policies.html
```

Amazon S3 Preventative Security Best Practices:

```
https://docs.aws.amazon.com/AmazonS3/latest/userguide/
security-best-practices.html#security-best-practices-prevent
```

Setting default server-side encryption behavior for Amazon S3 buckets:

```
https://docs.aws.amazon.com/AmazonS3/latest/userguide/bucket-
encryption.html
```

Consider encryption of data at rest:

```
https://docs.aws.amazon.com/AmazonS3/latest/userguide/
security-best-practices.html#server-side
```

Best practices for securing network access to Amazon S3

Because Amazon S3 is a managed service, it is located outside the customer's **Virtual Private Cloud** (**VPC**). It is important to protect access to the Amazon S3 service.

Here is a list of best practices to follow:

- Unless there is a business requirement to share data publicly (such as static web hosting), keep all Amazon S3 buckets (all tiers) private.

- To secure access from your VPC to the Amazon S3, use **AWS PrivateLink**. This keeps traffic internally inside the AWS backbone, through a secure channel, using the interface's VPC endpoint.

- For sensitive environments, use bucket policies to enforce access to an S3 bucket from a specific VPC endpoint or a specific VPC.

- Use bucket policies to enforce the use of transport encryption (HTTPS only).

- For sensitive environments, use bucket policies to require **TLS version 1.2** as the minimum.

- Encrypt data at rest using SSE-S3 (as explained in *Chapter 7, Applying Encryption in Cloud Services*).

- For sensitive environments, encrypt data at rest using SSE-C (as explained in *Chapter 7, Applying Encryption in Cloud Services*).

- Consider using presigned URLs for scenarios where you need to allow external user access (with specific permissions, such as file download) to an S3 bucket for a short period, without the need to create an IAM user.

For more information, please refer to the following resources:

Internetwork traffic privacy:

```
https://docs.aws.amazon.com/AmazonS3/latest/userguide/inter-
network-traffic-privacy.html
```

AWS PrivateLink for Amazon S3:

```
https://docs.aws.amazon.com/AmazonS3/latest/userguide/
privatelink-interface-endpoints.html
```

Protecting data using encryption:

`https://docs.aws.amazon.com/AmazonS3/latest/userguide/UsingEncryption.html`

Setting default server-side encryption behavior for Amazon S3 buckets:

`https://docs.aws.amazon.com/AmazonS3/latest/userguide/bucket-encryption.html`

Consider encryption of data at rest:

`https://docs.aws.amazon.com/AmazonS3/latest/userguide/security-best-practices.html#server-side`

Enforce encryption of data in transit:

`https://docs.aws.amazon.com/AmazonS3/latest/userguide/security-best-practices.html#transit`

Using S3 Object Lock:

`https://docs.aws.amazon.com/AmazonS3/latest/userguide/object-lock.html`

Using presigned URLs:

`https://docs.aws.amazon.com/AmazonS3/latest/userguide/using-presigned-url.html`

Best practices for conducting auditing and monitoring for Amazon S3

Auditing is a crucial part of data protection.

As with any other managed service, AWS allows you to enable logging and auditing using two built-in services:

- **Amazon CloudWatch**: This is a service that allows you to log object storage activities and raise the alarm according to predefined activities (such as excessive delete actions).
- **AWS CloudTrail**: This is a service that allows you to monitor API activities (essentially, any action performed on Amazon S3).

Here is a list of best practices to follow:

- Enable Amazon CloudWatch alarms for excessive S3 usage (for example, a high volume of GET, PUT, or DELETE operations on a specific S3 bucket).

- Enable AWS CloudTrail for any S3 bucket to log any activity performed on Amazon S3 by any user, role, or AWS service.

- Limit access to the CloudTrail logs to a minimum number of employees, preferably those with an AWS management account, outside the scope of your end users (including outside the scope of your users), to avoid possible deletion or changes to the audit logs.

- Enable S3 server access logs to record all access activities as complimentary to AWS CloudTrail API-based logging (for the purpose of future forensics).

- Use Access Analyzer for S3 to locate S3 buckets with public access or S3 buckets that have access from external AWS accounts.

- Enable file integrity monitoring to make sure files have not been changed.

- Enable object versioning to avoid accidental deletion (and to protect against ransomware).

- Use Amazon S3 inventory to monitor the status of S3 bucket replication (such as encryption on both the source and destination buckets).

For more information, please refer to the following resources:

Logging Amazon S3 API calls using AWS CloudTrail:

```
https://docs.aws.amazon.com/AmazonS3/latest/userguide/
cloudtrail-logging.html
```

Logging requests using server access logging:

```
https://docs.aws.amazon.com/AmazonS3/latest/userguide/
ServerLogs.html
```

Amazon S3 Monitoring and Auditing Best Practices:

```
https://docs.aws.amazon.com/AmazonS3/latest/userguide/
security-best-practices.html#security-best-practices-detect
```

Reviewing bucket access using Access Analyzer for S3:

```
https://docs.aws.amazon.com/AmazonS3/latest/userguide/access-
analyzer.html
```

Amazon S3 inventory:

```
https://docs.aws.amazon.com/AmazonS3/latest/userguide/storage-
inventory.html
```

Summary

In this section, we learned how to secure Amazon S3 services based on the AWS infrastructure. This included logging in, securing network access, data encryption (at both transit and rest), and logging and auditing.

Securing Azure Blob storage

Azure Blob storage is the Azure object storage service.

Best practices for conducting authentication and authorization for Azure Blob storage

Azure controls authorization for Blob storage using Azure Active Directory.

For temporary access to Azure Blob storage (that is, for an application or a non-human interaction), you have the option to use **shared access signatures** (**SAS**).

Here is a list of best practices to follow:

- Create an Azure AD group, add users to the AD group, and then grant the required permissions on the target Blob storage to the target AD group.
- Use shared key authorization (SAS) to allow applications temporary access to Blob storage.
- Grant minimal permissions to Azure Blob storage.
- For data that you need to retain for long periods (due to regulatory requirements), use an immutable Blob storage lock to protect the data from accidental deletion.

For more information, please refer to the following resources:

Authorize access to blobs using Azure Active Directory:

```
https://docs.microsoft.com/en-us/azure/storage/common/storage-
auth-aad
```

Prevent Shared Key authorization for an Azure Storage account:

```
https://docs.microsoft.com/en-us/azure/storage/common/shared-
key-authorization-prevent?tabs=portal
```

Grant limited access to Azure Storage resources using shared access signatures (SAS):

```
https://docs.microsoft.com/en-us/azure/storage/common/storage-
sas-overview
```

Security recommendations for Blob storage:

```
https://docs.microsoft.com/en-us/azure/storage/blobs/security-
recommendations
```

Best practices for securing network access to Azure Blob storage

Because Azure Blob storage is a managed service, it is located outside the customer's **Virtual Network (VNet)**. It is important to protect access to the Azure Blob storage service.

Here is a list of best practices to follow:

- Keep all Azure Blob storage (that is, all tiers) private.

- To secure access from your VNet to the Azure Blob storage, use an Azure private endpoint, which avoids sending network traffic outside your VNet through a secure channel.

- Unforce the use of transport encryption (HTTPS only) for all Azure Blob storage.

- For sensitive environments, require a minimum of TLS version 1.2 for Azure Blob storage.

- Deny default network access to the Azure storage account and only allow access from predefined conditions such as the setting up of IP addresses.

- Encrypt data at rest using Azure Key Vault.

- For sensitive environments (for example, which contain PII, credit card details, healthcare data, and more), encrypt data at rest using **customer-managed keys (CMKs)** stored inside Azure Key Vault (as explained in *Chapter 7*, *Applying Encryption in Cloud Services*).

For more information, please refer to the following resources:

Configure Azure Storage firewalls and virtual networks:

```
https://docs.microsoft.com/en-us/azure/storage/common/
storage-network-security?toc=%2Fazure%2Fstorage%2Fblobs%2Ftoc.
json&tabs=azure-portal
```

Tutorial: Connect to a storage account using an Azure Private Endpoint:

```
https://docs.microsoft.com/en-us/azure/private-link/tutorial-
private-endpoint-storage-portal
```

Require secure transfer to ensure secure connections:

```
https://docs.microsoft.com/en-us/azure/storage/common/storage-
require-secure-transfer
```

Enforce a minimum required version of Transport Layer Security (TLS) for requests to a storage account:

```
https://docs.microsoft.com/en-us/azure/storage/common/
transport-layer-security-configure-minimum-version?toc=%2Fazur
e%2Fstorage%2Fblobs%2Ftoc.json&tabs=portal
```

Azure Storage encryption for data at rest:

```
https://docs.microsoft.com/en-us/azure/storage/common/storage-
service-encryption?toc=/azure/storage/blobs/toc.json
```

Customer-managed keys for Azure Storage encryption:

```
https://docs.microsoft.com/en-us/azure/storage/common/
customer-managed-keys-overview?toc=/azure/storage/blobs/toc.
json
```

Best practices for conducting auditing and monitoring for Azure Blob storage

Auditing is a crucial part of data protection.

Azure allows you to monitor blob storage using the following services:

- **Azure Monitor**: This service logs access and audit events from Azure Blob storage.
- **Azure Security Center**: This service allows you to monitor for compliance issues in the Azure Blob storage configuration.

Here is a list of best practices to follow:

- Enable log alerts using the Azure Monitor service to track access to the Azure Blob storage and raise alerts (such as multiple failed access attempts to Blob storage in a short period of time).
- Enable Azure storage logging to audit all authorization events for access to the Azure Blob storage.

- Log anonymous successful access attempts to locate an unauthorized access attempt to the Azure Blob storage.
- Enable Azure Defender for Storage to receive security alerts in the Azure Security Center console.

For more information, please refer to the following resources:

Monitoring Azure Blob storage:

```
https://docs.microsoft.com/en-us/azure/storage/blobs/monitor-
blob-storage?tabs=azure-portal
```

Azure Storage analytics logging:

```
https://docs.microsoft.com/en-us/azure/storage/common/storage-
analytics-logging
```

Log alerts in Azure Monitor:

```
https://docs.microsoft.com/en-us/azure/azure-monitor/alerts/
alerts-unified-log
```

Summary

In this section, we learned how to secure the Azure Blob storage service based on the Azure infrastructure. This included logging in, securing network access, data encryption (at both transit and rest), and logging and auditing.

Securing Google Cloud Storage

Google Cloud Storage is the GCP object storage service.

Best practices for conducting authentication and authorization for Google Cloud Storage

Access can be controlled at the entire bucket level (including all objects inside this bucket) or on a specific object level (for example, suppose you would like to share a specific file with several of your colleagues).

GCP supports the following methods to access a cloud storage bucket:

- **Uniform bucket-level access**: This method sets permissions based on the Google Cloud IAM role (that is, user, group, domain, or public).

- **Fine-grained**: This method sets permissions based on a combination of both Google Cloud IAM and an ACL – it applies to either the entire bucket level or to a specific object.

Here is a list of best practices to follow:

- Create an IAM group, add users to the IAM group, and then grant the required permissions on the target cloud storage bucket to the target IAM group.
- Use IAM policies for applications that require access to cloud storage buckets.
- Grant minimal permissions to cloud storage buckets.
- Use **Security Token Service (STS)** to allow temporary access to cloud storage.
- Use HMAC keys to allow the service account temporary access to cloud storage.
- Use signed URLs to allow an external user temporary access to cloud storage.
- For data that you need to retain for long periods (due to regulatory requirements), use the bucket lock feature to protect the data from accidental deletion.

For more information, please refer to the following resources:

Identity and Access Management:

https://cloud.google.com/storage/docs/access-control/iam

Cloud Storage authentication:

https://cloud.google.com/storage/docs/authentication

Access control lists (ACLs):

https://cloud.google.com/storage/docs/access-control/lists

Retention policies and retention policy locks:

https://cloud.google.com/storage/docs/bucket-lock

Security Token Service API:

https://cloud.google.com/iam/docs/reference/sts/rest

HMAC keys:

https://cloud.google.com/storage/docs/authentication/hmackeys

Signed URLs:

https://cloud.google.com/storage/docs/access-control/signed-urls

4 best practices for ensuring privacy and security of your data in Cloud Storage:

```
https://cloud.google.com/blog/products/storage-data-transfer/
google-cloud-storage-best-practices-to-help-ensure-data-
privacy-and-security
```

Best practices for securing network access to Google Cloud Storage

Because Google Cloud Storage is a managed service, it is located outside the customer's VPC. It is important to protect access to Google Cloud Storage.

Here is a list of best practices to follow:

- Use TLS for transport encryption (HTTPS only).
- Keep all cloud storage buckets (all tiers) private.
- Use VPC Service Controls to allow access from your VPC to Google Cloud Storage.
- Encrypt cloud storage buckets using Google-managed encryption keys inside Google Cloud KMS (as explained in *Chapter 7, Applying Encryption in Cloud Services*).
- For sensitive environments (for example, which contain PII, credit card information, healthcare data, and more), encrypt cloud storage buckets using a CMK inside Google Cloud KMS (as explained in *Chapter 7, Applying Encryption in Cloud Services*).

For more information, please refer to the following resources:

Security, ACLs, and access control:

```
https://cloud.google.com/storage/docs/best-practices#security
```

The security benefits of VPC Service Controls:

```
https://cloud.google.com/vpc-service-controls/docs/overview
```

Enabling VPC accessible services:

```
https://cloud.google.com/vpc-service-controls/docs/manage-
service-perimeters#add_a_service_to_the_vpc_accessible_
services
```

Customer-supplied encryption keys:

```
https://cloud.google.com/storage/docs/encryption/customer-
supplied-keys
```

Customer-managed encryption keys:

```
https://cloud.google.com/storage/docs/encryption/customer-
managed-keys
```

Best practices for conducting auditing and monitoring for Google Cloud Storage

Auditing is a crucial part of data protection.

As with any other managed service, GCP allows you to enable logging and auditing using Google Cloud Audit Logs.

Here is a list of best practices to follow:

- Admin activity audit logs are enabled by default and cannot be disabled.
- Explicitly enable **Data Access audit logs** to log activities performed on Google Cloud Storage.
- Limit the access to audit logs to a minimum number of employees to avoid possible deletion or any changes made to the audit logs.

For more information, please refer to the following resources:

Cloud Audit Logs with Cloud Storage:

```
https://cloud.google.com/storage/docs/audit-logging
```

Usage logs & storage logs:

```
https://cloud.google.com/storage/docs/access-logs
```

Summary

In this section, we learned how to secure Google Cloud Storage based on the GCP infrastructure. This included logging in, securing network access, data encryption (at both transit and rest), and logging and auditing.

Securing block storage

Block storage is a storage scheme like the on-premises **Storage Area Network** (**SAN**).

It allows you to mount a volume (disk), format it to a common filesystem (such as NTFS for Windows or Ext4 for Linux), and store various files, databases, or entire operating systems.

Next, we are going to examine what the best practices are for securing block storage from AWS, Azure, and GCP.

For more information, please refer to the following resource:

Block-level storage:

`https://en.wikipedia.org/wiki/Block-level_storage`

Best practices for securing Amazon Elastic Block Store

Amazon Elastic Block Store (**Amazon EBS**) is the AWS block storage.

It is common when working with EC2 instances, to attach an additional volume to store your data (separately from the operating system volume). This is also known as block storage.

Amazon EBS can be attached to a single EC2 instance and can be accessed from within the operating system.

The traffic between your EC2 instance and your attached EBS volume is encrypted at transit (and is automatically configured and controlled by AWS).

Additionally, an EBS volume can be configured to encrypt data at rest for the rare scenario in which a potential attacker gains access to your EBS volume and wishes to access your data. The data itself (on the EBS volume and its snapshots) is only accessible by the EC2 instance that is connected to the EBS volume.

The following command uses the AWS CLI tool to create an encrypted EBS volume in a specific AWS availability zone:

```
aws ec2 create-volume \
    --size 80 \
    --encrypted \
    --availability-zone <AWS_AZ_code>
```

The following command uses the AWS CLI tool to enable EBS encryption by default in a specific AWS region:

```
aws ec2 enable-ebs-encryption-by-default --region <Region_Code>
```

Here is a list of best practices for EBS volumes:

- Configure encryption by default for each region you are planning to deploy EC2 instances.

- Encrypt both boot and data volumes.

- Encrypt each EBS volume at creation time.

- Encrypt EBS volume snapshots.

- Use AWS Config to detect unattached EBS volumes.

- Use an IAM policy to define who can attach, detach, or create a snapshot for EBS volumes to minimize the risk of data exfiltration.

- Avoid configuring public access to your EBS volume snapshots – make sure all snapshots are encrypted.

- For highly sensitive environments, encrypt EBS volumes using the *customer master key* (as explained in *Chapter 7, Applying Encryption in Cloud Services*).

- Set names and descriptions for EBS volumes to better understand which EBS volume belongs to which EC2 instance.

- Use tagging (that is, *labeling*) for EBS volumes to allow a better understanding of which EBS volume belongs to which EC2 instance.

For more information, please refer to the following resource:

Amazon EBS encryption:

```
https://docs.aws.amazon.com/AWSEC2/latest/UserGuide/
EBSEncryption.html
```

Best practices for securing Azure managed disks

Azure-managed disks are Azure managed block level storage.

It is common when working with VMs, to attach an additional volume to store your data (that is, separately from the operating system volume). This is also known as block storage.

The following command uses the Azure CLI tool to encrypt a specific VM, in a specific resource group, using a unique customer *key vault*:

```
az vm encryption enable -g MyResourceGroup --name MyVM --disk-
encryption-keyvault myKV
```

The following command uses the Azure CLI tool to show the encryption status of a specific VM in a specific resource group:

```
az vm encryption show --name "myVM" -g "MyResourceGroup"
```

Here is a list of best practices to follow:

- Create encryption keys (inside the Azure Key Vault service) for each region you are planning to deploy VMs in.
- For Windows machines, encrypt your data using BitLocker technology.
- For Linux machines, encrypt your data using dm-crypt technology.
- Encrypt both the OS and data volumes.
- Encrypt each data volume at creation time.
- Encrypt the VM snapshots.
- Use an Azure private link service to restrict the export and import of managed disks to your Azure network.
- For highly sensitive environments, encrypt data volumes using a *CMK* (as explained in *Chapter 7, Applying Encryption in Cloud Services*).
- Set names for the Azure disk volumes to allow a better understanding of which disk volume belongs to which VM.
- Use tagging (that is, *labeling*) for disk volumes to allow a better understanding of which disk volume belongs to which VM.

For more information, please refer to the following resource:

Server-side encryption of Azure Disk Storage:

https://docs.microsoft.com/en-us/azure/virtual-machines/disk-encryption

Best practices for securing Google Persistent Disk

Google Persistent Disk is a part of the GCP block storage.

The following command uses the Google Cloud SDK to encrypt a persistent disk, in a specific GCP project, in a specific region, using a specific encryption key:

```
gcloud compute disks \
    create encrypted-disk \
```

```
--kms-key \ projects/[KMS_PROJECT_ID]/locations/[REGION]/
keyRings/[KEY_RING]/cryptoKeys/[KEY]
```

Here is a list of best practices to follow:

- Encrypt both the OS and data volumes.

- Encrypt each data volume at creation time.

- Encrypt the machine instance snapshots.

- For highly sensitive environments, encrypt persistent disks using a *CMK* inside Google Cloud KMS (as explained in *Chapter 7, Applying Encryption in Cloud Services*).

- Set names for Google's persistent disks to allow you to have a better understanding of which persistent disk belongs to which machine instance.

- Use tagging (that is, *labeling*) for persistent disks or snapshots to allow you to have a better understanding of which disk or snapshot belongs to which machine instance.

For more information, please refer to the following resource:

Protect resources by using Cloud KMS keys:

https://cloud.google.com/compute/docs/disks/customer-managed-encryption

Summary

In this section, we learned how to secure block storage. Since block storage volumes are part of the common compute services (such as Amazon EC2, Azure VM, Google Compute Engine, and more), the only way to protect block storage volumes (and their snapshots) is to encrypt them, prior to using them.

Access to block storage volumes is done from within the guest operating system, and auditing is part of the capabilities of guest operating systems.

Securing file storage

File storage is a piece of storage such as the on-premises **network-attached storage** (**NAS**).

Each cloud provider has its own implementation of file storage, but at the end of the day, the basic idea of file storage are described as follows:

- They offer support for common file sharing protocols (such as NFS and SMB/CIFS).

- They have the ability to mount a volume from a managed file service into an operating system to store and retrieve files, for multiple VMs, in parallel.

- They have the ability to control access permissions to the remote filesystem.

- They enable automatic filesystem growth.

Next, we are going to examine the best practices for securing file storage services from AWS, Azure, and GCP.

For more information, please refer to the following resource:

Network-attached storage:

`https://en.wikipedia.org/wiki/Network-attached_storage`

Securing Amazon Elastic File System

Amazon Elastic File System (**Amazon EFS**) is the Amazon file storage service based on the NFS protocol.

Best practices for conducting authentication and authorization for Amazon EFS

AWS IAM is the supported service in which to manage permissions to access Amazon EFS.

Here is a list of best practices to follow:

- Avoid using the AWS root account to access AWS resources such as Amazon EFS.

- Create an IAM group, add users to the IAM group, and then grant the required permissions on the target Amazon EFS to the target IAM group.

- Use IAM roles for federated users, AWS services, or applications that need access to Amazon EFS.

- Use IAM policies to grant the minimal required permissions to create EFS volumes or access and use Amazon EFS.

- When using IAM policies, specify conditions (such as the source IP) and what actions an end user can, along with the mentioned condition, take on the target filesystem.

- Use resource-based policies to configure who can access the EFS volume and what actions this end user can take on the filesystem (for example, mount, read, write, and more).

For more information, please refer to the following resources:

Identity and access management for Amazon EFS:

https://docs.aws.amazon.com/efs/latest/ug/auth-and-access-control.html

Working with users, groups, and permissions at the Network File System (NFS) Level:

https://docs.aws.amazon.com/efs/latest/ug/accessing-fs-nfs-permissions.html

AWS managed policies for Amazon EFS:

https://docs.aws.amazon.com/efs/latest/ug/security-iam-awsmanpol.html

Security in Amazon EFS:

https://docs.aws.amazon.com/efs/latest/ug/security-considerations.html

Overview of managing access permissions to your Amazon EFS resources:

https://docs.aws.amazon.com/efs/latest/ug/access-control-overview.html

Best practices for securing network access to Amazon EFS

Because Amazon EFS is a managed service, it is located outside the customer's VPC. It is important to protect access to the Amazon EFS service.

Here is a list of best practices to follow:

- Keep Amazon EFS (that is, all storage classes) private.
- Use VPC security groups to control the access between your Amazon EC2 machines and the Amazon EFS mount volumes.
- To secure access from your VPC to the Amazon EFS, use AWS PrivateLink, which avoids sending network traffic outside your VPC, through a secure channel, using an interface's VPC endpoint.
- Use Amazon EFS access points to manage application access to the EFS volume.

- Use STS to allow temporary access to Amazon EFS.

- Use an IAM policy to enforce encryption at rest for Amazon EFS filesystems. You can do this by setting the value of `elasticfilesystem:Encrypted` to `True` inside the IAM policy condition.

- For sensitive environments, use the EFS mount helper to enforce the use of encryption in transit using TLS version 1.2 when mounting an EFS volume.

- Encrypt data at rest using AWS-managed CMK for Amazon EFS (as explained in *Chapter 7, Applying Encryption in Cloud Services*).

- For sensitive environments, encrypt data at rest using a CMK (as explained in *Chapter 7, Applying Encryption in Cloud Services*).

For more information, please refer to the following resources:

Controlling network access to Amazon EFS file systems for NFS clients:

`https://docs.aws.amazon.com/efs/latest/ug/NFS-access-control-efs.html`

Working with Amazon EFS Access Points:

`https://docs.aws.amazon.com/efs/latest/ug/efs-access-points.html`

Amazon Elastic File System Network Isolation:

`https://docs.aws.amazon.com/efs/latest/ug/network-isolation.html`

Data encryption in Amazon EFS:

`https://docs.aws.amazon.com/efs/latest/ug/encryption.html`

Using IAM to enforce creating encrypted file systems:

`https://docs.aws.amazon.com/efs/latest/ug/using-iam-to-enforce-encryption-at-rest.html`

Best practices for conducting auditing and monitoring for Amazon EFS

Auditing is a crucial part of data protection.

As with any other managed service, AWS allows you to enable logging and auditing using two built-in services:

- **Amazon CloudWatch**: This is a service that allows you to log access activities and raise the alarm according to predefined activities (such as excessive delete actions).

- **AWS CloudTrail**: This is a service that allows you to monitor API activities (essentially, any action performed on Amazon EFS).

Here is a list of best practices to follow:

- Enable Amazon CloudWatch alarms for excessive Amazon EFS usage (for example, a high volume of store or delete operations on a specific EFS volume).

- Enable the use of AWS CloudTrail for any EFS volume to log any activity performed on the Amazon EFS API, including any activity conducted by a user, role, or AWS service.

- Create a trail, using AWS CloudTrail, on any EFS volume to log events, such as a requested action, date, and time, requested parameters, and more, for access to objects stored inside AWS EFS.

- Limit the access to the CloudTrail logs to a minimum number of employees, preferably those with an AWS management account, outside the scope of your end users (including outside the scope of your users), to avoid possible deletion or changes to the audit logs.

For more information, please refer to the following resource:

Logging and Monitoring in Amazon EFS:

```
https://docs.aws.amazon.com/efs/latest/ug/logging-monitoring.
html
```

Summary

In this section, we learned how to secure the Amazon EFS service based on the AWS infrastructure. This included logging in, securing network access, data encryption (at both transit and rest), and logging and auditing.

Securing Azure Files

Azure Files is an Azure file storage service based on the SMB protocol.

Best practices for conducting authentication and authorization for Azure Files

Azure supports the following authentication and authorization mechanisms to control access to Azure Files:

- **Active Directory Domain Services (AD DS)**: This is like the on-premises Active Directory using Kerberos authentication.

- **Azure Active Directory Domain Services (Azure AD DS)**: This is an add-on service to Azure AD, which allows you to authenticate to legacy services (SMB in the case of Azure Files) and protocols (Kerberos in the case of Azure Files).

Here is a list of best practices to follow:

- Use identity-based authentication to grant minimal permissions for sharing, directory, or file level access on the Azure Files service.

- For a cloud-native environment in Azure (with no on-premises VMs), make sure all VMs are joined to an Azure AD domain and that all VMs are connected to the same VNet as Azure AD DS.

- Enable Active Directory authentication over SMB to allow domain joined VMs access to Azure Files.

- Avoid using storage account keys for authenticating to Azure Files.

For more information, please refer to the following resources:

Overview of Azure Files identity-based authentication options for SMB access:

```
https://docs.microsoft.com/en-us/azure/storage/files/storage-
files-active-directory-overview
```

Planning for an Azure Files deployment:

```
https://docs.microsoft.com/en-us/azure/storage/files/storage-
files-planning
```

Best practices for securing network access to Azure Files

Because Azure Files is a managed service, it is located outside the customer's VNet. It is important to protect access to the Azure Files service.

Here is a list of best practices to follow:

- Since SMB is considered a non-secure protocol, make sure all access to Azure Files services from the on-premises network pass through a secured channel such as a VPN tunnel or an ExpressRoute service.

- To secure access from your VNet to Azure Files, use an Azure private endpoint, which avoids sending network traffic outside your VNet, through a secure channel.

- Remove the need for the use of transport encryption (HTTPS only) for all Azure Files shares.

- For sensitive environments, require a minimum TLS version of 1.2 for Azure Blob storage.

- Deny default network access to the Azure storage account and only allow access from a predefined set of IP addresses.

- For data that you need to retain for long periods (due to regulatory requirements), enable the Azure Files soft delete feature to protect the data from accidental deletion.

- Encrypt data at rest using Azure Key Vault (as explained in *Chapter 7, Applying Encryption in Cloud Services*).

- For sensitive environments, encrypt data at rest using customer-managed keys stored inside Azure Key Vault (as explained in *Chapter 7, Applying Encryption in Cloud Services*).

For more information, please refer to the following resources:

Azure Files networking considerations:

```
https://docs.microsoft.com/en-us/azure/storage/files/storage-
files-networking-overview
```

Prevent accidental deletion of Azure file shares:

```
https://docs.microsoft.com/en-us/azure/storage/files/storage-
files-prevent-file-share-deletion
```

Require secure transfer to ensure secure connections:

```
https://docs.microsoft.com/en-us/azure/storage/common/storage-
require-secure-transfer?toc=/azure/storage/files/toc.json
```

Enforce a minimum required version of Transport Layer Security (TLS) for requests to a storage account:

```
https://docs.microsoft.com/en-us/azure/storage/common/
transport-layer-security-configure-minimum-version?toc=%2Fazur
e%2Fstorage%2Ffiles%2Ftoc.json&tabs=portal
```

Azure Storage encryption for data at rest:

```
https://docs.microsoft.com/en-us/azure/storage/common/storage-
service-encryption?toc=/azure/storage/files/toc.json
```

Customer-managed keys for Azure Storage encryption:

```
https://docs.microsoft.com/en-us/azure/storage/common/
customer-managed-keys-overview?toc=/azure/storage/files/toc.
json
```

Best practices for conducting auditing and monitoring for Azure Files

Auditing is a crucial part of data protection.

Azure allows you to monitor Azure Files using the following services:

- **Azure Monitor**: This logs access and audit events from Azure Files.
- **Advanced Threat Protection for Azure Storage**: This allows you to detect an anomaly or any unusual activity in the Azure Files and Azure storage account.

Here is a list of best practices to follow:

- Enable log alerts using the Azure Monitor service to track access to Azure Files and raise alerts (such as multiple failed access attempts to Azure Files in a short period of time).
- Enable Azure Defender for Storage to receive security alerts inside the Azure Security Center console.
- Enable Azure storage logging to audit all authorization events for access to the Azure storage.

For more information, please refer to the following resources:

Requests logged in logging:

```
https://docs.microsoft.com/en-us/azure/storage/common/storage-
analytics-logging?toc=/azure/storage/files/toc.json
```

Monitoring Azure Files:

```
https://docs.microsoft.com/en-us/azure/storage/files/storage-
files-monitoring?tabs=azure-portal
```

Summary

In this section, we learned how to secure Azure Files based on the Azure infrastructure. This included logging in, securing network access, data encryption (at both transit and rest), and logging and auditing.

Securing Google Filestore

Google Filestore is a GCP file storage service based on the NFS protocol.

Best practices for conducting authentication and authorization for Google Filestore

Google Cloud IAM is the supported service in which to manage permissions to access Google Filestore.

Here is a list of best practices to follow:

- Keep your Google Filestore instances private.
- Create an IAM group, add users to the IAM group, and then grant the required permissions on the target Google Filestore instance to the target IAM group.
- Use IAM roles to configure minimal permissions to any Google Filestore instance.
- Use Cloud Firestore Security Rules to allow mobile clients, web clients, or serverless authentication to Google Filestore.

For more information, please refer to the following resources:

Security for server client libraries:

```
https://cloud.google.com/firestore/docs/security/iam
```

Get started with Cloud Firestore Security Rules:

```
https://firebase.google.com/docs/firestore/security/
get-started
```

Writing conditions for Cloud Firestore Security Rules:

```
https://firebase.google.com/docs/firestore/security/rules-
conditions
```

Best practices for securing network access to Google Filestore

Because Google Filestore is a managed service, it is located outside the customer's VPC. It is important to protect access to Google Filestore.

Here is a list of best practices to follow:

- Use IP-based access control to restrict access to Google Filestore.
- Create a Google Filestore instance on the same VPC as your clients.
- If the Google Filestore instance is located outside your VPC, use VPC firewall rules to restrict access between your VPC and Google Filestore.

For more information, please refer to the following resources:

- *Access Control*:

  `https://cloud.google.com/filestore/docs/access-control`
- *Configuring IP-based access control*:

  `https://cloud.google.com/filestore/docs/creating-instances#configuring_ip-based_access_control`
- *Configuring Firewall Rules*:

  `https://cloud.google.com/filestore/docs/configuring-firewall`
- *Architecture*:

  `https://cloud.google.com/filestore/docs/architecture`

Summary

In this section, we learned how to secure the Google Filestore service based on the GCP infrastructure – from logging in to securing network access.

Securing the CSI

A CSI is a standard driver for connecting container orchestration systems such as Kubernetes to block and file storage from various cloud providers.

For more information, please refer to the following resource:

Kubernetes Container Storage Interface (CSI) Documentation:

`https://kubernetes-csi.github.io/docs/introduction.html`

Securing CSI on AWS

Amazon **Elastic Kubernetes Service (EKS)** has a CSI driver for the following storage types:

- **Block storage**: EBS
- **Managed NFS**: EFS
- **Parallel filesystem (for HPC workloads)**: **Amazon FSx for Lustre**

Here is a list of best practices to follow:

- When creating an IAM policy to connect to a CSI driver, specify the storage resource name instead of using wildcard.
- Use IAM roles for service accounts to restrict access to your pod.
- Always use the latest CSI version for your chosen storage type.
- When using the CSI driver for EBS and its snapshots, always set (in the YAML configuration file) the value of `encrypted` to `True` and specify the **Amazon KMS key ID** (`KmsKeyId`). This allows the CSI driver to use a key from Amazon KMS.
- When using the CSI driver for EFS, always set (in the YAML configuration file) the value of `encryptInTransit` to `True`.
- Use Amazon Secrets Manager with the secret store CSI driver to store and retrieve secrets (such as tokens, SSH authentication keys, Docker configuration files, and more) to/from your EKS pods.

For more information, please refer to the following resources:

Amazon Elastic Block Store (EBS) CSI driver:

```
https://github.com/kubernetes-sigs/aws-ebs-csi-driver
```

Amazon EFS CSI Driver:

```
https://github.com/kubernetes-sigs/aws-efs-csi-driver
```

Amazon FSx for Lustre CSI Driver:

```
https://github.com/kubernetes-sigs/aws-fsx-csi-driver
```

How do I use persistent storage in Amazon EKS?:

```
https://aws.amazon.com/premiumsupport/knowledge-center/
eks-persistent-storage/
```

How to use AWS Secrets & Configuration Provider with your Kubernetes Secrets Store CSI driver:

```
https://aws.amazon.com/blogs/security/how-to-use-aws-secrets-
configuration-provider-with-kubernetes-secrets-store-csi-
driver/
```

Introducing Amazon EFS CSI dynamic provisioning:

```
https://aws.amazon.com/blogs/containers/introducing-efs-csi-
dynamic-provisioning/
```

Securing CSI on Azure

Azure Kubernetes Service (**AKS**) has a CSI driver for the following storage types:

- **Block storage**: Azure Disk
- **Managed SMB and NFS**: Azure Files

Here is a list of the best practices to follow:

- Always use the latest CSI version for your chosen storage type.
- Use Azure Key Vault with the secret store CSI driver to store and retrieve secrets (such as tokens, SSH authentication keys, Docker configuration files, and more) to/ from your AKS pods.
- Use a private endpoint to connect your AKS cluster to Azure Files.

For more information, please refer to the following resources:

Azure Disk CSI driver for Kubernetes:

```
https://github.com/kubernetes-sigs/azuredisk-csi-driver
```

Azure Key Vault Provider for Secrets Store CSI Driver:

```
https://github.com/Azure/secrets-store-csi-driver-provider-
azure
```

Use the Azure disk Container Storage Interface (CSI) drivers in Azure Kubernetes Service (AKS):

```
https://docs.microsoft.com/en-us/azure/aks/azure-disk-csi
```

Use Azure Files Container Storage Interface (CSI) drivers in Azure Kubernetes Service (AKS):

`https://docs.microsoft.com/en-us/azure/aks/azure-files-csi`

Securing CSI on GCP

Google Kubernetes Engine has a CSI driver for the following storage types:

- **Block storage**: Google Compute Engine Persistent Disk
- **Object storage**: Google Cloud Storage
- **Managed NFS**: Google Cloud Filestore

Here is a list of best practices to follow:

- Always use the latest CSI version for your chosen storage type.
- When using the CSI driver for Google Persistent Disk, specify (in the YAML file) the `disk-encryption-kms-key` key to allow the CSI driver to use a customer-managed encryption key from Google Cloud KMS.
- Use Cloud IAM roles to restrict access from your GKE cluster to Google Cloud Filestore.
- Use Google Secret Manager with the Secret Store CSI driver to store and retrieve secrets (such as tokens, SSH authentication keys, Docker configuration files, and more) to/from your GKE pods.

For more information, please refer to the following resources:

Google Compute Engine Persistent Disk CSI Driver:

`https://github.com/kubernetes-sigs/gcp-compute-persistent-disk-csi-driver`

Google Cloud Filestore CSI driver:

`https://github.com/kubernetes-sigs/gcp-filestore-csi-driver`

Google Cloud Storage CSI driver:

`https://github.com/ofek/csi-gcs`

Using the Compute Engine persistent disk CSI Driver:

`https://cloud.google.com/kubernetes-engine/docs/how-to/persistent-volumes/gce-pd-csi-driver`

Create a CMEK protected attached disk:

```
https://cloud.google.com/kubernetes-engine/docs/how-to/using-
cmek#create_a_cmek_protected_attached_disk
```

Google Secret Manager Provider for Secret Store CSI Driver:

```
https://github.com/GoogleCloudPlatform/secrets-store-csi-
driver-provider-gcp
```

Summary

In this section, we learned how to secure a CSI, based on the AWS, Azure, and GCP infrastructures – from permissions and encryption to secret management.

Summary

In this chapter, we focused on the various storage services in AWS, Azure, and GCP, ranging from object storage to block storage, file storage, and, finally, container storage.

In each section, we learned how to manage identity management (for authentication and authorization), how to control network access (from access controls to network encryption), and how to configure auditing and logging.

In the next chapter, we will review the various network services in the cloud (including virtual networking, security groups and ACLs, DNS, CDN, VPN, DDoS protection, and WAF).

4
Securing Networking Services

In *Chapter 2*, *Securing Compute Services*, and *Chapter 3*, *Securing Storage Services*, we covered securing compute and storage services, respectively.

Now, it's time to talk about securing *networking services*. We'll discuss virtual networking services, **Domain Name System (DNS)** services, **content delivery networks (CDNs)**, **virtual private networks (VPNs)**, **distributed denial of service (DDoS)** protection services, and **web application firewalls (WAFs)**.

This chapter will cover various networking services and provide you with the best practices on how to securely connect to and use each of them.

In this chapter, we will cover the following topics:

- Securing virtual networking
- Securing DNS services
- Securing CDN services
- Securing VPN services
- Securing DDoS protection services
- Securing WAF services

Technical requirements

For this chapter, the reader needs to have a fundamental understanding of networking services, such as **virtual private cloud (VPC)/VNET** services and security groups (or **access control lists (ACLs)**), and a solid understanding of VPN, DDoS protection, and WAF services.

Securing virtual networking

Each cloud provider has its own implementation of virtual networking.

According to the **shared responsibility model**, responsibility for the network is split between the cloud provider and the customer. The physical network layer (that is, access between the physical network equipment and physical host servers and storage inside the cloud provider's data centers) is the cloud provider's responsibility.

Virtual networking (such as **Amazon VPC**, **Azure VNet**, or **Google Cloud Platform (GCP) VPC**) is a network layer that is the responsibility of the customers (this layer enables access between virtual servers, managed storage services, managed databases, and more).

Traditional on-premises networking deals with the physical connections between devices in a system: for example, concepts such as **virtual local area networks (VLANs)** or subnetting, to split a network (with the devices connected to a network) and create network security barriers.

In the cloud, a network is software-based (this is also known as **software-defined networking (SDN)**). In the cloud, you have micro-segmentation, which means you can configure *allow* and *deny* access control rules between two instances (even if they are located on the same subnet). You will also be able to audit and control access to a resource such as an API.

A virtual network is a network area inside your cloud environment where most of the common cloud resources reside (such as virtual servers, managed databases, and so on). These resources are split into multiple network segments called *subnets*.

There can be one or more virtual networks in each customer's cloud environment, but at the end of the day, the basic idea is the same. Following are some important points regarding virtual networks:

- Access to subnets is controlled by access controls (such as Layer 4 firewalls).
- Subnets can be *private* (no direct access from the internet) or *public* (access from the internet is allowed).

- If you need to allow access to the internet for private subnet resources, you need to configure a NAT gateway.

- Virtual networks can be connected with each other via peer connections.

Since each cloud provider has its own network access control mechanism, the following table compares the differences between access control mechanisms:

	AWS Network ACLs	AWS security groups	Azure network security groups	GCP VPC firewall rules
Stateless / Stateful	Stateless	Stateful	Stateless	Stateful
Location	Subnet level	Instance level	VM, subnet, tagging level	Instance level

Table 4.1 – Access control mechanisms

Next, we are going to see what the best practices are for securing virtual networking services from Amazon, Azure, and GCP.

Securing Amazon Virtual Private Cloud

Amazon Virtual Private Cloud (**Amazon VPC**) is the Amazon virtual networking service.

Best practices for securing network access to Amazon VPC

AWS supports the following mechanisms to protect access to resources inside a VPC:

- **Network ACLs**: A stateless mechanism for protecting access to/from resources at a subnet level. You need to configure both inbound and outbound rules. Network ACLs support both *allow* and *deny* rules.

- **Security groups**: A stateful mechanism for protecting access to resources at an instance level. You need to configure inbound rules. Security groups support only *allow* rules.

- Network access to a resource is granted by a combination of the network ACLs on a subnet level with an aggregation of all the security groups, effective on a resource such as a virtual machine (in case several security groups allow different access to a resource such as a virtual machine).

Here are some best practices for securing network access to Amazon VPC:

- When creating custom network ACLs, create a final deny rule for both inbound and outbound traffic for better protection.

- Create subnets according to the resource's function (for example, public subnets for web servers, private subnets for database servers, and so on).

- For remote access protocols (SSH/RDP), limit the source IP address (or **Classless Inter-Domain Routing (CIDR)**) to well-known sources.

- For file sharing protocols (CIFS/SMB/FTP), limit the source IP address (or CIDR) to well-known sources.

- Use security groups to control access between public resources (such as load balancers or publicly facing web servers) and private resources (such as databases) and limit the access to the minimum required ports/protocols.

- Set names and descriptions for security groups to allow a better understanding of any security group's purpose.

- Use *tagging* (also known as *labeling*) for security groups to allow a better understanding of which security groups belong to which AWS resources.

- For large-scale environments with multiple AWS accounts, use **AWS Firewall Manager** to centrally create and enforce VPC security groups.

- For secure access from resources inside your VPC to **AWS Managed Services** (such as AWS S3, Amazon RDS and more), and to keep traffic inside the AWS backbone, use **AWS PrivateLink**, and configure your VPC security groups to allow traffic from your VPC to AWS managed services.

- To allow outbound access from internal resources inside private subnets to destinations on the internet (based on the IPv4 protocol), use NAT gateways or any self-hosted NAT proxy.

- To allow outbound access from internal resources inside private subnets to destinations on the internet (based on the IPv6 protocol), use an *egress-only* internet gateway.

For more information, please refer to the following resources:

Network ACLs:

```
https://docs.aws.amazon.com/vpc/latest/userguide/vpc-network-acls.html
```

Security groups for your VPC:

```
https://docs.aws.amazon.com/vpc/latest/userguide/VPC_
SecurityGroups.html
```

AWS Firewall Manager:

```
https://aws.amazon.com/firewall-manager/
```

Interface VPC endpoints (AWS PrivateLink):

```
https://docs.aws.amazon.com/vpc/latest/privatelink/vpce-
interface.html
```

NAT gateways:

```
https://docs.aws.amazon.com/vpc/latest/userguide/vpc-nat-
gateway.html
```

Egress-only internet gateways:

```
https://docs.aws.amazon.com/vpc/latest/userguide/egress-only-
internet-gateway.html
```

Best practices for monitoring Amazon VPC

AWS allows you to monitor Amazon VPC using the following built-in services:

- **Amazon CloudWatch**: This is a service that allows you to monitor your VPC components (such as ingress/egress traffic volumes).

- **VPC Flow Logs**: This is a service that allows you to log network activity inside your VPC (for example, traffic metadata such as source, destination, port, timestamp, size, and allow and deny network events). This is useful for both troubleshooting and investigating security-related events.

Here are some best practices for monitoring Amazon VPC:

- Enable **CloudWatch Logs** to monitor your VPC components' activity and the traffic between your VPC resources and the VPC endpoint (AWS managed services).

- Use **AWS CloudTrail** to monitor VPC configuration.

- Enable **VPC Flow Logs** to log and further analyze allowed and denied traffic activity. Combined with **Amazon GuardDuty**, you will be able to detect anomalous network behavior, such as interaction with **command and control** (**C&C**) networks, malicious IP addresses, and more.

> **Note**
>
> For large-scale production environments, enable VPC Flow Logs only for short periods of time, for troubleshooting purposes only (due to high storage cost and large amounts of data generated by VPC Flow Logs).

- Use **AWS Config** or **AWS Security Hub** to detect inbound access to resources inside your VPC via unencrypted protocols (such as HTTP instead of HTTPS, or LDAP instead of LDAPS).

- In case you need to troubleshoot network issues by capturing network traffic without interrupting production systems, use **Traffic Mirroring** in Amazon VPC to copy live network traffic from a network interface of an **Amazon Elastic Compute Cloud (EC2)** instance, or from a network load balancer to an out-of-band security appliance.

For more information, please refer to the following resources:

Using CloudWatch Logs with interface VPC endpoints:

```
https://docs.aws.amazon.com/AmazonCloudWatch/latest/logs/
cloudwatch-logs-and-interface-VPC.html
```

Log and monitor your VPC:

```
https://docs.aws.amazon.com/vpc/latest/userguide/logging-
monitoring.html
```

VPC Flow Logs:

```
https://docs.aws.amazon.com/vpc/latest/userguide/flow-logs.
html
```

What is Traffic Mirroring:

```
https://docs.aws.amazon.com/vpc/latest/mirroring/what-is-
traffic-mirroring.html
```

Summary

In this section, we have learned how to secure the Amazon VPC network environment by relying on the AWS infrastructure and using everything from network ACLs for inbound and outbound traffic to monitoring and capturing network traffic.

Securing Azure VNet

Azure Virtual Network (**Azure VNet**) is the Azure virtual networking service.

Best practices for securing network access to Azure VNet

To protect resources inside a VNet, Azure supports **network security groups** (**NSGs**) – a stateless mechanism for protecting access to resources, at a virtual machine, subnet, or tagging level. You need to configure both inbound and outbound rules for VNet NSGs.

Here are some best practices to follow:

- Create subnets according to the resource function (for example, public subnets for web servers, private subnets for database servers, and so on).

- For remote access protocols (SSH/RDP), limit the source IP address (or CIDR) to well-known sources.

- For file sharing protocols (CIFS/SMB/FTP), limit the source IP address (or CIDR) to well-known sources.

- Use NSGs to control access between public resources (such as load balancer or publicly facing web servers) and private resources (such as databases) and limit the access to the minimum required ports/protocols.

- Set names and descriptions for NSGs to allow a better understanding of any NSG's purpose.

- Use *tagging* (also known as *labeling*) for NSGs to allow a better understanding of which network security groups belong to which Azure resources.

- Use **application security groups** to define access rules at the application layer (for example, rules for allowing inbound HTTP access).

- Use service tags to configure rules for pre-defined service (for example, **Azure Load Balancer**), instead of using IP addresses.

- To allow outbound access from internal resources inside private subnets to destinations on the internet, use **Azure Virtual Network NAT** (or use a NAT gateway).

- For large-scale environments with multiple Azure subscriptions, use **Azure Firewall** to centrally create, enforce, and log network policies across multiple subscriptions.

For more information, please refer to the following resources:

Azure Virtual Network concepts and best practices:

```
https://docs.microsoft.com/en-us/azure/virtual-network/
concepts-and-best-practices
```

Network security groups:

```
https://docs.microsoft.com/en-us/azure/virtual-network/
network-security-groups-overview
```

Application security groups:

```
https://docs.microsoft.com/en-us/azure/virtual-network/
application-security-groups
```

Virtual network service tags:

```
https://docs.microsoft.com/en-us/azure/virtual-network/
service-tags-overview
```

What is Virtual Network NAT:

```
https://docs.microsoft.com/en-us/azure/virtual-network/
nat-overview
```

What is Azure Firewall:

```
https://docs.microsoft.com/en-us/azure/firewall/overview
```

Best practices for monitoring Azure VNet

Azure allows you to monitor network activity using **Azure Network Watcher** – a service for capturing NSG Flow Logs.

Here are some best practices for monitoring Azure VNet:

- Enable Azure Network Watcher **NSG Flow Logs** to log and further analyze allowed and denied traffic activity.

> **Note**
>
> For large-scale production environments, enable NSG Flow Logs only for short periods of time, for troubleshooting purposes only (due to high storage cost and large amounts of data generated by NSG Flow Logs).

- If you need to troubleshoot network issues by capturing network traffic, use the Azure Network Watcher **packet capture** extension to copy live network traffic from a virtual machine to an Azure storage account.

> **Note**
>
> For large-scale production environments, enable the Network Watcher packet capture extension only for short periods of time, for troubleshooting purposes only (due to the performance impact on the target VM).

- For large-scale environments, use **Azure Traffic Analytics** to locate security threats (such as open ports, application outbound internet traffic, and so on).
- Use **Azure Policy** to detect inbound access to resources inside your VNet via unencrypted protocols (such as HTTP instead of HTTPS, or LDAP instead of LDAPS).

For more information, please refer to the following resources:

Log network traffic to and from a virtual machine using the Azure portal:

```
https://docs.microsoft.com/en-us/azure/network-watcher/
network-watcher-nsg-flow-logging-portal
```

Introduction to flow logging for network security groups:

```
https://docs.microsoft.com/en-us/azure/network-watcher/
network-watcher-nsg-flow-logging-overview
```

What is Azure Network Watcher:

```
https://docs.microsoft.com/en-us/azure/network-watcher/
network-watcher-monitoring-overview
```

Manage packet captures with Azure Network Watcher using the portal:

```
https://docs.microsoft.com/en-us/azure/network-watcher/
network-watcher-packet-capture-manage-portal
```

Traffic Analytics:

```
https://docs.microsoft.com/en-us/azure/network-watcher/
traffic-analytics
```

Summary

In this section, we have learned how to secure the Azure VNet environment by relying on the Azure infrastructure and using everything from access control lists for inbound and outbound traffic to monitoring and capturing network traffic.

Securing Google Cloud VPC

Google Cloud VPC is the Google virtual networking service.

Best practices for securing network access to Google Cloud VPC

To protect resources inside a VPC, Google supports **VPC firewall rules** – a stateful mechanism for protecting access to resources. You need to configure either inbound and outbound rules, and for each rule, you can configure either an action of *allow* or *deny*.

Here are some best practices for securing network access to Google Cloud VPC:

- Create subnets according to the resource function (for example, public subnets for web servers, private subnets for database servers, and so on).

- For remote access protocols (SSH/RDP), limit the source IP address (or CIDR) to well-known sources.

- For file sharing protocols (CIFS/SMB/FTP), limit the source IP address (or CIDR) to well-known sources.

- Use VPC firewall rules to control access between public resources (such as load balancers or publicly facing web servers) and private resources (such as databases) and limit the access to the minimum required ports/protocols.

- Set names and descriptions for VPC firewall rules to allow a better understanding of any firewall rule's purpose.

- Use *tagging* (also known as *labeling*) for VPC firewall rules to allow a better understanding of which VPC firewall rule belongs to which VPC resources.

- Use network tags to configure rules to groups of resources (such as a group of compute engine instances) instead of using IP addresses.

- To allow outbound access from internal resources inside private subnets to destinations on the internet, use a **Cloud NAT gateway**.

- For large-scale environments with multiple Google Cloud VPC projects, use VPC Service Controls to enforce access restrictions over your VPC resources, based on the identity of the IP address.

For more information, please refer to the following resources:

- *VPC firewall rules overview*:

  `https://cloud.google.com/vpc/docs/firewalls`

- *Using firewall rules*:

  `https://cloud.google.com/vpc/docs/using-firewalls`

- *Configuring network tags*:

  `https://cloud.google.com/vpc/docs/add-remove-network-tags`

- *NAT overview*:

  `https://cloud.google.com/nat/docs/overview`

- *Overview of VPC Service Controls*:

  `https://cloud.google.com/vpc-service-controls/docs/overview`

Best practices for monitoring Google Cloud VPC

Google allows you to monitor Google Cloud VPC using the following built-in services:

- **Google Cloud Logging**: This is a service that allows you to monitor your VPC components.

- **VPC Flow Logs**: This is a service that allows you to log network activity inside your VPC (for example, *allow* and *deny* network events).

Here are some best practices for monitoring Google Cloud VPC:

- Enable VPC audit logs to monitor your VPC components' activity and the traffic between your VPC resources.

- Note that admin activity audit logs are enabled by default and cannot be disabled.

- Explicitly enable **data access audit logs** to log activities in your Google Cloud VPC.

- Limit access to audit logs to the minimum number of employees (to avoid unwanted changes to the audit logs).

- Enable **Firewall Rules Logging** to audit the functionality of your VPC firewall rules.

- Enable **VPC Flow Logs** to log and further analyze allowed and denied traffic activity.

> **Note**
>
> For large-scale production environments, enable VPC Flow Logs only for short periods of time, for troubleshooting purposes only (due to the high storage cost and large amounts of data generated by VPC Flow Logs).

- In case you need to troubleshoot network issues by capturing network traffic, use **Packet Mirroring** to copy live network traffic from a compute engine VM instance to an instance group behind an internal load balancer.

> **Note**
>
> For large-scale production environments, enable Packet Mirroring only for short periods of time, for troubleshooting purposes only (due to high performance impact on the target VM).

For more information, please refer to the following resources:

Firewall Rules Logging overview:

https://cloud.google.com/vpc/docs/firewall-rules-logging

VPC Flow Logs overview:

https://cloud.google.com/vpc/docs/flow-logs

Using VPC Flow Logs:

https://cloud.google.com/vpc/docs/using-flow-logs

VPC audit logging information:

https://cloud.google.com/vpc/docs/audit-logging

Packet Mirroring overview:

https://cloud.google.com/vpc/docs/packet-mirroring

Summary

In this section, we have learned how to secure Google Cloud VPC by relying on the Google Cloud VPC infrastructure and using everything from VPC firewall rules for inbound and outbound traffic to monitoring and capturing network traffic.

Securing DNS services

Each cloud provider has its own implementation of managed DNS services – these include services for translating hostnames into IP addresses, different types of DNS records services (such as **Alias, CNAME**, and more), resolving hostname to load-balance IP, and more.

Securing Amazon Route 53

Amazon Route 53 is the Amazon managed DNS service.

Best practices for securing Amazon Route 53

The following are some of the best practices to follow:

- Create an **Identity and Access Management (IAM)** group, add users to the group, and grant the required permissions on the Route 53 service for the target group.

- Enable **Domain Name System Security Extensions (DNSSEC signing)** on any public-hosted zone to protect against DNS spoofing attacks.

- Use a new **customer master key** (**CMK**) to sign any newly created public-hosted zone.

- Make sure privacy protection is enabled for any domain you manage using Route 53 to protect the privacy of domain owners' contact information.

- Enable the Route 53 domain transfer lock to prevent your domains from being transferred to another registrar.

- Create a **sender policy framework** (**SPF**) record on your Route 53 hosted domain to publicly specify which mail servers are authorized to send emails on behalf of your email domain.

- Use the Route 53 **Resolver DNS Firewall** to block DNS-level threats originating from your VPC.

- Remove unassigned DNS records from your hosted zones (records of resources such as IP addresses that connected to a resource that was removed).

- Use private hosted zones to manage DNS records for internal resources (such as resources located inside private subnets).

- Enable public DNS query logging to be able to analyze which public DNS queries were submitted to Route 53 about your domains.

- Enable **Resolver query logging** to be able to analyze information such as the Route 53 Resolver DNS Firewall block rules.

- Enable Amazon GuardDuty to analyze DNS logs and raise alerts about suspicious activity, such as C&C activity, Bitcoin mining, and more.

For more information, please refer to the following resources:

Security in Amazon Route 53:

```
https://docs.aws.amazon.com/Route53/latest/DeveloperGuide/
security.html
```

Overview of managing access permissions to your Amazon Route 53 resources:

```
https://docs.aws.amazon.com/Route53/latest/DeveloperGuide/
access-control-overview.html
```

Configuring DNSSEC for a domain:

```
https://docs.aws.amazon.com/Route53/latest/DeveloperGuide/
domain-configure-dnssec.html
```

Enabling or disabling privacy protection for contact information for a domain:

```
https://docs.aws.amazon.com/Route53/latest/DeveloperGuide/
domain-privacy-protection.html
```

Locking a domain to prevent unauthorized transfer to another registrar:

```
https://docs.aws.amazon.com/Route53/latest/DeveloperGuide/
domain-lock.html
```

SPF record type:

```
https://docs.aws.amazon.com/Route53/latest/DeveloperGuide/
ResourceRecordTypes.html#SPFFormat
```

How Route 53 Resolver DNS Firewall works:

```
https://docs.aws.amazon.com/Route53/latest/DeveloperGuide/
resolver-dns-firewall-overview.html
```

Working with private hosted zones:

```
https://docs.aws.amazon.com/Route53/latest/DeveloperGuide/
hosted-zones-private.html
```

Summary

In this section, we have learned how to secure Amazon Route 53 by relying on the AWS infrastructure and using access controls, DNS record protection, threat detection for DNS-related activities, and more.

Securing Azure DNS

Azure DNS is the Azure managed DNS service.

Best practices for securing Azure DNS:

The following are some of the best practices to follow:

- Grant minimal permissions for accessing and managing the Azure DNS using Azure **role-based access controls** (**RBACs**).

- Remove unassigned DNS records from your hosted zones (records of resources such as IP addresses that connected to a resource that was removed).

- Enable the **ReadOnly** lock for any hosted zone you manage using Azure DNS to protect from accidental changes to DNS records.

- Use private DNS zones to manage DNS records for internal resources (such as resources located inside private subnets).

- Use **Azure Defender** for DNS to detect and send alerts about suspicious DNS-related activities.

- Enable DNS logging and forward the logs to **Azure Sentinel** to detect suspicious behavior on the Azure DNS service.

For more information, please refer to the following resources:

Azure security baseline for Azure DNS:

```
https://docs.microsoft.com/en-us/security/benchmark/azure/
baselines/dns-security-baseline
```

How to protect DNS zones and records:

```
https://docs.microsoft.com/en-us/azure/dns/dns-protect-zones-
recordsets#resource-locks
```

How to protect private DNS zones and records:

```
https://docs.microsoft.com/en-us/azure/dns/dns-protect-
private-zones-recordsets
```

Introduction to Azure Defender for DNS:

```
https://docs.microsoft.com/en-us/azure/security-center/
defender-for-dns-introduction
```

Summary

In this section, we have learned how to secure Azure DNS by relying on the Azure infrastructure and using access controls, DNS record protection, threat detection for DNS-related activities, and more.

Securing Google Cloud DNS

Google Cloud DNS is the Google managed DNS service.

Best practices for securing Google Cloud DNS

The following are some of the best practices to follow:

- Create an IAM group, add users to the group, and grant the required permissions on the Google Cloud DNS service for the target group.

- Enable DNSSEC signing on any public-hosted zone to protect against DNS spoofing attacks.

- Remove unassigned DNS records from your hosted zones (records of resources such as IP addresses that connected to a resource that was removed).

- Use Google Cloud DNS private zones to manage DNS records for internal resources (such as resources located inside private subnets).

- Enable Google Cloud DNS audit logs to monitor DNS activity.

- Note that admin activity audit logs are enabled by default and cannot be disabled.

- Explicitly enable data access audit logs to log activities in Google Cloud DNS.

- Limit access to audit logs to the minimum number of employees to avoid unwanted changes to the audit logs.

For more information, please refer to the following resources:

Cloud DNS overview:

```
https://cloud.google.com/dns/docs/overview
```

DNS best practices:

```
https://cloud.google.com/dns/docs/best-practices
```

Managing DNSSEC configuration:

`https://cloud.google.com/dns/docs/dnssec-config`

DNS Security Extensions (DNSSEC) overview:

`https://cloud.google.com/dns/docs/dnssec`

Cloud DNS audit logging information:

`https://cloud.google.com/dns/docs/audit-logging`

Logging and monitoring:

`https://cloud.google.com/dns/docs/monitoring`

Summary

In this section, we have learned how to secure Google Cloud DNS by relying on the Google Cloud infrastructure and using access controls, DNS record protection and more.

Securing CDN services

Each cloud provider has its own implementation of a CDN service – that is, a service for distributing content closer to the customer throughout the entire world.

A CDN caches content (such as images, videos, or static web pages) in multiple locations around the world, allowing customers to receive the content quickly from a location close to the customer.

CDNs also serve as an extra defense mechanism against DDoS attacks by being one of the first services that serves a customer's request, even before the request reaches the servers or applications.

Securing Amazon CloudFront

Amazon CloudFront is the AWS managed CDN service.

Best practices for securing Amazon CloudFront

The following are some of the best practices to follow:

- Restrict access to origin servers (where your original content is stored) from CDN segments only (allow traffic only from the CDN segments towards servers or services that store content).

- Share content via the HTTPS protocol to preserve the confidentiality of the content and to assure the authenticity of the content.

- When distributing content over HTTPS, use TLS 1.2 over older protocols, such as SSL v3.

- If you have a requirement to distribute private content, use CloudFront signed URLs.

- If you have a requirement to distribute sensitive content, use field-level encryption as an extra protection layer.

- Use **AWS Web Application Firewall (WAF)** to protect content on Amazon CloudFront from application-layer attacks (such as detecting and blocking bot traffic, *OWASP Top 10 application attacks*, and more).

- Enable CloudFront standard logs for audit logging purposes. Store the logs in a dedicated **Amazon S3** bucket, with strict access controls, to avoid log tampering.

For more information, please refer to the following resources:

Using HTTPS with CloudFront:

```
https://docs.aws.amazon.com/AmazonCloudFront/latest/
DeveloperGuide/using-https.html
```

Configuring secure access and restricting access to content:

```
https://docs.aws.amazon.com/AmazonCloudFront/latest/
DeveloperGuide/SecurityAndPrivateContent.html
```

Serving private content with signed URLs and signed cookies:

```
https://docs.aws.amazon.com/AmazonCloudFront/latest/
DeveloperGuide/PrivateContent.html
```

Using AWS WAF to control access to your content:

```
https://docs.aws.amazon.com/AmazonCloudFront/latest/
DeveloperGuide/distribution-web-awswaf.html
```

Using field-level encryption to help protect sensitive data:

```
https://docs.aws.amazon.com/AmazonCloudFront/latest/
DeveloperGuide/field-level-encryption.html
```

Configuring and using standard logs (access logs):

```
https://docs.aws.amazon.com/AmazonCloudFront/latest/
DeveloperGuide/AccessLogs.html
```

Logging and monitoring in Amazon CloudFront:

```
https://docs.aws.amazon.com/AmazonCloudFront/latest/
DeveloperGuide/logging-and-monitoring.html
```

Summary

In this section, we have learned how to secure Amazon CloudFront by relying on the AWS infrastructure and using secure transport protocols (such as TLS), protection for private or sensitive content, logging, and protection from application-layer attacks.

Securing Azure CDN

Azure Content Delivery Network (**CDN**) is the Azure managed CDN service.

Best practices for securing Azure CDN

The following are some of the best practices to follow:

- Restrict access to origin servers (where your original content is stored) from CDN segments only (allow traffic only from the CDN segments towards servers or services that store content).

- Prefer sharing content via the HTTPS protocol to preserve the confidentiality of the content and to ensure the authenticity of the content.

- When distributing content over HTTPS, prefer using TLS 1.2 over older protocols such as SSL v3.

- Enable Azure CDN logs for audit logging purposes. Forward the logs to **Azure Security Center** for further investigation.

- Forward Azure CDN logs to **Azure Sentinel** (the Azure managed SIEM service) for threat detection.

For more information, please refer to the following resource:

Azure security baseline for Content Delivery Network:

```
https://docs.microsoft.com/en-us/security/benchmark/azure/
baselines/content-delivery-network-security-baseline
```

Summary

In this section, we have learned how to secure Azure CDN by relying on the Azure infrastructure and using secure transport protocols, logging, threat detection, and more.

Securing Google Cloud CDN

Google Cloud CDN is the Google managed CDN service.

Best practices for securing Google Cloud CDN

The following are some of the best practices to follow:

- Restrict access to origin servers (where your original content is stored) from CDN segments only (allow traffic only from CDN segments towards servers or services that store content).

- Share content via HTTPS protocol to preserve the confidentiality of the content and to assure the authenticity of the content.

- When distributing content over HTTPS, use TLS 1.2 over older protocols such as SSL v3.

- If you have a requirement to distribute content such as individual files for a short period of time, use signed URLs.

- Enable Google Cloud CDN audit logs to monitor CDN activity.

- Note that admin activity audit logs are enabled by default and cannot be disabled.

- Explicitly enable data access audit logs to log activities in Google Cloud CDN.

- Limit access to audit logs to the minimum number of employees to avoid unwanted changes to the audit logs.

For more information, please refer to the following resources:

Cloud CDN features:

`https://cloud.google.com/cdn/docs/features`

Signed URLs and signed cookies overview:

`https://cloud.google.com/cdn/docs/private-content`

Cloud CDN audit logging information:

`https://cloud.google.com/cdn/docs/audit-logging`

Logging and monitoring

`https://cloud.google.com/cdn/docs/logging`

Summary

In this section, we have learned how to secure Google Cloud CDN by relying on the Google Cloud CDN infrastructure and using secure transport protocols, logging, and more.

Securing VPN services

Each cloud provider has its own implementation of a VPN service. VPNs allow network-based access to private resources over untrusted networks.

Following are some of the common VPN services concepts:

- Combined with a firewall, a VPN allows organizations to access and manage their internal resources (both sides of the VPN tunnel) in a secure manner.

- A VPN allows corporate users to connect to their organization's cloud environment from either the corporate network or from home.

- The connection between the VPN and the cloud environment is encrypted.

- The connection to the cloud environment is transparent (that is, the same as working locally from the corporate network).

- The VPN can enforce the use of **multi-factor authentication** (**MFA**) for end users connecting using a client VPN.

In this section, we will review how site-to-site VPN services and client VPN services can allow connectivity to your cloud environment.

Securing AWS Site-to-Site VPN

AWS Site-to-Site VPN is a managed service that allows you to connect your corporate network to the AWS environment in a secure IPsec channel.

Best practices for securing AWS Site-to-Site VPN

The following are some of the best practices to follow:

- Restrict access to AWS resources inside your AWS environment using Amazon VPC security groups and authorization rules.

- For non-sensitive environments, use pre-shared keys to authenticate to the site-to-site VPN tunnel.

- For highly sensitive environments, use a private certificate from the **AWS Certificate Manager (ACM) Private Certificate Authority (CA)** service.

- Create an IAM group, add users to the group, and grant the required permissions on the AWS Site-to-Site VPN connection for the target group an example of an IAM role would be the ability to invoke an API action through the VPN).

- It is recommended to schedule a maintenance window and rotate the pre-shared keys or the certificate for the AWS Site-to-Site VPN connection once a year, to avoid potential compromise.

- Use Amazon CloudWatch to monitor the VPN tunnels (for example, it could send an alarm when the amount of traffic in bytes is above a pre-defined threshold).

- Use AWS CloudTrail to monitor users' activity on the AWS VPN service.

For more information, please refer to the following resources:

Site-to-Site VPN tunnel authentication options:

```
https://docs.aws.amazon.com/vpn/latest/s2svpn/vpn-tunnel-
authentication-options.html
```

Identity and access management for AWS Site-to-Site VPN:

```
https://docs.aws.amazon.com/vpn/latest/s2svpn/
vpn-authentication-access-control.html
```

Replacing compromised credentials:

```
https://docs.aws.amazon.com/vpn/latest/s2svpn/
CompromisedCredentials.html
```

Logging and monitoring:

```
https://docs.aws.amazon.com/vpn/latest/s2svpn/logging-
monitoring.html
```

Monitoring your Site-to-Site VPN connection:

```
https://docs.aws.amazon.com/vpn/latest/s2svpn/monitoring-
overview-vpn.html
```

Securing AWS Client VPN

AWS Client VPN allows you to connect to the AWS environment from anywhere on the internet using an **OpenVPN** client in a secure TLS channel.

Best practices for securing AWS Client VPN

The following are some of the best practices to follow:

- Restrict access to AWS resources inside your AWS environment using VPC security groups and authorization rules.

- If you are managing your user identities with **AWS Directory Service**, use AWS Client VPN **Active Directory** authentication.

- If you are using the **SAML 2.0** federated authentication service, use AWS Client VPN **single sign-on** authentication (SAML authentication).

- For highly sensitive environments, use AWS Client VPN **certificate-based** authentication using the **ACM** service.

- If you are using AWS Client VPN certificate-based authentication, use client certificate revocation lists to revoke access to employees who have left the organization or do not need access through the VPN.

- Use Amazon CloudWatch to monitor the VPN tunnels (for example, it could send an alarm when the amount of traffic in bytes is above a pre-defined threshold).

- Use AWS CloudTrail to monitor users' activity on the AWS VPN service.

For more information, please refer to the following resources:

Restrict access to your network:

```
https://docs.aws.amazon.com/vpn/latest/clientvpn-admin/
scenario-restrict.html
```

AWS Client VPN authentication:

```
https://docs.aws.amazon.com/vpn/latest/clientvpn-admin/client-
authentication.html
```

Client certificate revocation lists:

```
https://docs.aws.amazon.com/vpn/latest/clientvpn-admin/cvpn-
working-certificates.html
```

Authorization rules:

```
https://docs.aws.amazon.com/vpn/latest/clientvpn-admin/cvpn-
working-rules.html
```

Logging and monitoring:

```
https://docs.aws.amazon.com/vpn/latest/clientvpn-admin/
logging-monitoring.html
```

Monitoring Client VPN:

```
https://docs.aws.amazon.com/vpn/latest/clientvpn-admin/
monitoring-overview.html
```

Summary

In this section, we have learned how to secure the AWS VPN services (both site-to-site and client-based) by relying on the AWS infrastructure and using network access controls, authentication mechanisms, logging, and more.

Securing Azure VPN Gateway (Site-to-Site)

Azure VPN Gateway (*Site-to-Site*) is a managed service that allows you to connect your corporate network to the Azure environment in a secure channel.

Best practices for securing Azure VPN Gateway (Site-to-Site)

The following are some of the best practices to follow:

- Restrict access to Azure resources inside your Azure environment using NSGs.

- Use the **GCMAES256** algorithm for both encryption of the IPsec tunnel and ensuring the integrity of the traffic passing through the tunnel.

- Use pre-shared keys to authenticate to the site-to-site VPN tunnel.

- For large-scale environments with multiple Azure subscriptions and multiple site-to-site VPN gateways, use Azure Firewall to centrally create, enforce, and log network policies across multiple subscriptions.

- Use Azure Monitor to monitor the VPN tunnels (for example, it could send alerts when the amount of traffic in bytes is above a pre-defined threshold).

- Enable **Azure DDoS Protection** to protect your VPN gateway from DDoS attacks.

For more information, please refer to the following resources:

Azure security baseline for VPN Gateway:

```
https://docs.microsoft.com/en-us/security/benchmark/azure/
baselines/vpn-gateway-security-baseline
```

About cryptographic requirements and Azure VPN gateways:

```
https://docs.microsoft.com/en-us/azure/vpn-gateway/
vpn-gateway-about-compliance-crypto
```

Tutorial: Create a Site-to-Site connection in the Azure portal:

```
https://docs.microsoft.com/en-us/azure/vpn-gateway/tutorial-
site-to-site-portal
```

Monitoring VPN Gateway:

```
https://docs.microsoft.com/en-us/azure/vpn-gateway/monitor-
vpn-gateway
```

Securing Azure VPN Gateway (Point-to-Site)

Azure VPN Gateway (*Point-to-Site*) allows you to connect from anywhere on the internet to the Azure environment in a secure channel using an OpenVPN client, **Secure Socket Tunneling Protocol (SSTP)**, or **Internet Key Exchange version 2 (IKEv2)** VPN client.

Best practices for securing Azure VPN Gateway (Point-to-Site)

The following are some of the best practices to follow:

- If you are managing your user identities inside Azure Active Directory, use Azure Active Directory to authenticate users to the VPN gateway, combined with Azure RBACs to provide minimal access to resources on your Azure environment.

- If you are authenticating users through Azure Active Directory, enforce MFA for your end users.

- For highly sensitive environments, use certificates to authenticate to the point-to-site VPN tunnel.

- Restrict access to Azure resources inside your Azure environment using NSGs.

- Use the **GCMAES256** algorithm for both encryption of the IPSec tunnel and ensuring the integrity of the traffic passing through the tunnel.

- Use Azure Monitor to monitor the VPN tunnels (for example, it could send alerts when the amount of traffic in bytes is above a pre-defined threshold) and to log audit-related events (an example of suspicious behavior could be a user attempting to log in in the middle of the night for the first time).

- Enable Azure DDoS Protection to protect your VPN gateway from DDoS attacks.

- Use **Azure Advanced Threat Protection** to identify anomalous behavior of users connecting through the point-to-site VPN tunnel.

- Use Azure Security Center to detect security-related events through the VPN gateway.

For more information, please refer to the following resources:

Azure security baseline for VPN Gateway:

```
https://docs.microsoft.com/en-us/security/benchmark/azure/
baselines/vpn-gateway-security-baseline
```

About cryptographic requirements and Azure VPN gateways:

```
https://docs.microsoft.com/en-us/azure/vpn-gateway/
vpn-gateway-about-compliance-crypto
```

About Point-to-Site VPN:

```
https://docs.microsoft.com/en-us/azure/vpn-gateway/point-to-
site-about
```

Configure a Point-to-Site VPN connection using Azure certificate authentication: Azure portal:

```
https://docs.microsoft.com/en-us/azure/vpn-gateway/
vpn-gateway-howto-point-to-site-resource-manager-portal
```

Enable Azure AD Multi-Factor Authentication (MFA) for VPN users:

```
https://docs.microsoft.com/en-us/azure/vpn-gateway/openvpn-
azure-ad-mfa
```

Monitoring VPN Gateway:

```
https://docs.microsoft.com/en-us/azure/vpn-gateway/monitor-
vpn-gateway
```

Summary

In this section, we have learned how to secure the Azure VPN services (both site-to-site and client-based VPN) by relying on the Azure infrastructure and using network access controls, authentication mechanisms, logging, and more.

Securing Google Cloud VPN

Google Cloud VPN is a managed service that allows you to connect your corporate network to the GCP environment in a secure channel (using an IPSec tunnel).

Best practices for securing Google Cloud VPN

The following are some of the best practices to follow:

- Restrict access to GCP resources inside your Google Cloud VPC using VPC firewall rules.

- Use the **AES-GCM-16-256** algorithm for both encryption of the IPSec tunnel and ensuring the integrity of the traffic passing through the tunnel.

- Use a strong, 32-character, pre-shared key to authenticate to the Google Cloud VPN tunnel.

- Create an IAM group, add users to the group, and grant the required permissions on the Google Cloud VPN connection for the target group.

- Use **Google Cloud Logging** to monitor activity on the Google Cloud VPN service.

For more information, please refer to the following resources:

Cloud VPN overview:

```
https://cloud.google.com/network-connectivity/docs/vpn/
concepts/overview
```

Generating a strong pre-shared key:

```
https://cloud.google.com/network-connectivity/docs/vpn/how-to/
generating-pre-shared-key
```

Supported IKE ciphers:

```
https://cloud.google.com/network-connectivity/docs/vpn/
concepts/supported-ike-ciphers
```

Configuring firewall rules:

```
https://cloud.google.com/network-connectivity/docs/vpn/how-to/
configuring-firewall-rules
```

Best practices for Cloud VPN:

```
https://cloud.google.com/network-connectivity/docs/vpn/
concepts/best-practices
```

Viewing logs and metrics:

```
https://cloud.google.com/network-connectivity/docs/vpn/how-to/
viewing-logs-metrics
```

Summary

In this section, we have learned how to secure Google Cloud VPN by relying on the GCP infrastructure and using network access controls, authentication mechanisms, logging, and more.

Securing DDoS protection services

Each cloud provider has its own implementation of a managed DDoS protection service.

Because cloud providers have very large bandwidth, they can offer (as a paid service) mechanisms to protect customers' environments from DDoS attacks.

The following services help to mitigate DDoS attacks:

- DDoS protection services (discussed in this section)
- Auto-scaling groups combined with load-balancing services
- CDN services (discussed earlier in this chapter)
- WAF services (discussed later in this chapter)

In this section, we will focus on DDoS protection services.

Securing AWS Shield

AWS Shield is the Amazon managed DDoS protection service.

It comes in two price models:

- **AWS Shield Standard**: This is the default and free Layer 7 DDoS protection (HTTP/HTTPS), provided for all customers.

- **AWS Shield Advanced**: This offers Layers 3/4 (Network layer) and Layer 7 (Application layer) DDoS protection, with additional protection for AWS services such as DNS (Route 53), CDN (CloudFront), **Elastic Load Balancing** (**ELB**), and virtual machine (EC2) services. This price tier also offers support from the AWS DDoS response team.

Best practices for securing AWS Shield

The following are some of the best practices to follow:

- Use AWS Shield Standard for any web-based production environment you expose to the internet.

- Use AWS Shield Advanced for large-scale production environments you expose to the internet for better insights into the attacks.

- When using AWS Shield Advanced, register an **Elastic IP** (**EIP**) address as a protected source to allow quicker detection of attacks.

- When using AWS Shield Advanced, you can generate near real-time reports about attacks on resources in your AWS account(s).

- When combining AWS Shield and the AWS WAF service, use Amazon CloudWatch to monitor incoming requests and alert you when there is a spike in incoming requests, to have preliminary alerts on incoming DDoS attacks.

- Use **AWS Identity and Access Management** (**IAM**) to limit the permissions to the AWS Shield Console.

- Use AWS CloudTrail to log actions in the AWS Shield Console.

For more information, please refer to the following resources:

How AWS Shield works:

```
https://docs.aws.amazon.com/waf/latest/developerguide/ddos-
overview.html
```

Best practices for DDoS resiliency:

```
https://d0.awsstatic.com/whitepapers/Security/DDoS_White_
Paper.pdf
```

Reviewing DDoS events:

```
https://docs.aws.amazon.com/waf/latest/developerguide/using-
ddos-reports.html
```

Overview of managing access permissions to your AWS Shield resources:

```
https://docs.aws.amazon.com/waf/latest/developerguide/
shd-access-control-overview.html
```

Logging and monitoring in Shield:

```
https://docs.aws.amazon.com/waf/latest/developerguide/
shd-incident-response.html
```

Monitoring tools:

```
https://docs.aws.amazon.com/waf/latest/developerguide/
monitoring_automated_manual.html
```

AWS Shield Standard:

```
https://aws.amazon.com/shield/features/#AWS_Shield_Standard
```

AWS Shield Advanced:

```
https://aws.amazon.com/shield/features/#AWS_Shield_Advanced
```

Amazon says it mitigated the largest DDoS attack ever recorded:

```
https://www.theverge.com/2020/6/18/21295337/amazon-aws-
biggest-ddos-attack-ever-2-3-tbps-shield-github-netscout-arbor
```

Securing Azure DDoS Protection

Azure DDoS Protection is the Azure managed DDoS protection service.

It comes in two price models:

- **Azure DDoS Protection Basic**: This provides Layers 3/4 (Network layer) and Layer 7 DDoS protection (HTTP/HTTPS), offered at no cost.
- **Azure DDoS Protection Standard**: This provides Layers 3/4 (Network layer) and Layer 7 DDoS protection (HTTP/HTTPS), with additional protection at the VNet level, with extra logging and alerting capability.

Best practices for securing Azure DDoS Protection

The following are some of the best practices to follow:

- Enable Azure DDoS Protection Basic for any production environment you expose to the internet.

- Use Azure DDoS Protection Standard for large-scale production environments you expose to the internet for better insights into attacks.

- When using Azure DDoS Protection Standard, enable resource logs for public IP addresses to have quicker detection of attacks.

- When combining **Azure Application Gateway** with a WAF, you add protection against web application attacks.

- Use Azure Monitor to monitor and alert you when there is a spike in incoming requests to have a preliminary alert on incoming DoS attacks.

- Send Azure DDoS Protection logs to Azure Sentinel for further analysis of DDoS attacks.

- Use Azure Active Directory to limit the permissions to the Azure DDoS Protection Console.

- When using Azure DDoS Protection Standard, you can conduct simulations of DDoS attacks against your Azure staging or production Azure environments (at non-peak hours) by using a third-party solution from **BreakingPoint Cloud**. Simulations will allow you to have a better understanding of how effective the DDoS Protection plans are and help to train your teams.

For more information, please refer to the following resources:

Azure DDoS Protection Standard overview:

```
https://docs.microsoft.com/en-us/azure/ddos-protection/ddos-
protection-overview
```

View and configure DDoS protection alerts:

```
https://docs.microsoft.com/en-us/azure/ddos-protection/alerts
```

View and configure DDoS diagnostic logging:

```
https://docs.microsoft.com/en-us/azure/ddos-protection/
diagnostic-logging?tabs=DDoSProtectionNotifications
```

Azure DDoS Protection Standard features:

```
https://docs.microsoft.com/en-us/azure/ddos-protection/ddos-
protection-standard-features
```

Azure security baseline for Azure DDoS Protection Standard:

```
https://docs.microsoft.com/en-us/security/benchmark/azure/
baselines/ddos-protection-security-baseline
```

Test through simulations:

```
https://docs.microsoft.com/en-us/azure/ddos-protection/test-
through-simulations
```

Securing Google Cloud Armor

Google Cloud Armor is the Google managed DDoS protection and **Web Application Firewall (WAF)** service.

It comes in two price models:

- **Google Cloud Armor Standard**: This provides protection against volumetric DDoS attacks and includes preconfigured WAF rules.

- **Managed Protection Plus**: This provides protection against volumetric DDoS attacks, includes preconfigured WAF rules, and includes an adaptive protection mechanism. This price tier also offers support from the Google DDoS response team.

Cloud Armor protects applications located behind an external Google Cloud load balancer, which is based on HTTP/HTTPS and TCP/SSL proxy load balancers.

Best practices for securing Google Cloud Armor

The following are some of the best practices to follow:

- Create an IAM group, add users to the group, and grant the required permissions on the Cloud Armor for the target group.

- Note that Cloud Armor contains pre-configured protection rules against common web application attacks.

- If you need to configure your own rules to match your application, create custom Cloud Armor security policies to allow or deny traffic to your applications behind an external Google Cloud load balancer.

- Enable Cloud Armor logs for any backend service to detect allowed or denied HTTP/HTTPS requests.

- For critical production applications, it is recommended to subscribe to the Managed Protection Plus service.

- For critical production applications, it is recommended to enable the **Cloud Armor Adaptive Protection Mechanism** to detect anomalous activity and generate a custom signature for blocking application attacks using WAF rules (for application attacks).

- For scenarios where you would like to allow access to your production applications for third-party partners without them having to specify their external IP address or IP range, use Cloud Armor named IP address lists to configure a whitelist of allowed sources.

- Use the **Google Security Command Center** service to detect anomalous behavior in the Cloud Armor traffic activity (such as spikes in traffic).

For more information, please refer to the following resources:

Configuring Google Cloud Armor security policies:

```
https://cloud.google.com/armor/docs/configure-security-
policies
```

Google Cloud Armor Managed Protection overview:

```
https://cloud.google.com/armor/docs/managed-protection-
overview
```

Google Cloud Armor Adaptive Protection overview:

```
https://cloud.google.com/armor/docs/adaptive-protection-
overview
```

Google Cloud Armor named IP address lists:

```
https://cloud.google.com/armor/docs/armor-named-ip
```

New WAF capabilities in Cloud Armor for on-prem and cloud workloads:

```
https://cloud.google.com/blog/products/identity-security/
new-waf-capabilities-in-cloud-armor
```

Monitoring Google Cloud Armor security policies:

```
https://cloud.google.com/armor/docs/monitoring
```

Security Command Center findings:

```
https://cloud.google.com/armor/docs/cscc-findings
```

Summary

In this section, we have learned about the DDoS protection services from AWS, Azure, and Google. We also discussed their pricing models and the advanced reporting and alerting capabilities provided by the more advanced DDoS protection services.

Securing WAF services

Each cloud provider has its own implementation of a WAF service – that is, an application-layer firewall with capabilities to detect and mitigate common HTTP/HTTPS-based attacks against your publicly exposed web applications.

Securing AWS WAF

AWS WAF is the AWS managed web application firewall service.

AWS WAF offers protection against the following types of attacks:

- Layer 7 DDoS attacks (when combined with AWS Shield)
- Common web application attacks
- Bots (non-human generated traffic)

AWS WAF also allows you to protect the following Amazon services:

- **Amazon CloudFront**: The Amazon managed CDN service
- **Amazon API Gateway**: The Amazon managed API gateway service
- **Amazon ALB**: The Amazon managed **Application Load Balancer** service (Layer 7 load balancer)

Best practices for securing AWS WAF

The following are some of the best practices to follow:

- To protect an external web resource, create web ACLs, with either *allow* or *block* actions.
- When creating a new web ACL rule, change the default CloudWatch metric name to an informative name that will allow you to detect it later when reviewing the CloudWatch logs.
- Use Amazon CloudWatch to monitor your web ACL rule activity.
- For protection against non-standard types of web application attacks, create your own custom rules.
- For better protection, subscribe to the rules available on the **AWS Marketplace** (created by security vendors).
- For large-scale environments with multiple AWS accounts, use AWS Firewall Manager to centrally create and enforce WAF rules.

- Send AWS WAF logs to the **Amazon Kinesis Data Firehose** service to review near real-time logs of attacks.

- Use AWS Config to enable logging for every newly created web ACL.

- Use AWS IAM to limit the permissions to the AWS WAF Console.

- Use AWS CloudTrail to log actions in the AWS WAF Console.

For more information, please refer to the following resources:

Guidelines for Implementing AWS WAF:

```
https://d1.awsstatic.com/whitepapers/guidelines-implementing-
aws-waf.pdf
```

Getting started with AWS WAF:

```
https://docs.aws.amazon.com/waf/latest/developerguide/getting-
started.html
```

Overview of managing access permissions to your AWS WAF resources:

```
https://docs.aws.amazon.com/waf/latest/developerguide/access-
control-overview.html
```

Logging and monitoring in AWS WAF:

```
https://docs.aws.amazon.com/waf/latest/developerguide/
waf-incident-response.html
```

Securing Azure WAF

Azure Web Application Firewall (**WAF**) is the Azure managed web application firewall service.

Azure WAF is integrated with and can be deployed as part of the following services:

- **Azure Application Gateway**: A Layer 7 load balancer service

- **Azure Front Door**: A global web application threat protection service

- **Azure CDN**: A managed CDN

Best practices for securing Azure WAF

The following are some of the best practices to follow:

- Deploy Azure WAF v2 license on any newly exposed web application.

- For large-scale environments with multiple Azure subscriptions and multiple web applications, use Azure WAF with **Azure Front Door** to protect your web applications.

- After learning the traffic for your production web application (running WAF in learning mode), configure Azure WAF in prevention mode.

- For protection against non-standard types of web application attacks, create your own custom rules.

- Create custom rules to block traffic originating from known malicious IP addresses.

- Use Azure activity logs as part of the Azure Monitor service to monitor changes in Azure WAF rules.

- Send Azure WAF logs to Azure Sentinel to detect and remediate web-based attacks.

- Use Azure Active Directory to limit the permissions to the Azure WAF console.

For more information, please refer to the following resources:

Azure security baseline for Azure Web Application Firewall:

```
https://docs.microsoft.com/en-us/security/benchmark/azure/
baselines/web-application-firewall-security-baseline
```

Azure security baseline for Application Gateway:

```
https://docs.microsoft.com/en-us/security/benchmark/azure/
baselines/application-gateway-security-baseline
```

What is Azure Web Application Firewall on Azure Application Gateway:

```
https://docs.microsoft.com/en-us/azure/web-application-
firewall/ag/ag-overview
```

Azure Web Application Firewall and Azure Policy:

```
https://docs.microsoft.com/en-us/azure/web-application-
firewall/shared/waf-azure-policy
```

Summary

In this section, we have learned how to use managed WAF services from both AWS and Azure, covering everything from configuration best practices to monitoring and authorization.

Summary

In this chapter, we have focused on the various network services offered by AWS, Azure, and Google.

This has included virtual networking, DNS, CDN, VPN, DDoS protection, and WAF services.

In each section, we have reviewed the best practices for configuration, authentication, monitoring, and auditing.

Managing these services allows us to control who has access to them and to monitor their activity.

In the next chapter, we will review how to manage identities in the cloud (including directory services and cloud based SAML authentication) and how to enforce MFA.

Section 2: Deep Dive into IAM, Auditing, and Encryption

In this part of the book, we'll be exploring all the ins and outs of identity management, auditing, and encryption.

This part of the book comprises the following chapters:

- *Chapter 5, Effective Strategies to Implement IAM Solutions*
- *Chapter 6, Monitoring and Auditing Your Cloud Environments*
- *Chapter 7, Applying Encryption in Cloud Services*

5
Effective Strategies to Implement IAM Solutions

From *Chapter 2, Securing Compute Services,* to *Chapter 4, Securing Network Services,* we covered the fundamental building blocks of cloud services (from compute and storage to networking services).

However, we cannot talk about cloud services without also discussing identity management.

In this chapter, we will cover various concepts of identity management – from traditional directory services (based on the Kerberos protocol in the Microsoft environment, LDAP-based directory services, popular in non-Microsoft environments, and even Linux-based directory services) to modern directory services (based on the SAML or OAuth protocols) – and, finally, we will understand how to secure authentication mechanisms based on **Multi-Factor Authentication (MFA)**.

In this chapter, we will cover the following topics:

- Introduction to IAM
- Failing to manage identities

- Securing cloud-based IAM services
- Securing directory services
- Configuring MFA

Technical requirements

For this chapter, you are required to have a solid understanding of identity management and concepts such as **Active Directory** (**AD**), the Kerberos protocol, SAML versus OAuth 2.0, and MFA.

Following is a sample diagram which depicts the SAML authentication flow:

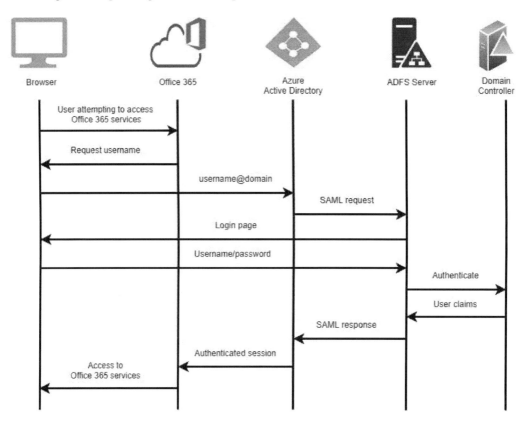

Figure 5.1 – Example of the SAML authentication flow to the Office 365 service

Now that you are aware of the basic concepts needed for the chapter, let's dive into the details.

Introduction to IAM

Identity and Access Management (**IAM**) refers to the concept of managing the entire user life cycle, including provisioning (that is, account creation), assigning permissions, and, finally, account deprovisioning (that is, when a person leaves the organization, or the account is no longer necessary).

Access management is made up of the following main concepts:

- **Identity**: This indicates a user, computer, service, or role that wishes to access a system or application and take actions (from accessing shared storage to querying a database and pulling information).

- **Authentication**: This is the process of proving that a specific identity (such as a user) is who they claim to be (for example, providing a username and password that match the user's records on a central user repository).

- **Authorization**: This is the process of granting an authenticated identity (such as a user) the permissions to take actions on a resource (such as allowing a user to upload a file to shared storage).

Cloud providers take a different approach to IAM:

- **AWS IAM**: By default, all requests are implicitly denied.

- **Azure Active Directory (Azure AD)**: By default, users have a minimal set of permissions in which to access resources.

- **GCP**: By default, service accounts have permission to call Google Cloud APIs.

The most common directory service deployed on most organizations' on-premises data centers is **Microsoft AD**. This is a central repository for storing objects such as user accounts, computer accounts, groups, and more.

The most used protocol when working on-premises on traditional Windows applications or services is the **Kerberos** protocol.

For more information, please refer to the following resources:

- AWS IAM – *Determining whether a request is allowed or denied within an account*:

  ```
  https://docs.aws.amazon.com/IAM/latest/UserGuide/
  reference_policies_evaluation-logic.html#policy-eval-
  denyallow
  ```

- *What are the default user permissions in Azure Active Directory?*:

  `https://docs.microsoft.com/en-us/azure/active-directory/`
  `fundamentals/users-default-permissions`

- GCP's default service accounts:

  `https://cloud.google.com/iam/docs/service-accounts#default`

- What Active Directory is:

  `https://en.wikipedia.org/wiki/Active_Directory`

- What the Kerberos protocol is:

  `https://en.wikipedia.org/wiki/Kerberos_(protocol)`

Failing to manage identities

Before we move on to **Identity Management** (**IdM**), let's look at a few examples of failing to manage identities:

- A new employee has joined the organization. Since we do not have a documented and automated **IdM** workflow, the employee's permissions were copied from a system administrator's profile. The new employee was not aware of which sites they should browse on the internet, and, as result, they were infected by ransomware. This, in turn, infected the sales database, which was encrypted, and caused downtime for the sales division.

- An employee was able to create an easy-to-guess password (because a complex password policy was not enforced at the organization level), and, as a result, a hacker was able to guess the employee's password and gain access to a confidential financial report.

- An employee has changed their role in the organization, from IT to the development team, and we forgot to update their privileges on the production servers. As a result, the employee is now over-privileged, and they can access and make changes to the production system.

- An employee has left the organization, and we forgot to disable their account. As a result, the employee had access to the corporate CRM system through a VPN, which he used to export the contact details of customers so that he could sell the products of his new employer.

Securing cloud-based IAM services

Each cloud provider has its own implementation of managed IAM services, in other words, a service for managing authentication and authorization requests.

Here is a list of AWS IAM terminology:

- **IAM user**: This is a person or application with permission to access AWS resources. An IAM user has credentials (such as a password, access keys, and MFA).

- **IAM group**: This refers to a group of IAM users to make the permissions management task easier.

- **IAM role**: This indicates an identity that has permission to access resources without any credentials. Usually, you assign an IAM role to an IAM group, IAM user, or a service account that requires temporary permissions.

- **Service account**: This refers to a special type of IAM user, and its purpose is to allow applications to have access to resources.

- **IAM policy**: This is a JSON-based definition that sets the permissions for accessing AWS resources. There are two types of IAM policies:

  - **Identity-based policies**: This is attached to a user, group, or role.

  - **Resource-based policies**: This is attached to the AWS resource (for example, the Amazon S3 bucket).

- **Identity provider**: This refers to the ability to manage identities outside of AWS while still being able to grant access to AWS resources to the external identities (such as a federation between AWS and Azure AD).

- **AWS IAM policy evaluation logic**:

  - **Identity-based policies with resource-based policies**: The result of both policies is the total permissions for both policies.

  - **Identity-based policies with permissions boundaries**: The result of identity-based policies with the restrictions from permissions boundaries becomes the effective permissions.

  - **Identity-based policies with AWS Organizations service control policies**: The result of both policies (for the account member of the organization) becomes the effective permissions.

Securing AWS IAM

AWS IAM is the Amazon-managed IAM service.

Best practices for securing AWS IAM

The following is a list of best practices:

- Disable and remove all access keys and secret access keys from the AWS account root user.

- Configure a strong password for the AWS account root user.

- Enable MFA for the AWS account root user.

- Avoid using the AWS account root user. Instead, create a random password for the AWS root account, and in the rare scenarios where a root account is required, reset the root account password.

- Create an IAM user with a full IAM admin role to only the AWS console, to manage the AWS account.

- Enable MFA for any IAM user with a full IAM admin role.

- Avoid creating access keys and secret access keys for an IAM user with a full IAM admin role.

- Create IAM users with IAM policies according to the principle of least privilege.

- Create IAM groups, assign permissions to the groups, and add IAM users to those groups for easier account and permission management.

- For limited user access, create custom-managed policies and assign the custom policies to a group of users.

- Configure a password policy (which includes the minimum and maximum password age, the minimum password length, and enforces the use of password history and complex passwords).

- Use IAM roles to allow applications that are deploying on EC2 instances access to AWS resources.

- Use IAM roles instead of creating access keys and secret access keys to allow temporary access to resources rather than permanent access.

- Avoid embedding access keys and secret access keys inside your code. Instead, use secret management solutions such as AWS Secrets Manager to store and retrieve access keys.

- Rotate access keys periodically to avoid key abuse by malicious internal or external users.

- For highly sensitive environments or resources, set an IAM policy to restrict access based on conditions such as data, time, MFA, and more.

- For highly sensitive environments or resources, set an IAM policy to only allow access to users with MFA enabled.

- Use the AWS IAM **AssumeRole** capability to switch between multiple AWS accounts using the same IAM identity.

- Use IAM permissions boundaries to restrict IAM user access to specific AWS resources.

For more information, please refer to the following resources:

Security best practices in IAM:

```
https://docs.aws.amazon.com/IAM/latest/UserGuide/best-
practices.html
```

Best practices for managing AWS access keys:

```
https://docs.aws.amazon.com/general/latest/gr/aws-access-keys-
best-practices.html
```

AWS: Allows access based on date and time:

```
https://docs.aws.amazon.com/IAM/latest/UserGuide/reference_
policies_examples_aws-dates.html
```

AssumeRole:

```
https://docs.aws.amazon.com/STS/latest/APIReference/API_
AssumeRole.html
```

Permissions boundaries for IAM entities:

```
https://docs.aws.amazon.com/IAM/latest/UserGuide/access_
policies_boundaries.html
```

Policy evaluation logic:

```
https://docs.aws.amazon.com/IAM/latest/UserGuide/reference_
policies_evaluation-logic.html#policy-eval-basics
```

Auditing AWS IAM

AWS allows you to monitor the AWS IAM using the following built-in services:

- **Amazon CloudWatch**: This is a service that allows you to have AWS CloudTrail audit logs and create alarms when a log passes a certain threshold; for example, after multiple failed logins.

- **AWS CloudTrail**: This is a service that allows you to audit actions done by either the AWS account root user or by any IAM user.

- **Amazon GuardDuty**: This is a service that uses machine learning to detect and alert you about identity misuse (based on the AWS CloudTrail logs).

Best practices for auditing AWS IAM

The following is a list of best practices:

- Enable AWS CloudTrail on all AWS regions.

- Limit the level of access to the CloudTrail logs to a minimum number of employees – preferably to those with an AWS management account, outside the scope of your end users (including outside the scope of your IAM users), to avoid possible deletion or changes to the audit logs.

- Use Amazon GuardDuty to audit the AWS account root user activity.

- Use AWS CloudTrail to audit IAM user activities.

- Use IAM credential reports to locate users that haven't logged in for a long period of time.

- Use an IAM policy simulator to check what the effective permissions for a specific IAM user are (that is, whether they are allowed or denied access to resources).

- Use AWS IAM Access Analyzer to detect unused permissions (from both your AWS account and cross-accounts) and fine-tune the permissions to your AWS resources.

- Use AWS IAM Access Analyzer to detect secrets that can be accessed from outside your AWS account and are stored inside the AWS Secrets Manager service.

- Use the IAMCTL tool to compare IAM policies between IAM user accounts to detect any changes (for example, by comparing template IAM user policies with one of your other IAM users).

For more information, please refer to the following resources:

AWS security audit guidelines:

`https://docs.aws.amazon.com/general/latest/gr/aws-security-audit-guide.html`

Logging IAM and AWS STS API calls with AWS CloudTrail:

`https://docs.aws.amazon.com/IAM/latest/UserGuide/cloudtrail-integration.html`

Monitor and control actions taken with assumed roles:

`https://docs.aws.amazon.com/IAM/latest/UserGuide/id_credentials_temp_control-access_monitor.html`

GuardDuty IAM finding types:

`https://docs.aws.amazon.com/guardduty/latest/ug/guardduty_finding-types-iam.html`

AWS IAM access analysis features:

`https://aws.amazon.com/iam/features/analyze-access/`

Automate resolution for IAM Access Analyzer cross-account access findings on IAM roles:

`https://aws.amazon.com/blogs/security/automate-resolution-for-iam-access-analyzer-cross-account-access-findings-on-iam-roles/`

Discover, review, and remediate unintended access to Secrets Manager secrets using IAM Access Analyzer:

`https://aws.amazon.com/about-aws/whats-new/2021/01/discover-review-remediate-unintended-access-secrets-manager-iam-access-analyzer/`

Getting credential reports for your AWS account:

`https://docs.aws.amazon.com/IAM/latest/UserGuide/id_credentials_getting-report.html`

Testing IAM policies with the IAM policy simulator:

`https://docs.aws.amazon.com/IAM/latest/UserGuide/access_policies_testing-policies.html`

New IAMCTL tool compares multiple IAM roles and policies:

```
https://aws.amazon.com/blogs/security/new-iamctl-tool-
compares-multiple-iam-roles-and-policies/
```

Summary

In this section, we learned how to secure Amazon IAM based on the AWS infrastructure. We examined how to protect the AWS account root user, access keys management, set password policies, audit user activities, and detect unused or over-privileged accounts.

Securing Azure AD

Azure AD is the Azure-managed directory service.

Azure AD supports the following types of identity models:

- **Cloud-only identity**: The user account is created inside the Azure AD tenant and only exists in the cloud (where access to on-premises is not required).

- **Hybrid identity**: The user account exists in both the Azure AD tenant and on-premises.

Here is a list of Azure AD terminology:

- **User**: This is a person or application with permission to access Azure resources. A user has credentials (such as a password or MFA).

- **Group**: This is a group of users to make the permissions management task easier.

- Azure **role-based access control** (**RBAC**): This is an authorization system with built-in permissions to access Azure resources (for example, *Owner*, *Contributor*, *Reader*, and more).

Best practices for securing Azure AD

The following is a list of best practices:

- Configure a strong password for the original Azure AD global administrator account.

- Enable MFA for the original Azure AD global administrator account.

- Avoid using the original Azure AD global administrator account – keep the user's password in a secured location.

- Create an Azure AD user with a global administrator role for the purpose of managing the Azure AD.

- Enable MFA for any user in your Azure AD (such as a global administrator role).

- Limit the number of global administrators to less than five.

- Use Azure RBAC to grant minimal permissions required for users to be able to access and use Azure resources.

- Enable the Azure AD **Privileged Identity Management (PIM)** service in your Azure AD to control just-in-time access to manage Azure AD resources.

- Create Azure AD groups, assign permissions to the groups, and add users to those groups for easier account and permission management.

- Configure a password policy (which includes the minimum and maximum password age, the minimum password length, and enforces the use of password history and complex passwords).

- Create an emergency account (these are special user accounts that shouldn't be used daily, have MFA enabled, and are a member of the global administrator role) to avoid getting locked out of your Azure AD.

- Use a conditional access policy to enforce the use of MFA and enforce the location from which a global administrator can have access to log in and manage your Azure AD (such as your office network).

For more information refer to the following resources:

- *Microsoft 365 identity models and Azure Active Directory*:

  https://docs.microsoft.com/en-us/microsoft-365/enterprise/
  about-microsoft-365-identity?view=o365-worldwide

- *Classic subscription administrator roles, Azure roles, and Azure AD roles*:

  https://docs.microsoft.com/en-us/azure/role-based-access-
  control/rbac-and-directory-admin-roles#azure-roles

- *Elevate access to manage all Azure subscriptions and management groups*:

  https://docs.microsoft.com/en-us/azure/role-based-access-
  control/elevate-access-global-admin

- *What is Azure AD Privileged Identity Management?*:

  https://docs.microsoft.com/en-us/azure/active-directory/
  privileged-identity-management/pim-configure

- *Overview of role-based access control in Azure Active Directory*:

  ```
  https://docs.microsoft.com/en-us/azure/active-directory/
  roles/custom-overview
  ```

- *Best practices for Azure AD roles*:

  ```
  https://docs.microsoft.com/en-us/azure/active-directory/
  roles/best-practices
  ```

- *Password policies and account restrictions in Azure Active Directory*:

  ```
  https://docs.microsoft.com/en-us/azure/active-directory/
  authentication/concept-sspr-policy
  ```

- *Manage emergency access accounts in Azure AD*:

  ```
  https://docs.microsoft.com/en-us/azure/active-directory/
  roles/security-emergency-access
  ```

- *Plan an Azure Active Directory Multi-Factor Authentication deployment*:

  ```
  https://docs.microsoft.com/en-us/azure/active-directory/
  authentication/howto-mfa-getstarted
  ```

Auditing Azure AD

Azure AD has audit logs which can provide an overview of different system activities to ensure compliance.

Best practices for auditing Azure AD

Here are the best practices for auditing Azure AD:

- Use Azure AD Identity Protection to detect any potential vulnerability activities of your Azure AD users and send the audit logs to your SIEM system.

- Use Azure AD reports to detect risky users or risky sign-in events.

- Use Azure AD audit logs to review and detect events in your Azure AD (such as changes to users or groups, sign-in events, and more).

- Send your Azure AD activity logs to the Azure Monitor service for further analysis.

- Limit the level of access to Azure Monitor service data to a minimum number of employees, to avoid possible deletion or changes to the audit logs.

- If you use the Azure AD PIM service in your Azure AD, create access reviews to detect who used PIM to request high privilege to carry out actions.

- For hybrid environments (that is, an on-premises Active Directory connected to Azure AD), use Microsoft Defender for Identity to detect suspicious activities in your on-premises Active Directory.

For more information refer to the following resources:

What is Identity Protection?:

```
https://docs.microsoft.com/en-us/azure/active-directory/
identity-protection/overview-identity-protection
```

What is Microsoft Defender for Identity?:

```
https://docs.microsoft.com/en-us/defender-for-identity/what-is
```

What are Azure Active Directory reports?:

```
https://docs.microsoft.com/en-us/azure/active-directory/
reports-monitoring/overview-reports
```

Audit logs in Azure Active Directory:

```
https://docs.microsoft.com/en-us/azure/active-directory/
reports-monitoring/concept-audit-logs
```

Analyze Azure AD activity logs with Azure Monitor logs:

```
https://docs.microsoft.com/en-us/azure/active-directory/
reports-monitoring/howto-analyze-activity-logs-log-analytics
```

Create an access review of Azure resource and Azure AD roles in PIM:

```
https://docs.microsoft.com/en-us/azure/active-directory/
privileged-identity-management/pim-how-to-start-security-
review
```

Summary

In this section, we learned how to secure Azure AD based on the Azure infrastructure. We examined how to protect privileged accounts, set password policies, and audit user activities to detect suspicious user behavior.

Securing Google Cloud IAM

Google Cloud IAM is the Google-managed IAM service.

Here is a list of Google Cloud IAM terminology:

- **Member**: This is a Google account (for example, a user), a service account (for applications and virtual machines), or Cloud Identity with access to GCP resources.

- **User**: This is a person or application (a service account) with permissions to access GCP resources. A user has credentials (such as a password and MFA).

- **Group**: This is a group of users to make the permissions management task easier.

- **Role**: This refers to a collection of permissions to access resources.

- **Service account**: This is a special type of IAM user to allow applications access to resources.

- **IAM policy**: This is a JSON-based definition that sets the permissions for accessing GCP resources.

  The GCP policy evaluation entails the following:

  - **No organization policy set**: The default access to resources is enforced.

  - **Inheritance**: If a resource node has set `inheritFromParent = true`, then the effective policy of the parent resource is inherited.

  - **Disallow inheritance**: If a resource hierarchy node has a policy that includes `inheritFromParent = false`, it doesn't inherit the organization policy from its parent.

  - **Reconciling policy conflicts**: By default, policies are inherited and merged; however, `DENY` values always take precedence.

Best practices for securing Google Cloud IAM

Here are the best practices for securing Google Cloud IAM:

- Use Google Workspace to create and manage user accounts.

- Configure a password policy (which includes the minimum and maximum password age, the minimum password length, and enforces the use of password history and complex passwords) from within your Google Workspace admin console.

- Enable MFA for any user with high privileges in your Google Cloud (such as the GCP project owner role).

- Create IAM groups, assign permissions to the groups, and add users to those groups for easier account and permission management.

- Use service accounts to grant applications minimal access to Google Cloud resources.

- Create a dedicated service account for each application.

- For scenarios where you only need an application to access resources for a short amount of time, use short-lived service account credentials.

- Disable unused service accounts.

- Use Google Managed Service accounts for services (such as Google Compute Engine) that require access to Google resources (such as Google Cloud Storage).

- Use role recommendations using IAM Recommender to enforce minimal permissions to Google resources.

- Limit the use of service account keys, or avoid them completely, to avoid having to expose access to your Google Cloud resources from outside your GCP environment.

- Use IAM conditions to enforce the location from which a user can access resources in your Google Cloud environment (such as your office network).

- Use the policy simulator to determine the effect of a policy on your users.

For more information, please refer to the following resources:

An overview of Google Cloud IAM:

```
https://cloud.google.com/iam/docs/overview#concepts_related_
identity
```

Understanding hierarchy evaluation:

```
https://cloud.google.com/resource-manager/docs/organization-
policy/understanding-hierarchy#hierarchy_evaluation_rules
```

Enforce and monitor password requirements for users:

```
https://support.google.com/a/answer/139399
```

Using IAM securely:

```
https://cloud.google.com/iam/docs/using-iam-securely
```

Achieve least privilege with less effort using IAM Recommender:

```
https://cloud.google.com/blog/products/identity-security/
achieve-least-privilege-with-less-effort-using-iam-recommender
```

Policy Simulator:

`https://cloud.google.com/iam/docs/understanding-simulator`

Best practices for securing service accounts:

`https://cloud.google.com/iam/docs/best-practices-for-securing-service-accounts`

Restricting service account usage:

`https://cloud.google.com/resource-manager/docs/organization-policy/restricting-service-accounts`

Creating short-lived service account credentials:

`https://cloud.google.com/iam/docs/creating-short-lived-service-account-credentials`

Overview of IAM Conditions:

`https://cloud.google.com/iam/docs/conditions-overview`

Google-managed service accounts:

`https://cloud.google.com/compute/docs/access/service-accounts#google-managed_service_accounts`

Auditing Google Cloud IAM

Google allows you to monitor the Google Cloud IAM using Google Cloud Logging.

Best practices for auditing Google Cloud IAM

Here are the best practices for auditing Google Cloud IAM:

- Enable Cloud IAM audit logs for further log analysis, such as tracking failed Active Directory logins.
- Admin activity audit logs are enabled by default and cannot be disabled.
- Explicitly enable **Data access audit logs** to log activities performed on Google Cloud IAM.
- Limit the level of access to the audit logs to a minimum number of employees, to avoid possible deletion or changes to the audit logs using IAM roles.
- Use Policy Analyzer to determine which identity (for example, a user or a service account) has access to which Google Cloud resource and the type of access.

- Use service account insights to identify unused service accounts and service account keys.

For more information, please refer to the following resources:

IAM audit logging:

```
https://cloud.google.com/iam/docs/audit-logging
```

Analyzing IAM policies:

```
https://cloud.google.com/asset-inventory/docs/analyzing-iam-policy
```

Monitoring usage patterns for service accounts and keys:

```
https://cloud.google.com/iam/docs/service-account-monitoring
```

Manage service account insights:

```
https://cloud.google.com/iam/docs/manage-service-account-insights
```

Summary

In this section, we learned how to secure Google Cloud IAM based on the GCP infrastructure. We examined how to protect privileged accounts, set password policies, manage and work with service accounts, and audit user and service account activities.

Securing directory services

Each cloud provider has its own implementation of a managed Active Directory service. This service allows you to centrally manage your user and computer identities, join Windows machines to the Active Directory domain, set password policies (such as the password length, password complexity, and more), and control access to traditional resources (such as Windows file shares, SQL servers, IIS servers, and more).

It is important to note that as a customer, you always have the option to deploy Active Directory domain controllers based on virtual machines and maintain them yourself, as organizations are doing on-premises (this is also known as a self-hosted solution). However, the goal of this book is to show you how things are done using managed services, where, as a customer, you can focus on consuming the IAM service (that is, authenticate and create identities and then grant them permissions) without having to maintain servers (such as availability, patch management, backups, and more).

In the next section, we are going to examine what the best practices are for securing managed directory services from AWS, Azure, and GCP.

Securing AWS Directory Service

AWS Directory Service is the Amazon-managed Active Directory service.

Best practices for securing AWS Directory Service

The following is a list of best practices:

- Configure a password policy (which includes the minimum and maximum password age, the minimum password length, and enforces the use of password history and complex passwords).

- Configure an account lockout policy (including the number of failed login attempts, the account lockout duration, and whether to allow a reset of the account lockout after a certain amount of time).

- To avoid using a privileged account for a password reset, use the **AWS Delegated Fine Grained Password Policy Administrators** group to allow your support team permission to reset passwords.

- Use MFA for accounts with high privileges to manage the AWS Directory Service using a RADIUS server.

- Create Active Directory groups, add users to the groups, and grant permissions over resources (such as access to files servers, login servers, and more) to groups instead of granting permissions to specific users.

- Use VPC security groups to restrict access from your EC2 instances to your AWS Directory Service domain controllers.

- Use a complex password for the built-in admin account of your AWS Directory Service.

For more information, please refer to the following resources:

Secure your AWS Managed Microsoft AD directory:

```
https://docs.aws.amazon.com/directoryservice/latest/admin-
guide/ms_ad_security.html
```

Best practices for AWS Managed Microsoft AD:

```
https://docs.aws.amazon.com/directoryservice/latest/admin-
guide/ms_ad_best_practices.html
```

Security in AWS Directory Service:

https://docs.aws.amazon.com/directoryservice/latest/admin-guide/security.html

New whitepaper – *Active Directory Domain Services on AWS*:

https://d1.awsstatic.com/whitepapers/adds-on-aws.pdf

Best practices for monitoring AWS Directory Service

AWS allows you to monitor AWS Directory Service using the following built-in services:

- **Amazon CloudWatch**: This service allows you to monitor your AWS Directory Service logs.
- **AWS CloudTrail**: This service allows you to audit API actions done through the AWS Directory Service console, SDK, or **command line interface** (**CLI**).

Here are the best practices:

- Enable AWS Directory Service log forwarding and forward the Active Directory logs to Amazon CloudWatch for further Active Directory log analysis, such as tracking failed Active Directory logins.
- Use AWS CloudTrail to audit a user's activity inside the AWS Directory Service using an API.

For more information, please refer to the following resources:

Enable log forwarding:

https://docs.aws.amazon.com/directoryservice/latest/admin-guide/ms_ad_enable_log_forwarding.html

How to monitor and track failed logins for your AWS Managed Microsoft AD:

https://aws.amazon.com/blogs/security/how-to-monitor-and-track-failed-logins-for-your-aws-managed-microsoft-ad/

Logging AWS Directory Service API Calls with CloudTrail:

https://docs.aws.amazon.com/directoryservice/latest/devguide/cloudtrail_logging.html

Summary

In this section, we learned how to secure AWS Directory Service based on the AWS infrastructure. We examined how to set password policies, configure permissions, network access, and, finally, monitor and audit Active Directory.

Securing Azure Active Directory Domain Services (Azure AD DS)

Azure AD DS is the Azure-managed Active Directory service.

Best practices for securing Azure AD DS

The following is a list of best practices:

- Configure a password policy (which includes the minimum and maximum password age, the minimum password length, and enforces the use of password history and complex passwords).

- Configure an account lockout policy (including the number of failed login attempts, the account lockout duration, and whether to allow a reset of the account lockout after a certain amount of time).

- Disable the use of vulnerable protocols such as **Windows New Technology LAN Manager (NTLM)**.

- Disable the use of weak password encryption using the RC4 algorithm.

- Enforce the use of TLS 1.2 transport encryption.

- Enable the use of the Kerberos armoring capability to protect the traffic flowing between the client and the domain controllers.

- If you have a requirement to allow impersonation on behalf of another user to access resources (for example, an application that needs access to a file server), enable the use of **Kerberos constrained delegation (KCD)**.

- Use Azure network security groups to restrict access from your virtual machines to your Azure AD DS.

- Use MFA for accounts with high privileges to manage the Azure AD DS service.

- Use a complex password for the built-in global administrator account of your Azure AD.

- If you have a requirement to allow access to legacy applications deployed on-premises from the internet, use Azure AD Application Proxy together with Azure AD DS.

For more information, please refer to the following resources:

Harden an Azure Active Directory Domain Services managed domain:

```
https://docs.microsoft.com/en-us/azure/active-directory-
domain-services/secure-your-domain
```

Configure Kerberos constrained delegation (KCD) in Azure Active Directory Domain Services:

```
https://docs.microsoft.com/en-us/azure/active-directory-
domain-services/deploy-kcd
```

Azure security baseline for Azure Active Directory Domain Services:

```
https://docs.microsoft.com/en-us/security/benchmark/azure/
baselines/aad-ds-security-baseline
```

Deploy Azure AD Application Proxy for secure access to internal applications in an Azure Active Directory Domain Services managed domain:

```
https://docs.microsoft.com/en-us/azure/active-directory-
domain-services/deploy-azure-app-proxy
```

Best practices for monitoring Azure AD DS

Azure allows you to send Azure AD DS audit logs to the following destinations:

- **Azure Storage**: This is for archive purposes only.
- **Azure Event Hubs**: This is for sending audit logs to an external SIEM system for further analysis.
- **Azure Log Analytics Workspace**: This is for further analysis from within the Azure portal.

Here are the best practices:

- Enable Azure AD DS auditing and select where to store the audit logs (for example, Azure Storage, Azure Event Hubs, or the Azure Log Analytics Workspace).
- If you chose to send Azure AD DS audit logs to the Azure Log Analytics Workspace, use the Azure Monitor service to query the logs (such as failed logins, account lockouts, and more).

For more information, please refer to the following resource:

Enable security audits for Azure Active Directory Domain Services:

```
https://docs.microsoft.com/en-us/azure/active-directory-
domain-services/security-audit-events
```

Summary

In this section, we learned how to secure Azure AD DS, based on Azure infrastructure. We examined how to set password policies, configure permissions, network access, and, finally, monitor and audit Active Directory.

Securing Google Managed Service for Microsoft AD

Google Managed Service for Microsoft AD is the GCP-managed Active Directory service.

Best practices for securing Google Managed Service for Microsoft AD

The following is a list of best practices:

- Deploy Google Managed Microsoft AD in a shared VPC to allow access from multiple GCP projects to Active Directory.

- Configure a password policy (which includes the minimum and maximum password age, the minimum password length, and enforces the use of password history and complex passwords).

- Configure an account lockout policy (including the number of failed login attempts, the account lockout duration, and whether to allow a reset of the account lockout after a certain amount of time).

- To avoid using a privileged account for a password reset, use the **Compute Instance Admin** role to allow your support team permission to reset passwords.

- Create Active Directory groups, add users to the groups, and grant permissions over resources (such as access to files servers, login servers, and more) to those groups instead of granting permissions to specific users.

- Use VPC firewall rules to restrict access from your virtual machine instances to your Managed Microsoft AD domain controllers.

- Use authorized networks to control which VPC networks are allowed to access your Managed Microsoft AD.

- For large-scale environments with multiple GCP projects, use VPC Service Controls to enforce access restrictions to your Managed Microsoft AD based on the identity of the IP address.

- Use a complex password for the built-in admin account of your Managed Microsoft AD.

For more information, please refer to the following resources:

Best practices for running Active Directory on Google Cloud:

```
https://cloud.google.com/managed-microsoft-ad/docs/best-
practices
```

Managed Service for Microsoft AD:

```
https://cloud.google.com/managed-microsoft-ad/docs/how-to
```

Managing authorized networks:

```
https://cloud.google.com/managed-microsoft-ad/docs/managing-
authorized-networks
```

Accessing Managed Microsoft AD from within your VPC:

```
https://cloud.google.com/managed-microsoft-ad/docs/
firewalls#accessing_from_within_your_vpc
```

Using VPC Service Controls:

```
https://cloud.google.com/managed-microsoft-ad/docs/how-to-use-
vpc-service-controls
```

Best practices for monitoring Google Managed Service for Microsoft AD

Google allows you to monitor the Google Managed Microsoft AD using Google Cloud Logging.

The following is a list of best practices:

- Enable **Managed Microsoft AD audit logs** for further Active Directory log analysis, such as tracking failed Active Directory logins.

- Admin activity audit logs are enabled by default and cannot be disabled.

- Explicitly enable **Data access audit logs** to log activities performed on Google Managed Microsoft AD.

- Limit the level of access to the audit logs to a minimum number of employees, to avoid possible deletion or changes to the audit logs, using IAM roles.

For more information, please refer to the following resources:

Using Cloud Audit Logs for Managed Microsoft AD:

```
https://cloud.google.com/managed-microsoft-ad/docs/audit-
logging
```

Using Managed Microsoft AD Audit Logs:

```
https://cloud.google.com/managed-microsoft-ad/docs/using-ad-
audit-logs
```

Summary

In this section, we learned how to secure Google Managed Microsoft AD based on the GCP infrastructure. We examined how to set password policies, configure permissions, network access, and, finally, monitor and audit Active Directory.

Configuring MFA

Each cloud provider has its own mechanism to enforce the use of MFA to protect authentication attempts against potential account breaches.

Best practices for configuring MFA using AWS IAM

The following is a list of best practices:

- Enable MFA on the AWS account root user.
- Enable MFA on any IAM user with high privileges to the AWS console (such as an admin role).
- Enable MFA for AWS console access and so that users must authenticate themselves using MFA before programmatically calling for API access requests.
- For non-sensitive environments, use a virtual MFA device (such as Google Authenticator) for better protection of your IAM users' access.
- For sensitive environments, use a hardware MFA device or U2F security key (such as *Yubikey*).
- Avoid using SMS as part of MFA (due to vulnerabilities in the SMS protocol).

For more information, please refer to the following resources:

Using multi-factor authentication (MFA) in AWS:

```
https://docs.aws.amazon.com/IAM/latest/UserGuide/id_
credentials_mfa.html
```

Enabling a virtual multi-factor authentication (MFA) device (console):

```
https://docs.aws.amazon.com/IAM/latest/UserGuide/id_
credentials_mfa_enable_virtual.html
```

Enabling MFA devices for users in AWS:

```
https://docs.aws.amazon.com/IAM/latest/UserGuide/id_
credentials_mfa_enable.html
```

Configuring MFA-protected API access:

```
https://docs.aws.amazon.com/IAM/latest/UserGuide/id_
credentials_mfa_configure-api-require.html
```

Multi-factor Authentication:

```
https://aws.amazon.com/iam/features/mfa/
```

Best practices for configuring MFA using Azure Active Directory

The following is a list of best practices:

- Enable MFA on the original global administrator account.
- Enable MFA on any user with high privileges (such as the global administrator role).
- Enable a conditional access policy to enforce the use of MFA for any attempts to connect to the Azure portal outside your corporate network.
- For non-sensitive environments, use the Microsoft Authenticator app for better protection of your Azure AD users' access.
- For sensitive environments, use a hardware MFA device such as *FIDO2 security key* or *Windows Hello*.
- Avoid using SMS as part of MFA (due to vulnerabilities in the SMS protocol).
- Configure an account lockout when there are multiple failed login attempts using MFA.

For more information, please refer to the following resources:

How it works: Azure AD Multi-Factor Authentication:

```
https://docs.microsoft.com/en-us/azure/active-directory/
authentication/concept-mfa-howitworks
```

Tutorial: Secure user sign-in events with Azure AD Multi-Factor Authentication:

```
https://docs.microsoft.com/en-us/azure/active-directory/
authentication/tutorial-enable-azure-mfa
```

Plan an Azure Active Directory Multi-Factor Authentication deployment:

```
https://docs.microsoft.com/en-us/azure/active-directory/
authentication/howto-mfa-getstarted
```

What authentication and verification methods are available in Azure Active Directory?:

```
https://docs.microsoft.com/en-us/azure/active-directory/
authentication/concept-authentication-methods
```

Configure Azure AD Multi-Factor Authentication settings:

```
https://docs.microsoft.com/en-us/azure/active-directory/
authentication/howto-mfa-mfasettings
```

Enable per-user Azure AD Multi-Factor Authentication to secure sign-in events:

```
https://docs.microsoft.com/en-us/azure/active-directory/
authentication/howto-mfa-userstates
```

Overview of Azure AD Multi-Factor Authentication for your organization:

```
https://docs.microsoft.com/en-us/azure/active-directory/
fundamentals/concept-fundamentals-mfa-get-started
```

Best practices for configuring MFA using Google Cloud:

GCP doesn't directly control MFA settings since it doesn't create or manage user identities.

Identities in Google Cloud are managed by Google Workspace or Gmail accounts, where you can control the MFA settings before granting the identities account to GCP resources.

The following is a list of best practices for configuring MFA with Google Cloud:

- Enable MFA on any user with high privileges (such as the GCP project owner role).
- For non-sensitive environments, use the Google Authenticator app for better protection of your users' access.

- For sensitive environments, use a hardware MFA device (such as Titan Security Keys).
- Avoid using SMS as part of MFA (due to vulnerabilities in the SMS protocol).

For more information, please refer to the following resources:

Enforce uniform MFA to company-owned resources:

`https://cloud.google.com/identity/solutions/enforce-mfa`

Protect your business with 2-Step Verification:

`https://support.google.com/a/answer/175197?hl=en`

Protect your account with 2-Step Verification:

`https://support.google.com/accounts/answer/185839`

Deploy 2-Step Verification:

`https://support.google.com/a/answer/9176657?hl=en`

Summary

In this section, we learned how to configure MFA based on the AWS, Azure, and GCP infrastructures – from software-based MFA to hardware-based MFA devices.

Summary

In this chapter, we focused on the various IAM services in AWS, Azure, and GCP.

We discussed everything from managed Active Directory services to modern IAM services, and, finally, we provided recommendations regarding how to use MFA for extra protection of your identities.

In each section, we reviewed best practices for configuration, account management, monitoring, and auditing.

IdM services allow us to control access to resources and services in our cloud environment. They provide least privilege access to resources and monitor what actions were performed using identities in our cloud environments.

In the next chapter, we will review how to conduct security monitoring and auditing in the cloud (from audit trails and threat detection to digital forensics in the cloud).

6
Monitoring and Auditing Your Cloud Environments

In chapters 2–5, we covered the fundamental building blocks of cloud services (from compute, storage, and networking services to identity and access management services).

Following previous chapters where we reviewed various network security-related services, the following diagram demonstrates traffic flow from external customers, through security controls (**Distributed Denial of Service (DDoS) protection**, **Web Application Firewall (WAF)**, and access control lists such as AWS NACL and security groups), till the customer reaches a resource:

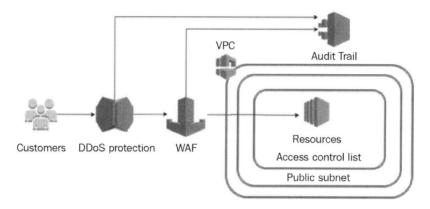

Figure 6.1 – Customer traffic flow

> **Important Note**
>
> AWS, Azure, and **Google Cloud Platform (GCP)** have similar capabilities to control traffic flow and audit events.

All services and security controls send their audit logs to a central audit service for alerts and further analysis.

This chapter will cover various concepts of monitoring and auditing from a security perspective – from audit trails and threat detection to digital forensics in cloud environments.

In this chapter, we will cover the following topics:

- Conducting security monitoring and audit trails
- Conducting threat detection and response
- Conducting incident response and digital forensics

Technical requirements

For this chapter, you need to have a solid understanding of audit trails and security monitoring, threat detection, and digital forensics.

Conducting security monitoring and audit trails

Monitoring is a crucial part of security in the cloud. Monitoring in the context of cloud security is about logging activities done on your cloud environments, such as user login events (both success and failure), actions taken (who did what and when, and what was the end result – success or failure), documenting all actions done (also known as an audit trail), storing events in a central repository with limited access to logs (according to the *need to know* concept), raising alerts according to pre-configured rules (for example, *only alert me when the root account or administrator managed to successfully log in to the management console*), and being able to take actions.

In cloud environments, all resources are based on APIs, which allows us to deploy the resources and make changes to them. We control cloud resources (as we have seen in previous chapters) using security controls (from security groups through a **WAF**. All cloud resources can send their audit logs to a central logging service for further analysis (sometimes by default and sometimes by manually enabling audit logging).

Next, we are going to see what the best practices are for conducting security monitoring and audit trails using AWS, Azure, and GCP built-in managed services.

Security monitoring and audit trails using AWS CloudTrail

AWS provides the following monitoring and auditing services:

- **AWS CloudTrail** is the Amazon-managed audit trail service. It enables you to track all user activity based on an AWS API from both the AWS Management Console and through the API for further analysis and correlation (mostly management-related API events).

- **Amazon CloudWatch** is the Amazon-managed service for collecting cloud endpoint-related events (such as EC2 and **Relational Database Service** (**RDS**).

- **AWS Config** is a service that allows you to monitor configuration changes in various AWS services.

- **DNS logs** allow you to detect DNS queries from your **Virtual Private Cloud** (**VPC**) to a **Command and Control** (**C&C**) server.

- **VPC Flow Logs** allows you to detect malicious traffic from your VPC to a C&C server.

In this section, we will focus on AWS CloudTrail.

Best practices for using AWS CloudTrail

Here is a list of best practices to follow:

- Enabling AWS CloudTrail on all AWS accounts and all AWS regions

- Enabling the logging of data events (such as S3 object-level activity, AWS Lambda executions, and DynamoDB object-level events)

> **Important Note**
>
> It is recommended to conduct risk analysis on the target service (such as a service that stores or processes credit card information, healthcare data, and more) prior to enabling data event logging due to the cost of event storage versus the value that can be achieved from data event logs.

- Enable CloudTrail insights to detect unusual activity related to write API events

- Limit access to the CloudTrail logs to a minimum number of employees – preferred in an AWS management account, outside the scope of your end users, to avoid possible deletion or changes to the audit logs

- Enforce the use of **Multi-Factor Authentication** (**MFA**) for users with access to the CloudTrail console

- Send events to CloudWatch logs for further analysis on user activity (such as file deletion from an S3 bucket, changes to a security group, or shutting down an EC2 instance

- Limit access to CloudTrail logs stored in S3, using S3 bucket policy

- According to your industry regulation, you can configure log retention by using S3 object life cycle management rules – archive necessary logs for the required period and delete logs if no longer necessary

- Enable log file integrity validation for CloudTrail logs to make sure your logs haven't been tampered with

- When storing CloudTrail logs inside an S3 bucket, enabling the MFA delete feature to avoid accidental deletion of CloudTrail logs

- Create an AWS Configuration rule that makes sure CloudTrail logs are sent to Amazon CloudWatch Logs

- Encrypt all CloudTrail logs stored inside a dedicated S3 bucket using a customer master key CMK (as explained in *Chapter 7, Applying Encryption in Cloud Services*)

For more information, please refer to the following resources:

Security best practices in AWS CloudTrail:

```
https://docs.aws.amazon.com/awscloudtrail/latest/userguide/
best-practices-security.html
```

Logging data events for trails:

```
https://docs.aws.amazon.com/awscloudtrail/latest/userguide/
logging-data-events-with-cloudtrail.html
```

Logging Insights events for trails:

```
https://docs.aws.amazon.com/awscloudtrail/latest/userguide/
logging-insights-events-with-cloudtrail.html
```

Sending events to CloudWatch Logs:

```
https://docs.aws.amazon.com/awscloudtrail/latest/userguide/
send-cloudtrail-events-to-cloudwatch-logs.html
```

How can I view and track account activity history for specific IAM users, roles, and AWS access keys?

```
https://aws.amazon.com/premiumsupport/knowledge-center/view-
iam-history/
```

Enabling log file integrity validation for CloudTrail:

```
https://docs.aws.amazon.com/awscloudtrail/latest/userguide/
cloudtrail-log-file-validation-enabling.html
```

Deleting an object from an MFA delete-enabled bucket:

```
https://docs.aws.amazon.com/AmazonS3/latest/userguide/
UsingMFADelete.html
```

cloud-trail-cloud-watch-logs-enabled:

```
https://docs.aws.amazon.com/config/latest/developerguide/
cloud-trail-cloud-watch-logs-enabled.html
```

Configure AWS KMS key policies for CloudTrail:

```
https://docs.aws.amazon.com/awscloudtrail/latest/userguide/
create-kms-key-policy-for-cloudtrail.html
```

Amazon S3 bucket policy for CloudTrail:

```
https://docs.aws.amazon.com/awscloudtrail/latest/userguide/
create-s3-bucket-policy-for-cloudtrail.html
```

Security monitoring using AWS Security Hub

AWS Security Hub is a managed service that allows you to aggregate events and configurations from multiple sources (such as *Amazon GuardDuty, Amazon Inspector, Amazon Macie, AWS IAM Access Analyzer, AWS Systems Manager,* and *AWS Firewall Manager*) into a single console, which enables you to prioritize the work on security events coming from the various sources. Let's discuss each of them:

- **Amazon GuardDuty** – A service that continuously monitors CloudTrail logs, VPC Flow Logs, and DNS logs, and uses machine learning capabilities to detect malicious activities in your AWS environment

- **Amazon Inspector** – A vulnerability assessment service for EC2 instances (such as misconfiguration and missing patches)

- **Amazon Macie** – A service that discovers and protects sensitive information (such as **Personally Identifiable Information (PII)**) on S3 buckets

- **AWS IAM Access Analyzer** – A service for detecting unnecessary IAM permissions (such as over-privileges) on resources by external entities

- **AWS Systems Manager** – A service for allowing automated tasks on EC2 or RDS instances from a central location (such as logging-in and changing a setting on a farm of EC2 instances)

- **AWS Firewall Manager** – A service for configuring WAF rules on large environments centrally

Best practices for using AWS Security Hub

Here is a list of best practices to follow:

- Enable AWS Security Hub on all AWS accounts and all AWS regions from a single master AWS account in your AWS organization

- Grant minimal privileges to the AWS Security Hub console and enforce MFA for users with access to it
- Enable AWS Config for tracking configuration changes and sending events to the AWS Security Hub

> **Important Note**
>
> AWS Config can function independently from AWS Security Hub, allows you to track resource configuration history, and provides both a real-time and history inventory of your cloud environment.

- Enable AWS Foundational Security Best Practices standards in AWS Security Hub

> **Important Note**
>
> Using AWS Foundational Security Best Practices, you can detect services in your environment that deviate from security best practices that appear in well-known CIS benchmarks, such as usage of a root account, failure to configure MFA, and the failure to encrypt data at rest (such as RDS databases and S3 buckets).

- Use AWS Security Hub insights to review Security Hub findings and deciding on proper actions
- Follow remediation instructions inside the AWS Security Hub console to fix security events raised on the console

> **Important Note**
>
> It is recommended to decide whether you want to use the AWS Security Hub console to fix security events or, in a mature cloud environment, send events from Security Hub to an external **Security Information and Event Management** (**SIEM**) or ticketing system to be handled by a security operations team.

For more information, please refer to the following resources:

Nine AWS Security Hub best practices:

https://aws.amazon.com/blogs/security/nine-aws-security-hub-best-practices/

AWS Foundational Security Best Practices controls:

https://docs.aws.amazon.com/securityhub/latest/userguide/securityhub-standards-fsbp-controls.html

Insights in AWS Security Hub:

```
https://docs.aws.amazon.com/securityhub/latest/userguide/
securityhub-insights.html
```

Automated Response and Remediation with AWS Security Hub:

```
https://aws.amazon.com/blogs/security/automated-response-and-
remediation-with-aws-security-hub/
```

Summary

In this section, we have learned how to conduct auditing of your AWS accounts using AWS CloudTrail and how to monitor for security and compliance best practices using AWS Security Hub in a centralized console.

Security monitoring and audit trails using Azure Monitor

Azure allows you to monitor and log user activity logs inside Azure Monitor, a managed log collection and monitoring service.

Azure offers a tiered licensing model:

- **Azure AD Free** – Support for basic security and usage reports
- **Azure AD Premium P1** – Support for both Azure Active Directory basic security reports and advanced security and usage reports
- **Azure AD Premium P2** – Support for the preceding type of reports, and the ability to detect risky accounts and investigate risk events in an SIEM system (such as Azure Sentinel)

Best practices for using Azure Monitor

Here is a list of best practices to follow:

- Enable Azure activity logging by sending activity logs to a Log Analytics workspace
- Enable Azure resource logging by creating diagnostic settings for each Azure resource and sending the logs to a Log Analytics workspace
- Use Azure Monitor Private Link to secure access from your **Virtual Network (VNet)** to the Azure Monitor, which avoids sending network traffic outside your VNET through a secure channel

- Limit access to the Azure monitor logs to a minimum number of employees – preferred in a dedicated storage account, outside the scope of your end users, to avoid possible deletion or changes to the audit logs

- Send Azure Monitor activity logs to Azure Sentinel for further security analysis

- For highly sensitive environments, store your Log Analytics data inside a customer-managed storage account and encrypting Azure Monitor logs using a **Customer-Managed Encryption Key** (**CMEK**) (as explained in *Chapter 7, Applying Encryption in Cloud Services*)

- Use **Azure Monitor Private Link Scope** (**AMPLS**) to connect your VNETs to Azure Monitor without passing through the public internet

For more information, please refer to the following resources:

Azure security logging and auditing:

```
https://docs.microsoft.com/en-us/azure/security/fundamentals/
log-audit
```

Azure Activity log:

```
https://docs.microsoft.com/en-us/azure/azure-monitor/
essentials/activity-log
```

Azure resource logs:

```
https://docs.microsoft.com/en-us/azure/azure-monitor/
essentials/resource-logs
```

Roles, permissions, and security in Azure Monitor:

```
https://docs.microsoft.com/en-us/azure/azure-monitor/roles-
permissions-security#security-considerations-for-monitoring-
data
```

View activity logs to monitor actions on resources:

```
https://docs.microsoft.com/en-us/azure/azure-resource-manager/
management/view-activity-logs
```

Connect data from the Azure Activity log:

```
https://docs.microsoft.com/en-us/azure/sentinel/connect-azure-
activity
```

Azure Monitor customer-managed key:

```
https://docs.microsoft.com/en-us/azure/azure-monitor/logs/
customer-managed-keys
```

Using customer-managed storage accounts in Azure Monitor Log Analytics:

```
https://docs.microsoft.com/en-us/azure/azure-monitor/logs/
private-storage
```

Use Azure Private Link to connect networks to Azure Monitor:

```
https://docs.microsoft.com/en-us/azure/azure-monitor/logs/
private-link-security
```

Azure Private Link introduces new modes and enforces Network Isolation strictly:

```
https://techcommunity.microsoft.com/t5/azure-monitor/azure-
monitor-private-links-introduces-new-modes-and-enforces/
ba-p/2519136
```

Security monitoring and approval process using Customer Lockbox

When talking about cloud services and the *shared responsibility model*, we understood that as customers of **Infrastructure as a Service (IaaS)**, we control everything inside a virtual machine and, among others, we are responsible for monitoring activity done above the operating system layer.

On **Platform as a Service (PaaS)**, we are responsible for monitoring activity done above the platform (such as a managed database) layer, and on **Software as a Service (SaaS)**, we are responsible for monitoring activity done at the managed service layer (assuming the SaaS vendor supports it).

What happens when a cloud vendor employee needs access to our tenant, for example, in a scenario where support personnel would like to resolve a ticket we have submitted as customers to restore an object from a mailbox or a deleted file from an object store?

Where do we see audit trails of such an event, and how can we approve it in the first place?

Microsoft offers us a way to intervene in the process by enabling a license for a feature called **Customer Lockbox**.

Customer Lockbox works as per the following steps:

1. We submit a ticket to Microsoft support and ask for assistance that requires access to our tenant.

2. The ticket is assigned to a support engineer, and since they don't have access to our tenant, they escalate the ticket to a support manager.

3. After the support manager approves the request, an email is sent to a designated approver from our organization, who is asked to grant the support engineer access to our tenant.

4. Once the process is approved, the support engineer gets *just enough time and just enough access* to accomplish the requested task.

5. The entire process is logged into our tenant logs (for example, in our **exchange online logs**) and temporary permissions are removed.

Best practices for using Customer Lockbox

Here is a list of best practices to follow:

- Purchase a license and enabling Customer Lockbox

- Review the audit logs recorded for Customer Lockbox activities

- Connect the activity logs of Customer Lockbox to Azure Sentinel for audit purposes

- Enable alerts for anomaly behavior of Customer Lockbox

- Limit access to Customer Lockbox logs to a minimum number of employees – preferred in a dedicated storage account, outside the scope of your end users, to avoid possible deletion or changes to the audit logs

- Enforce the use of MFA for users with access to Customer Lockbox logs

- Designate an employee with the Customer Lockbox Approver role, instead of using the Global Admin role for the approval process

For more information, please refer to the following resources:

Customer Lockbox in Office 365:

```
https://docs.microsoft.com/en-us/microsoft-365/compliance/
customer-lockbox-requests?view=o365-worldwide
```

Customer Lockbox for Microsoft Azure:

```
https://docs.microsoft.com/en-us/azure/security/fundamentals/
customer-lockbox-overview
```

Azure security baseline for Customer Lockbox for Microsoft Azure:

```
https://docs.microsoft.com/en-us/security/benchmark/azure/
baselines/lockbox-security-baseline
```

Approve audit support access requests to VMs using Customer Lockbox for Azure:

```
https://azure.microsoft.com/en-us/blog/approve-audit-support-
access-requests-to-vms-using-customer-lockbox-for-azure/
```

Customer Lockbox Approver Role Now Available:

```
https://techcommunity.microsoft.com/t5/security-compliance-
and-identity/customer-lockbox-approver-role-now-available/
ba-p/223393
```

Summary

In this section, we have learned how to conduct auditing of your Azure accounts using Azure Monitor and how to approve and monitor Microsoft support engineers' access to our tenant.

Security monitoring and audit trail using Google Cloud Logging

GCP allows you to monitor and log user activity logs inside Google Cloud Logging, a managed log collection and monitoring service.

Best practices for using Google Cloud Logging

Here is a list of best practices to follow:

- Admin activity audit logs are enabled by default and cannot be disabled.
- Explicitly enabling **data access audit logs** to log activities performed on Google services.

> **Important Note**
>
> It is recommended to conduct risk analysis on the target service (such as a service that stores or processes credit card information or healthcare data) prior to enabling data event logging due to the cost of event storage versus the value that can be achieved from data event logs.

- Limit access to the **Cloud Logging logs** to a minimum number of employees – preferably in a dedicated GCP project, outside the scope of your end users, to avoid possible deletion or changes to the audit logs.

- Limit access to audit logs to a minimum number of employees to avoid possible deletion or changes to the audit logs, using IAM roles (a **Logs Viewer** for admin activity logs and a **Private Logs Viewer** for data access logs).

- Encrypt all **Cloud Logging logs** using CMEKs (as explained in *Chapter 7, Applying Encryption in Cloud Services*).

For more information, please refer to the following resources:

Best practices for Cloud Audit Logs:

```
https://cloud.google.com/logging/docs/audit/best-practices
```

Best practices for working with Google Cloud Audit Logs:

```
https://cloud.google.com/blog/products/it-ops/best-practices-
for-working-with-google-cloud-audit-logging
```

Enabling customer-managed encryption keys for Logs Router:

```
https://cloud.google.com/logging/docs/routing/managed-
encryption
```

Configuring Data Access audit logs:

```
https://cloud.google.com/logging/docs/audit/configure-data-
access
```

Storing your organization's logs in a log bucket:

```
https://cloud.google.com/logging/docs/central-log-storage
```

IAM roles for auditing-related job functions:

```
https://cloud.google.com/iam/docs/job-functions/auditing
```

Security monitoring using Google Security Command Center

Google Security Command Center is a managed service that allows you to aggregate logs and configuration from multiple sources (such as *Google App Engine, BigQuery, Cloud SQL, Cloud Storage, Cloud IAM*, and **Google Kubernetes Engine** (GKE) into a single console, which enables you to prioritize the work on security configuration, compliance, and threats.

Best practices for using Google Security Command Center

Here is a list of best practices to follow:

- Use Cloud IAM roles to grant minimal access to the Google Security Command Center console.

- Admin activity audit logs are enabled by default and cannot be disabled.

- Explicitly enable data access audit logs to log activities performed on Google Security Command Center.

> **Important Note**
>
> It is recommended to conduct risk analysis on the target service (such as a service that stores or processes credit card information or healthcare data) prior to enabling data event logging due to the cost of event storage versus the value that can be achieved from data event logs.

- Use Google Security Command Center to detect and fix misconfigurations in various GCP services (such as firewall rules, public Cloud Storage buckets, virtual machines with public IP, or instances without **Secure Socket Layer** (SSL).

- Subscribe to **Security Command Center** to receive anomalous behavior from outside your environment (such as leaked credentials or anomalous virtual machine behavior.

- For environments that are built on containers, enabling Google Security Command Center premium tier and using the **Container Threat Detection** service to detect runtime attacks on containers and send the logs to Google Cloud Logging.

- Use the **Cloud DLP Data Discovery** capability to view the result of Google Cloud DLP scans.

- Use **Web Security Scanner** on test environments before moving an application (such as Google App Engine, GKE, or Compute Engine applications) to detect application vulnerabilities.

- Use Google Security Command Center to detect vulnerabilities and mis-compliance according to CIS Benchmarks.

For more information, please refer to the following resources:

Security Command Center conceptual overview:

```
https://cloud.google.com/security-command-center/docs/
concepts-security-command-center-overview
```

Using Security Health Analytics:

```
https://cloud.google.com/security-command-center/docs/how-to-
use-security-health-analytics
```

Security Command Center audit logging information:

```
https://cloud.google.com/security-command-center/docs/audit-
logging
```

Container Threat Detection conceptual overview:

```
https://cloud.google.com/security-command-center/docs/
concepts-container-threat-detection-overview
```

Overview of Web Security Scanner:

```
https://cloud.google.com/security-command-center/docs/
concepts-web-security-scanner-overview#best_practices
```

Vulnerabilities findings:

```
https://cloud.google.com/security-command-center/docs/
concepts-vulnerabilities-findings
```

Find and fix misconfigurations in your Google Cloud resources:

```
https://cloud.google.com/blog/products/identity-security/find-
and-fix-misconfigurations-in-your-google-cloud-resources
```

Security monitoring and approval process using Access Transparency and Access Approval

Google Access Transparency allows you to review access attempts to your GCP project and resources by Google employees inside Google Cloud Logging.

Google Access Approval allows you to control any request by Google support engineers to access your GCP project and resources.

Best practices for using Access Transparency and Access Approval

Here is a list of best practices to follow:

- Enable **Access Transparency** to begin logging actions done by Google employees on your tenant

- Grant a **Private Logs Viewer** role to a user who needs minimal access to review the Access Transparency logs

- Create a **Pub/Sub** topic for **Access Approval**

- Create a service account for the Access Approval process, with a Pub/Sub Publisher role, and contacting Google support, providing them the name of the Pub/Sub topic you have previously created and the GCP Project details and GCP organization ID for which you wish to receive notifications

- Grant an **Access Approvals Approver** role to a user who needs minimal access to approve requests by Google support engineers

- Enforce the use of MFA for users with access to either **Access Transparency** or the **Access Approval console/logs**

For more information, please refer to the following resources:

Access Transparency:

```
https://cloud.google.com/logging/docs/audit/access-
transparency-overview
```

Enabling Access Transparency:

```
https://cloud.google.com/logging/docs/audit/enable-access-
transparency
```

Understanding and using Access Transparency logs:

```
https://cloud.google.com/logging/docs/audit/reading-access-
transparency-logs
```

Access Approval QuickStart:

```
https://cloud.google.com/access-approval/docs/quickstart
```

Approving Access Approval requests:

```
https://cloud.google.com/access-approval/docs/approve-requests
```

Summary

In this section, we have learned how to conduct auditing of your GCP projects using **Google Cloud Logging**, how to centrally detect and respond to security-related events and compliance issues using Google Security Command Center, and how to approve and monitor Google support engineers' access to our tenant using **Access Transparency** and **Access Approval**.

Conducting threat detection and response

In the previous section, we spoke about a way to log activity in our cloud environment (what was done, when, and by whom).

In this section, we will review managed services that allow us to review our logs and pinpoint actual threats and our response to the threats.

Using Amazon Detective for threat detection

Amazon Detective connects to services such as AWS CloudTrail and Amazon VPC Flow Logs to detect login events, API calls, and network traffic.

It then uses machine learning to detect activities outside normal behavior to assist you in finding the root cause of suspicious activities in your AWS environment.

Amazon Detective is the cloud-native equivalent of third-party tools such as Splunk, which allows you to query a large number of logs and detect security-related incidents.

Best practices for using Amazon Detective for threat detection

Here is a list of best practices to follow:

- Allow access to the **Amazon Detective** findings to a limited number of employees
- Enforce the use of MFA for employees with access to the Amazon Detective console and logs
- Use Amazon Detective to analyze AWS IAM roles' activities and sending the results to **Amazon GuardDuty**
- Use AWS CloudTrail to log activities done on the Amazon Detective console
- Use Amazon Detective as part of incident response threat hunting to detect security-related incidents in your AWS environment

For more information, please refer to the following resources:

Security best practices for Amazon Detective:

```
https://docs.aws.amazon.com/detective/latest/adminguide/
security-best-practices.html
```

Logging Amazon Detective API calls with AWS CloudTrail:

```
https://docs.aws.amazon.com/detective/latest/adminguide/
logging-using-cloudtrail.html
```

Analyze and understand IAM role usage with Amazon Detective:

```
https://aws.amazon.com/blogs/security/analyze-and-understand-
iam-role-usage-with-amazon-detective/
```

Using Amazon GuardDuty for threat detection

Amazon GuardDuty is a monitoring service that pulls data from VPC Flow Logs, AWS CloudTrail, CloudTrail S3 data event logs, and DNS logs.

It uses machine learning to review the logs and alerts you only on events that require further investigation and sometimes actions (such as replacing privileged account credentials or configuring MFA if credentials were compromised).

Amazon GuardDuty combines machine learning capabilities with signature-based detection (such as API action blacklists or detecting bot activity in your AWS environment). Examples of events include privilege escalation events, stolen credentials, and outbound traffic from your environment to an external malicious IP address.

Amazon GuardDuty works on a single AWS account or in an entire AWS organization. To avoid blind spots in your AWS organization (such as AWS accounts or regions that have not enabled GuardDuty), it is recommended to aggregate all GuardDuty logs using CloudWatch events to a central S3 bucket.

Best practices for using Amazon GuardDuty for threat detection

Here is a list of best practices to follow:

- Use IAM roles to grant minimal access to the GuardDuty console
- Enforce the use of MFA for users with access to the GuardDuty console

- Enable S3 protection on an entire AWS organization level and on S3 buckets that contain sensitive information (such as credit card information healthcare data) to allow GuardDuty to monitor and search for malicious activity against an S3 bucket, such as a bucket made public

- Use CloudWatch Events to get notifications about GuardDuty findings

- As remediation activities, you can choose one of the following alternatives:

  - A. Use CloudWatch to trigger AWS Lambda functions as remediation activities to GuardDuty findings

  - B. Send events from Security Hub to AWS Systems Manager and running actions (such as changing the setting on remote EC2 instances)

  - C. Send events from Security Hub to AWS Lambda functions to run actions (such as closing an open port on a security group)

- Use AWS CloudTrail to log activities done on the Amazon GuardDuty console

- Enable integration between Amazon GuardDuty and AWS Security Hub to get a central view of all compliance and security incidents inside a central console

- Enable integration between Amazon Detective and Amazon GuardDuty to get findings from Amazon Detective into the Amazon GuardDuty console

For more information, please refer to the following resources:

What is Amazon GuardDuty?:

```
https://docs.aws.amazon.com/guardduty/latest/ug/guardduty_
managing_access.html#guardduty_user-access
```

Amazon S3 protection in Amazon GuardDuty:

```
https://docs.aws.amazon.com/guardduty/latest/ug/s3_detection.
html
```

Creating custom responses to GuardDuty findings with Amazon CloudWatch Events:

```
https://docs.aws.amazon.com/guardduty/latest/ug/guardduty_
findings_cloudwatch.html
```

Logging Amazon GuardDuty API calls with AWS CloudTrail:

```
https://docs.aws.amazon.com/guardduty/latest/ug/logging-using-
cloudtrail.html
```

Enabling and configuring integration with AWS Security Hub:

```
https://docs.aws.amazon.com/guardduty/latest/ug/securityhub-
integration.html#securityhub-integration-enable
```

Integration with Amazon Detective:

```
https://docs.aws.amazon.com/guardduty/latest/ug/detective-
integration.html
```

Remediating security issues discovered by GuardDuty:

```
https://docs.aws.amazon.com/guardduty/latest/ug/guardduty_
remediate.html
```

Automatically block suspicious traffic with AWS Network Firewall and Amazon GuardDuty:

```
https://aws.amazon.com/blogs/security/automatically-block-
suspicious-traffic-with-aws-network-firewall-and-amazon-
guardduty/
```

How you can use Amazon GuardDuty to detect suspicious activity within your AWS account:

```
https://aws.amazon.com/blogs/security/how-you-can-use-amazon-
guardduty-to-detect-suspicious-activity-within-your-aws-
account/
```

Security monitoring using Microsoft Defender for Cloud

Microsoft Defender for Cloud is a centralized service for threat detection and protection.

Best practices for using Microsoft Defender for Cloud

Here is a list of best practices to follow:

- Use Azure **Role-Based Access Control** (**RBAC**) to grant minimal permissions for users to be able to use the Microsoft Defender for Cloud console

- Use MFA for users with permissions to access the Microsoft Defender for Cloud console

- Use Microsoft Defender for Cloud recommendations from within the Security Center console to find out what actions should be done to resolve compliance issues in your Azure environment and remediating them

- Reduce the attack surface in your applications using Microsoft Defender for Cloud adaptive application controls (such as malware detection, unsupported applications, and applications containing sensitive data)

- Configure an email address to get notifications from the **Microsoft Security Response Center** (**MSRC**) when resources were detected as compromised by Microsoft Defender for Cloud

- Automatically deploy a monitoring agent on all your virtual machines to allow monitoring of Microsoft Defender for Cloud

- Use Microsoft Defender for Cloud to review all the assets in your Azure environment

- Use Microsoft Defender for Cloud to monitor compliance against CIS Benchmarks

- Use Microsoft Defender for Cloud to monitor for compliance, such as DDoS protection at VNET level, full disk encryption, endpoint protection, and patch management on virtual machines, SQL configuration such as auditing and encryption at rest, Azure storage encryption at rest, and others

- Use an Microsoft Defender for Cloud feature called **File Integrity Monitoring** (**FIM**) to detect changes to files in sensitive environments that cannot be tampered with (such as **Payment Card Industry Data Security Standard** (**PCI DSS**) environments).

For more information, please refer to the following resources:

Permissions in Microsoft Defender for Cloud:

```
https://docs.microsoft.com/en-us/azure/security-center/
security-center-permissions
```

Review your security recommendations:

```
https://docs.microsoft.com/en-us/azure/security-center/
security-center-recommendations
```

Remediate recommendations in Microsoft Defender for Cloud:

```
https://docs.microsoft.com/en-us/azure/security-center/
security-center-remediate-recommendations
```

Automate responses to Security Center triggers:

```
https://docs.microsoft.com/en-us/azure/security-center/
workflow-automation
```

Use adaptive application controls to reduce your machines' attack surfaces:

```
https://docs.microsoft.com/en-us/azure/security-center/
security-center-adaptive-application
```

Configure email notifications for security alerts:

```
https://docs.microsoft.com/en-us/azure/security-center/
security-center-provide-security-contact-details
```

Configure auto-provisioning for agents and extensions from Microsoft Defender for Cloud:

```
https://docs.microsoft.com/en-us/azure/security-center/
security-center-enable-data-collection
```

Explore and manage your resources with asset inventory:

```
https://docs.microsoft.com/en-us/azure/security-center/asset-
inventory
```

Azure Security Benchmark – 90 security and compliance best practices for your workloads in Azure:

```
https://www.microsoft.com/security/blog/2020/01/23/azure-
security-benchmark-90-security-compliance-best-practices-
azure-workloads/
```

File integrity monitoring in Microsoft Defender for Cloud:

```
https://docs.microsoft.com/en-us/azure/security-center/
security-center-file-integrity-monitoring
```

Using Azure Sentinel for threat detection

Azure Sentinel is a cloud-native SIEM service, built upon Azure Log Analytics workspaces.

It uses **artificial intelligence** (**AI**) to detect threats in your Azure environment and assist you in responding to detected threats.

Best practices for using Azure Sentinel for threat detection

Here is a list of best practices to follow:

- Use Azure RBAC to grant minimal permissions for users to be able to use Azure Sentinel and investigate incidents inside the console.
- Use MFA for users with permissions to access the Azure Sentinel console.

- Use Azure Monitor to send Azure Sentinel audit logs to the Azure Log Analytics workspace for further analysis.

- Create a Log Analytics workspace for both Azure Sentinel and Microsoft Defender for Cloud.

- Use the Azure Sentinel console to review incidents and investigate them and using the investigation graph to take a deeper look at the incident and the resources that were part of the incident itself.

- Use the Azure Sentinel repository of pre-configured playbooks to automatically remediate an incident (such as blocking an IP address, blocking an Azure AD user, or isolating a virtual machine).

- Send Microsoft 365 defender logs to Azure Sentinel for further analysis.

- Integrate third-party threat intelligence platform products into Azure Sentinel for data enrichment.

- Enable Azure Sentinel **User and Entity Behavior Analytics** (**UEBA**) to detect anomalous behavior of users, hosts, IP addresses, and applications in your Azure environment.

- For sensitive environments, add an extra layer of protection by encrypting your Azure Sentinel data using a CMEK (as explained in *Chapter 7, Applying Encryption in Cloud Services*).

For more information, please refer to the following resources:

`https://docs.microsoft.com/en-us/azure/sentinel/best-practices`

Azure security baseline for Azure Sentinel:

`https://docs.microsoft.com/en-us/security/benchmark/azure/baselines/sentinel-security-baseline`

Permissions in Azure Sentinel:

`https://docs.microsoft.com/en-us/azure/sentinel/roles`

Tutorial: Investigate incidents with Azure Sentinel:

`https://docs.microsoft.com/en-us/azure/sentinel/tutorial-investigate-cases`

Tutorial: Use playbooks with automation rules in Azure Sentinel:

`https://docs.microsoft.com/en-us/azure/sentinel/tutorial-respond-threats-playbook`

Microsoft 365 Defender integration with Azure Sentinel:

`https://docs.microsoft.com/en-us/azure/sentinel/microsoft-365-defender-sentinel-integration`

Pre-deployment activities and prerequisites for deploying Azure Sentinel:

`https://docs.microsoft.com/en-us/azure/sentinel/prerequisites`

Understand threat intelligence in Azure Sentinel:

`https://docs.microsoft.com/en-us/azure/sentinel/understand-threat-intelligence`

Identify advanced threats with User and Entity Behavior Analytics (UEBA) in Azure Sentinel:

`https://docs.microsoft.com/en-us/azure/sentinel/identify-threats-with-entity-behavior-analytics`

Set up an Azure Sentinel customer-managed key:

`https://docs.microsoft.com/en-us/azure/sentinel/customer-managed-keys`

Audit Azure Sentinel queries and activities :

`https://docs.microsoft.com/en-us/azure/sentinel/audit-sentinel-data`

Using Azure Defender for threat detection

Azure Defender is a threat protection service for various types of Azure resources, such as virtual machines, SQL databases, containers, and Azure App services.

Best practices for using Azure Defender for threat detection

Here is a list of best practices to follow:

- Since Azure Defender is integrated into Microsoft Defender for Cloud, use Azure RBAC to grant minimal permissions for users to be able to use the Microsoft Defender for Cloud console
- Since Azure Defender is integrated into Microsoft Defender for Cloud, use MFA for users with permissions to access the Microsoft Defender for Cloud console
- Enable Azure Defender to protect your services (according to Azure Defender-supported services)

- Enable Azure Defender at the subscription level for all the subscriptions in your Azure environment

- Use Azure Defender's built-in vulnerability scanner to detect vulnerabilities on your virtual machines

For more information, please refer to the following resources:

Introduction to Azure Defender:

```
https://docs.microsoft.com/en-us/azure/security-center/azure-
defender
```

Introduction to Azure Defender for servers:

```
https://docs.microsoft.com/en-us/azure/security-center/
defender-for-servers-introduction
```

QuickStart: Enable Azure Defender:

```
https://docs.microsoft.com/en-us/azure/security-center/enable-
azure-defender
```

The Azure Defender dashboard:

```
https://docs.microsoft.com/en-us/azure/security-center/azure-
defender-dashboard
```

Summary

In this section, we have learned how to conduct threat detection and remediation based on both AWS and Azure-managed services, including getting insights from a large number of logs to detect anomalous behavior of users, virtual machines, network, and application services, how to investigate the incidents, and how to run actions for automatic remediation in large environments.

Using Google Security Command Center for threat detection and prevention

Google Security Command Center is a threat detection service for virtual machines and containers.

This service can scan web servers for vulnerabilities and data exfiltration and prevent them.

Best practices for using Google Security Command Center for threat detection and prevention

Here is a list of best practices to follow:

- Use the latest supported **Google Kubernetes Engine (GKE)** version.

- Enable Container Threat Detection.

- Enable VM Threat Detection.

- Use Cloud IAM roles to grant minimal access to the Google Security Command Center console.

- Enable admin activity audit logs by default.

- Explicitly enable data access audit logs to log activities performed on Google Security Command Center.

> **Important Note**
> It is recommended to conduct risk analysis on the target service (such as a service that stores or processes credit card information, healthcare data, and so on) prior to enabling data event logging due to the cost of event storage versus the value that can be achieved from data event logs.

- Use Cloud Logging to review Google Security Command Center findings.

For more information, please refer to the following resources:

- *Using Container Threat Detection*:

  https://cloud.google.com/security-command-center/docs/how-to-use-container-threat-detection

- *Use Virtual Machine Threat Detection*:

  https://cloud.google.com/security-command-center/docs/how-to-use-vm-threat-detection

- *Investigating and responding to threats*:

  https://cloud.google.com/security-command-center/docs/how-to-investigate-threats

- *Remediating Web Security Scanner findings*:

  https://cloud.google.com/security-command-center/docs/how-to-remediate-web-security-scanner-findings

Conducting incident response and digital forensics

Incident response and forensics are challenging in cloud environments for several reasons:

- Our entire environment is stored at a physical location, managed by an external service provider.

- Our entire environment is split between our on-premises and a cloud provider (also known as a hybrid cloud environment).

- Our entire environment is split between multiple cloud providers (also known as a multi-cloud environment).

- Our cloud environment is in multiple regions or multiple cloud accounts (such as across an AWS account, Azure subscriptions, and GCP projects), and we might lack visibility to all resources deployed in our cloud environment or information about who owns or manages those accounts.

- According to the shared responsibility model, we may not have visibility for actions done by our cloud provider (such as a cloud engineer making changes to a managed database or performing a backup or restore from an SaaS application).

- Our cloud environment may contain cloud services that our central IT or security department is not aware of or are managed by business-division IT personnel or a third-party company we are not aware of.

- Virtual servers (and containers) are ephemeral – they might exist for short periods of time before being decommissioned and erased.

National Institute of Standards and Technology (**NIST**) defines the following stages for conducting incident response:

- **Preparation** – Prepare up-to-date contact person information (taking part in the incident response process), prepare a system to document incident response activities, prepare a workstation for forensics purposes, and so on.

- **Detection and analysis** – Collect audit logs and change management logs to detect anomalies (such as multiple failed logons or changes to configuration files, and analyze gathered information from IDS/IPS logs to website defacement events, and so on).

- **Containment, eradication, and recovery** – Identify the attacking host, conduct removal actions (such as removing malware from an infected host), and return systems to normal activity (return clean hosts to production).

- **Post-incident activity** – Conduct lessons-learned and update procedures to minimize the chances of similar attacks happening again.

For more information, please refer to the following resource:

NIST – Computer Security Incident Handling Guide:

```
https://nvlpubs.nist.gov/nistpubs/specialpublications/nist.
sp.800-61r2.pdf
```

Conducting incident response in AWS

AWS offers several services to assist in going through the incident response life cycle:

- **Preparation phase**:

  - Use NACL and security groups to set the proper network access rules to access your AWS environment.

  - Use AWS Shield to protect your environment from DDoS attacks.

  - Use AWS WAF to protect your environment from application-layer attacks.

  - Use AWS Config to monitor for configuration changes.

  - Use Amazon Inspector to detect compliance issues, such as vulnerabilities originating from non-hardened virtual servers or unpatched systems.

- **Detection phase**:

  - Use AWS CloudTrail to log actions done through API for future analysis.

  - Use Amazon CloudWatch logs to send alerts on behavior outside the regular pattern (such as a spike in failed logins).

  - Use Amazon GuardDuty to detect suspicious activity from AWS CloudTrail logs, VPC Flow Logs, or DNS logs.

  - Use VPC Flow Logs to monitor network activity.

> **Important Note**
>
> For production environments, enable VPC Flow Logs only for troubleshooting purposes.

  - Use Amazon Macie to detect any leakage of sensitive information (such as credit card information) stored in S3 buckets.

- **Respond phase**:

  - Use AWS Config rules to automatically return configuration settings to the desired state.

  - Use Amazon CloudWatch Events to trigger AWS Lambda functions as guardrails to automatically respond to events (such as blocking a security group rule or shutting down an EC2 instance).

  - Use AWS Systems Manager to run commands on multiple remote EC2 instances.

- **Recover phase**:

  - Use AWS Backup to restore an EC2 instance from an older backup.

  - Use **Elastic Block Store (EBS)** snapshots to restore EBS volumes.

  - Use CloudFormation templates to rebuild an entire AWS environment from scratch.

For more information, please refer to the following resources:

How to get started with security response automation on AWS:

```
https://aws.amazon.com/blogs/security/how-get-started-
security-response-automation-aws/
```

AWS Security Incident Response Guide:

```
https://d1.awsstatic.com/whitepapers/aws_security_incident_
response.pdf
```

Incident Response in the Cloud:

```
https://docs.aws.amazon.com/whitepapers/latest/aws-security-
incident-response-guide/incident-response-in-the-cloud.html
```

How to perform automated incident response in a multi-account environment:

```
https://aws.amazon.com/blogs/security/how-to-perform-
automated-incident-response-multi-account-environment/
```

AWS Cloud: Proactive Security and Forensic Readiness – Part 5:

```
https://blog.cloudsecurityalliance.org/2019/05/02/aws-cloud-
proactive-security-part-5/
```

AWS Incident Response:

```
https://github.com/easttimor/aws-incident-response
```

AWS Incident Response Playbook Samples:

`https://github.com/aws-samples/aws-incident-response-playbooks`

AWS-security-automation:

`https://github.com/awslabs/aws-security-automation`

Conducting incident response in Azure

Azure offers several services to assist in going through the incident response life cycle:

- **Preparation phase**:

  - Use network security groups to set the proper network access rules to access your Azure environment.

  - Use Azure DDoS protection to protect your environment from DDoS attacks.

  - Use Azure WAF (or Azure Application Gateway) to protect your environment from application-layer attacks.

  - Use Azure Monitor and Azure Log Analytics to monitor for configuration changes.

- **Detection phase**:

  - Use Azure Monitor and Azure Log Analytics to log actions done through API for future analysis.

  - Use Microsoft Defender for Cloud to detect compliance issues, such as vulnerabilities originating from non-hardened virtual servers or unpatched systems.

  - Use Azure Sentinel to detect attacks and respond to incidents raised from other Azure services (such as Azure Log Analytics or Azure Defender).

  - Use Azure Network Watcher to monitor network activity.

  > **Important Note**
  > For production environments, enable Azure Network Watcher only for troubleshooting purposes.

  - Use Azure Information Protection to classify data and detect leakage of sensitive information (such as credit card information).

- **Respond phase**:

  - Use Azure Automation to trigger scripts to automatically respond to events (such as a block security group rule or shutting down a virtual server).

- **Recover phase**:

  - Use Azure Backup to restore an Azure VM from an older backup.

  - Use Azure disk snapshots to restore an Azure VM disk.

  - Use Azure Resource Manager to rebuild an entire Azure environment from scratch.

For more information, please refer to the following resources:

Incident management overview:

```
https://docs.microsoft.com/en-us/compliance/assurance/
assurance-incident-management
```

Computer forensics Chain of Custody in Azure:

```
https://docs.microsoft.com/en-us/azure/architecture/example-
scenario/forensics/
```

Conducting incident response in Google Cloud Platform

GCP offers several services to assist in going through the incident response life cycle:

- **Preparation phase**:

  - Use firewall rules to set the proper network access rules to access your GCP environment.

  - Use Google Cloud Armor to protect your environment from DDoS attacks and from application-layer attacks.

- **Detection phase**:

  - Use Google Cloud Logging to log actions done through the API for future analysis.

  - Use Google Security Command Center to detect compliance issues, such as vulnerabilities originating from non-hardened virtual servers or unpatched systems.

  - Use Google VPC Flow Logs to monitor network activity.

> **Important Note**
> For production environments, enable Google VPC Flow Logs only for
> troubleshooting purposes.

- Use Google Cloud DLP to classify data and detect any leakage of sensitive
  information (such as credit card information).

- **Recover phase**:

  - Use Google Persistent Disk snapshots to restore a GCP VM disk.

  - Use Google Cloud Deployment Manager to rebuild an entire GCP environment
    from scratch.

For more information, please refer to the following resources:

Data incident response process:

`https://cloud.google.com/security/incident-response`

Incidents for metric-based alerts:

`https://cloud.google.com/monitoring/alerts/incidents-events`

Summary

In this chapter, we have focused on the various monitoring/auditing, threat management,
and incident response services in AWS, Azure, and GCP.

We learned how to enable auditing in our cloud environments. We also learned how to use
built-in security services to monitor compliance by gathering information from multiple
event sources. We reviewed the built-in services that enable us to detect and respond to
threats in large-scale environments.

In this chapter, we have also reviewed the steps to conduct incident response by using
built-in services (including preparation, detection, response, and finally recovery to
normal actions).

In the next chapter, we will review cryptography in various aspects (encryption
fundamentals, differences between symmetric and asymmetric algorithms, key
management services, secrets management, and encryption at transit and at rest).

7
Applying Encryption in Cloud Services

In *Chapter 2, Securing Compute Services*, to *Chapter 6, Monitoring and Auditing Your Cloud Environments*, we covered the fundamental building blocks of cloud services (from compute, storage, and networking services to **Identity and Access Management** (**IAM**) services, to auditing, threat management, and incident response).

This chapter will cover various concepts regarding encryption – including the differences between symmetric and asymmetric encryption, **Key Management Services** (**KMSes**), secrets management services, and using encryption in transit and at rest in cloud environments.

Since encryption is a common security best practice that is used to allow data confidentiality, and since many cloud services already have built-in support for encryption (unlike on-premises environments, which require a lot of effort to maintain encryption keys), it is crucial to understand how encryption works and how it is implemented in the various cloud services.

Failing to encrypt sensitive data (such as credit card information, healthcare data, **Personally Identifiable Information** (**PII**), and more) puts us at risk of data exposure, as well as potential lawsuits from customers and regulators.

Encryption in the cloud is also important because of multi-tenancy (encryption at rest) and public APIs (encryption in transit).

In this chapter, we will cover the following topics:

- Introduction to encryption
- Best practices for deploying KMSes
- Best practices for deploying secrets management services
- Best practices for using encryption in transit
- Best practices for using encryption at rest
- Encryption in use

Technical requirements

For this chapter, you need to have a solid understanding of cryptographic concepts such as symmetric algorithms, asymmetric algorithms, encryption in transit, and encryption at rest.

Introduction to encryption

Encryption is the process of converting plain text into cipher text. The easiest way to explain why we need encryption is to imagine a scenario where we wish to transfer a file containing sensitive information (such as patient medical records) between two computers over an untrusted network such as the public internet, without being revealed by an untrusted third party.

Another example is a retail website, which processes the credit card information of its customers when they purchase products from the website.

To follow the **Payment Card Industry Data Security Standard** (**PCI DSS**), a standard for storing and processing credit card information, the retail company must encrypt all credit card information in transit and at rest.

Let's use a common three-tier architecture as an example – with front web servers (behind the load balancer for high availability), an application server (for processing the business logic), and a backend database (for storing purchase information).

To protect credit card information, we need to do the following:

- Configure the SSL certificate on the load balancer (for encryption in transit).
- Configure the SSL certificate on the web servers (for encryption in transit).
- Configure the SSL certificate between the web servers and the application server (for encryption in transit).

- If the application server stores credit card information (even for a short period) in its local hard drive, we must configure full disk encryption (for encryption at rest).

- Configure full database encryption on the backend database (for encryption at rest).

- To make sure all the encryption keys are stored securely, we need to store them in a secured location (such as a KMS, as explained later in this chapter).

The following is the terminology we need to understand:

- **Plaintext**: The original human-readable form of information.

- **Ciphertext**: The result of encryption being done on plaintext – a non-human readable form of information.

- **Encryption**: The process of converting plaintext into ciphertext.

- **Decryption**: The process of converting ciphertext back into its original form of plaintext.

- **Encryption key**: A string that, together with an encryption algorithm, can encode or decode ciphertext.

- **Encryption algorithm**: A mathematical algorithm that's used in cryptography that, together with an encryption key, allows us to encrypt or decrypt a message.

For more information, please refer to the following resources:

Encryption (according to Wikipedia):

```
https://en.wikipedia.org/wiki/Encryption
```

Cryptographic Algorithm:

```
https://www.sciencedirect.com/topics/computer-science/
cryptographic-algorithm
```

Data Encryption:

```
https://www.sciencedirect.com/topics/computer-science/data-
encryption
```

An Overview of Cryptography:

```
https://www.garykessler.net/library/crypto.html
```

Symmetric encryption

Symmetric encryption is a way to transfer data between two parties while using the same encryption key for both the encryption and decryption processes.

Symmetric encryption is commonly used for the following purposes:

- Encrypting data at rest (such as PII, credit card information, and healthcare information)
- Validating that the sender of a message is who they claim to be
- Generating random numbers (as part of the cryptographic process)

The following diagram shows the process of converting plaintext into ciphertext and vice versa using symmetric encryption:

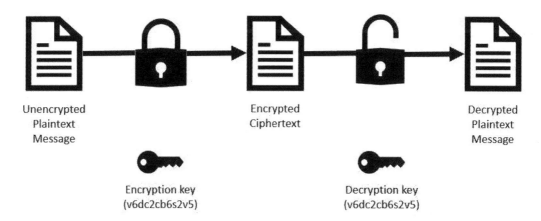

Figure 7.1 – Symmetric encryption

The following are the pros of symmetric encryption:

- Small ciphertext size
- Suitable for transferring large amounts of data
- Low CPU resources
- Small encryption key size
- Fast encryption time (compared to asymmetric encryption)

The following are the cons of symmetric encryption:

- Considered less secure than asymmetric encryption since both parties are using the same encryption key
- Considered less confidential than asymmetric encryption since both parties are using the same encryption key

Advanced Encryption Standard (AES)

AES is considered the de facto standard that's used today in both on-premises and the public cloud for encryption at rest. It was developed by NIST in 2001 and comes in variable key sizes – the most commonly used key size is 256-bit.

For more information, please refer to the following resources:

Symmetric-key algorithm:

`https://en.wikipedia.org/wiki/Symmetric-key_algorithm`

Advanced Encryption Standard:

`https://en.wikipedia.org/wiki/Advanced_Encryption_Standard`

Asymmetric encryption

Asymmetric encryption is a way to transfer data between two parties. However, unlike symmetric encryption, in asymmetric encryption (also known as **public-key cryptography** or **public-key encryption**), we use two different keys (private and public) that are linked together mathematically.

In asymmetric encryption, the public key can be shared with anyone and is used to encrypt a message. The private key must be safely guarded and is used for two purposes – decrypting the message and signing the message to ensure message integrity (the message was not tampered with in the process).

Asymmetric encryption is commonly used for the following purposes:

- Creating digital signatures
- Distributing sessions keys for use cases such as the TLS protocol

The following diagram shows the process of converting plaintext into ciphertext and vice versa using asymmetric encryption:

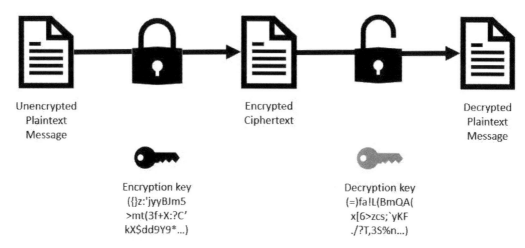

Figure 7.2 – Asymmetric encryption (public-key encryption)

The following are the pros of asymmetric encryption:

- Large ciphertext size (compared to symmetric encryption)

- Large encryption key size (for example, RSA 2,048-bit or higher)

- Considered much safer than symmetric encryption since there are two keys involved in the process and you cannot reveal the private key from the public key

- Considered more confidential than symmetric encryption since there are two keys and the private key (as implied, this must be kept private) is required to decrypt the message

The following are the cons of symmetric encryption:

- Suitable for transferring small amounts of data

- High CPU resources

- Slow encryption time (compared to symmetric encryption)

Rivest Shamir Adleman (RSA)

RSA is one of the most used protocols for encryption at transit, key establishment, and digital signatures. RSA security relies on factoring two large prime numbers (also known as the **factoring problem**). The recommended key size begins at 2,048-bit or higher.

Elliptical Curve Cryptography (ECC)

ECC is mostly used for key agreements, digital signatures, and pseudo-random generators.

It has a small key size (compared to the RSA algorithm) and is based on the algebraic structure of elliptic curves over finite fields.

The recommended key sizes for ECC are 256-bit (for NSA secret message classifications) and 384-bit (for NSA top-secret message classifications).

For more information, please refer to the following resources:

Public-key cryptography:

https://en.wikipedia.org/wiki/Public-key_cryptography

RSA (cryptosystem):

https://en.wikipedia.org/wiki/RSA_(cryptosystem)

Elliptic-curve cryptography:

https://en.wikipedia.org/wiki/Elliptic-curve_cryptography

Summary

In this section, we reviewed the fundamental concepts regarding encryption, what the differences are between symmetric and asymmetric encryption, and when to use each type of encryption (including common encryption algorithms).

Best practices for deploying KMSes

All major public cloud providers have implementations of a managed KMS – a secured location (or a vault) for generating, storing, and retrieving encryption keys.

The following are some important concepts in the key management field:

- **Key Encryption Key (KEK)**: This is used for generating other encryption keys. The KEK is stored inside the KMS and never leaves it since it wraps (encrypts) other keys in the hierarchy below it.

- **Data Encryption Key (DEK)**: This is used for encrypting the data itself. The DEK is stored near the data itself. KMSes keep a history of DEKs and keep this information in metadata near the data itself, which allows the encrypted service to know which DEK version to use.

- **Master Encryption Key (MEK)**: This is used for encrypting and decrypting the DEK in transit.

- **Key Generation**: The idea of regenerating new encryption keys to avoid the potential of the key being revealed by an external third party due to a static encryption key (a key that has not been replaced in a very long time) being used for a long time.

AWS Key Management Service (KMS)

AWS KMS is Amazon's key management service.

It allows you to generate and store cryptographic keys in a FIPS 140-2 standard.

AWS KMS generates AES256 symmetric encryption keys for encryption at rest, as well as RSA 2,048-bit (up to 4,096-bit) and ECC 256-bit (up to 512-bit), for encryption, digital signing, and signature verification.

The following are examples of common services that use AWS KMS:

- **Amazon S3 (object storage)**: Protects against unauthorized access to object storage

- **Amazon EBS (block storage)**: Protects against unauthorized access to block storage or snapshots

- **Amazon RDS (managed relational database)**: Protects against unauthorized access to managed databases (usually from within the operating system)

The following are some best practices regarding AWS KMS:

- Use IAM policies to grant access to a specific encryption key using an API (such as the ability to tag a resource, but not to read an encryption key).

- For better control over your encryption keys, specify the key's ARN inside the IAM policy.

- Use the AWS IAM Access Analyzer API to detect external entities with access to AWS KMS keys.

- Use Amazon S3 bucket keys to create unique data keys for objects inside an S3 bucket, which lower the number of requests between S3 and AWS KMS (offers better performance for encrypting/decrypting objects, caching encryption closer to data, and lowering the cost per total number of requests to AWS KMS).

- To secure access from your VPC to AWS KMS, use AWS PrivateLink, which avoids sending network traffic outside your VPC, through a secure channel, using an interface VPC endpoint.

- Use AWS CloudTrail to log all API calls that are made through AWS KMS.

- Use Amazon CloudWatch events to log events concerning CMK key imports, rotation, or deletion.

- Use Amazon CloudWatch alarms to send you notifications about CMK keys that are about to be deleted.

- Enforce the use of MFA for any user with access to AWS KMS (using the AWS console or using APIs).

- For services that support encryption at rest, use AWS managed keys, stored inside AWS KMS, to protect data at rest.

- For highly sensitive environments that support encryption at rest, use **Customer Master Keys** (**CMKs**) to protect data at rest while controlling the encryption keys.

- For highly sensitive environments, encrypt log data inside Amazon CloudWatch using an AWS KMS customer-managed key and grant CloudWatch service access to the encryption key.

- If you're using AWS CMKs, and if you have encryption keys that you are not using, disable them through either the AWS KMS console or through an API call.

- Make sure that KMS key rotation is enabled for all your CMKs.

- If you are using your own CMK, regularly rotate your keys. Keys that we leave unchanged increase the risk of key compromise by an unauthorized entity.

- As a best practice, rotate all encryption keys every 365 days (a balance between security and administrative overhead).

- Use tagging (also known as **labeling**) to have a better understanding of which CMK belongs to which AWS resource.

- Use symmetric encryption with AWS KMS to encrypt data at rest (such as objects inside Amazon S3). Use asymmetric encryption with AWS KMS to sign files and validate that they have not been changed.

- Use AWS Config to monitor for AWS KMS configuration changes.

- Before permanently closing an AWS account that contains sensitive data, delete the CMKs to avoid revealing your data to an unwanted third party.

- If you need to prove that you created the CMKs and not AWS, KMS lets you generate encryption keys on-premises and import them into the AWS KMS service (also known as "bring your own key"). The drawback of this is that AWS cannot rotate your imported keys.

For more information, please refer to the following resources:

Customer master keys (CMKs):

```
https://docs.aws.amazon.com/kms/latest/developerguide/
concepts.html#master_keys
```

Logging AWS KMS API calls with AWS CloudTrail:

```
https://docs.aws.amazon.com/kms/latest/developerguide/logging-
using-cloudtrail.html
```

Monitoring with Amazon CloudWatch:

```
https://docs.aws.amazon.com/kms/latest/developerguide/
monitoring-cloudwatch.html
```

Creating an Amazon CloudWatch alarm to detect usage of a customer master key that is pending deletion:

```
https://docs.aws.amazon.com/kms/latest/developerguide/
deleting-keys-creating-cloudwatch-alarm.html
```

Enabling and disabling keys:

```
https://docs.aws.amazon.com/kms/latest/developerguide/
enabling-keys.html
```

Using IAM policies with AWS KMS:

```
https://docs.aws.amazon.com/kms/latest/developerguide/
iam-policies.html
```

Connecting to AWS KMS through a VPC endpoint:

```
https://docs.aws.amazon.com/kms/latest/developerguide/kms-vpc-
endpoint.html
```

Multi-Factor Authentication:

```
https://docs.aws.amazon.com/whitepapers/latest/kms-best-
practices/multi-factor-authentication.html
```

AWS-managed and Customer-managed CMKs:

```
https://docs.aws.amazon.com/whitepapers/latest/kms-best-
practices/aws-managed-and-customer-managed-cmks.html
```

AWS Key Management Service Best Practices:

```
https://docs.aws.amazon.com/whitepapers/latest/kms-best-
practices/introduction.html
```

How to use AWS Config to determine compliance of AWS KMS key policies to your specifications:

```
https://aws.amazon.com/blogs/security/how-to-use-aws-config-
to-determine-compliance-of-aws-kms-key-policies-to-your-
specifications/
```

Reducing the cost of SSE-KMS with Amazon S3 Bucket Keys:

```
https://docs.aws.amazon.com/AmazonS3/latest/userguide/bucket-
key.html
```

How to use an AWS IAM Access Analyzer API to automate the detection of public access to AWS KMS keys:

```
https://aws.amazon.com/blogs/security/how-to-use-aws-iam-
access-analyzer-api-to-automate-detection-of-public-access-to-
aws-kms-keys/
```

Rotating AWS KMS keys:

```
https://docs.aws.amazon.com/kms/latest/developerguide/rotate-
keys.html
```

Importing key material in AWS KMS keys:

```
https://docs.aws.amazon.com/kms/latest/developerguide/
importing-keys.html
```

Encrypt log data in CloudWatch Logs using AWS Key Management Service:

```
https://docs.aws.amazon.com/AmazonCloudWatch/latest/logs/
encrypt-log-data-kms.html
```

AWS CloudHSM

AWS CloudHSM is the Amazon-managed cloud-based **Hardware Security Module (HSM)**. It is a FIPS 140-2 Level 3 validated HSM. It is meant to comply with regulated environments such as banks or government agencies. It is a single-tenant key for storage and acts as dedicated hardware for a single customer. The HSM device is tamper-resistant and tamper-proof, which means that any attempt to breach the physical device will cause all the keys to be erased. The **Federal Information Processing Standard (FIPS)** is a US government standard for cryptographic modules (both hardware and software).

AWS CloudHSM generates AES256 symmetric encryption keys for encryption at rest, as well as RSA 2,048-bit (up to 4,096-bit) and ECC 256-bit (up to 512-bit) for encryption, digital signing, and signature verification.

Since it is a hardware-based module, it contains TLS/SSL acceleration and Oracle **Transparent Database Encryption (TDE)** acceleration.

The following are some best practices regarding AWS CloudHSM:

- Use AWS CloudHSM to offload TLS processing from highly intensive web servers.
- Use AWS CloudHSM to store your organizational PKI **Certificate Authority (CA)** private key.
- Always deploy a cluster of AWS CloudHSM modules for high availability, in a different availability zone.
- To overcome the CloudHSM capacity to create new keys, add another CloudHSM module.
- Create an IAM group, add users to that IAM group, and grant the required permissions on AWS CloudHSM to the target IAM group.
- Enforce the use of MFA for any user with access to the AWS CloudHSM console.
- Use **CloudHSM Management Utility (CMU)** to generate local users that perform actions directly on the CloudHSM appliance (mostly for appliance maintenance).
- Enforce the use of MFA for local users with the **Crypto Officer (CO)** role.
- Use IAM policies to grant access to an encryption key.
- For better control over your encryption keys, specify the key ARN inside the IAM policy.
- Create a private subnet inside your VPC and deploy the AWS CloudHSM cluster nodes inside this private subnet.

- To secure access from your VPC to AWS CloudHSM, use AWS PrivateLink, which avoids sending network traffic outside your VPC, through a secure channel, using an interface VPC endpoint.

- Use a dedicated EC2 instance to connect to and manage AWS CloudHSM.

- Use security groups to control access between the EC2 instance and AWS CloudHSM.

- Generate an SSL certificate to connect to and manage AWS CloudHSM.

- Use tagging (also known as labeling) to have a better understanding of which CMK belongs to which AWS resource.

- Use symmetric encryption with AWS CloudHSM to encrypt data at rest (such as objects inside Amazon S3).

- Use asymmetric encryption with AWS CloudHSM to sign files and validate they have not been changed.

- Use AWS CloudTrail to log all API calls that have been made through AWS CloudHSM.

- Use Amazon CloudWatch Logs to monitor the events of AWS CloudHSM, such as creating/deleting/changing a password for local CloudHSM users or creating/deleting keys.

For more information, please refer to the following resources:

Create IAM Administrative Groups:

```
https://docs.aws.amazon.com/cloudhsm/latest/userguide/create-
iam-user.html
```

Identity and Access Management for AWS CloudHSM:

```
https://docs.aws.amazon.com/cloudhsm/latest/userguide/
identity-access-management.html
```

AWS CloudHSM and VPC endpoints:

```
https://docs.aws.amazon.com/cloudhsm/latest/userguide/
cloudhsm-vpc-endpoint.html
```

Create a Private Subnet:

```
https://docs.aws.amazon.com/cloudhsm/latest/userguide/create-
subnets.html
```

Reconfigure SSL with a New Certificate and Private Key:

https://docs.aws.amazon.com/cloudhsm/latest/userguide/getting-started-ssl.html

Best Practices for AWS CloudHSM:

https://docs.aws.amazon.com/cloudhsm/latest/userguide/best-practices.html

Managing Two-Factor Authentication (2FA) for Crypto Officers:

https://docs.aws.amazon.com/cloudhsm/latest/userguide/manage-2fa.html

Working With AWS CloudTrail and AWS CloudHSM:

https://docs.aws.amazon.com/cloudhsm/latest/userguide/get-api-logs-using-cloudtrail.html

Working With Amazon CloudWatch Logs and AWS CloudHSM:

https://docs.aws.amazon.com/cloudhsm/latest/userguide/get-hsm-audit-logs-using-cloudwatch.html

CloudHSM best practices to maximize performance and avoid common configuration pitfalls:

https://aws.amazon.com/blogs/security/cloudhsm-best-practices-to-maximize-performance-and-avoid-common-configuration-pitfalls/

AWS CloudHSM Clusters:

https://docs.aws.amazon.com/cloudhsm/latest/userguide/clusters.html

Improve Your Web Server's Security with SSL/TLS Offload in AWS CloudHSM:

https://docs.aws.amazon.com/cloudhsm/latest/userguide/ssl-offload.html

AWS CloudHSM FAQs:

https://aws.amazon.com/cloudhsm/faqs/

Azure Key Vault

Azure Key Vault is the Azure key management, secrets management, and certificate management service. It allows you to generate and store cryptographic keys in a FIPS 140-2 Level 2 standard.

Azure Key Vault generates RSA 2,048-bit (up to 4,096-bit) and ECC 256-bit (up to 512-bit) for encryption, digital signing, and signature verification.

The following are examples of common services that use Azure Key Vault:

- **Azure Blob storage** (**object storage**): Protects against unauthorized access to object storage
- **Azure Managed Disks** (**block storage**): Protects against unauthorized access to block storage or snapshots
- **Azure SQL** (**managed SQL database**): Protects against unauthorized access to managed databases (usually from within the operating system)

The following are some best practices regarding Azure Key Vault:

- Use Azure Key Vault to store Azure storage account keys.
- Use Azure Key Vault to store x509 certificates, such as your organizational PKI CA private key.
- Use Azure Key Vault to store passwords, instead of storing them in cleartext in code or scripts (such as PowerShell scripts).
- Use Azure Key Vault to store client application secrets, instead of storing them in cleartext in your code (such as Java or DotNet code).
- Use Azure Key Vault to store SSH keys for accessing VMs using SSH, without storing the SSH keys locally on a desktop.
- Use Azure Key Vault to store connection strings to databases (instead of storing cleartext credentials inside code or scripts).
- Use Azure Key Vault to store access keys for various Azure services (from the Redis Cache service, Azure Cosmos DB, Azure Event Hubs, and more).
- Use Azure **Role-Based Access Control** (**RBAC**) to configure minimal access to Azure Key Vault.
- Enforce the use of MFA for users with access to the Azure Key Vault console or through an API.

- Use Azure AD **Privileged Identity Management** (**PIM**) to control access to Azure Key Vault. For the highest level of access control to Azure Key Vault, create a different AD group for each Azure Key Vault (for example, split them between Prod and Dev) and use Azure PIM to control **Just-in-Time** (**JIT**) access to each Key Vault by different members of your organization, according to their job requirements (owner for creating new keys, reader for accessing keys, and so on).

- Use virtual network service endpoints to control access from your VNet to Azure Key Vault.

- Use tagging (that is, labeling) to have a better understanding of which key vault belongs to which Azure resource.

- As a best practice, rotate all the encryption keys every 365 days (a balance between security and administrative overhead).

- Enable Azure Key Vault logging and send the logs to Azure Log Analytics Workspace.

- Forward the logs from Azure Log Analytics Workspace to Azure Sentinel for further analysis.

- Use Key Vault insights (within Azure Monitor) to gather information about performance, failure, and latency issues.

- Enable Azure Defender for Key Vault for advanced threat protection for Azure Key Vault.

- Use Azure Security Center to monitor for compliance issues related to Azure Key Vault.

- Enable soft delete and purge protection to avoid accidental key deletion.

For more information, please refer to the following resources:

Best practices to use Key Vault:

```
https://docs.microsoft.com/en-us/azure/key-vault/general/best-
practices
```

Virtual network service endpoints for Azure Key Vault:

```
https://docs.microsoft.com/en-us/azure/key-vault/general/
overview-vnet-service-endpoints
```

Enable Key Vault logging:

```
https://docs.microsoft.com/en-us/azure/key-vault/general/
howto-logging?tabs=azure-cli
```

Monitoring and alerting for Azure Key Vault:

`https://docs.microsoft.com/en-us/azure/key-vault/general/alert`

Monitoring your key vault service with Key Vault insights:

`https://docs.microsoft.com/en-us/azure/azure-monitor/insights/`
`key-vault-insights-overview`

Introduction to Azure Defender for Key Vault:

`https://docs.microsoft.com/en-us/azure/security-center/`
`defender-for-key-vault-introduction`

Azure security baseline for Key Vault:

`https://docs.microsoft.com/en-us/security/benchmark/azure/`
`baselines/key-vault-security-baseline`

Key types, algorithms, and operations:

`https://docs.microsoft.com/en-us/azure/key-vault/keys/about-`
`keys-details`

Manage storage account keys with Key Vault and the Azure CLI:

`https://docs.microsoft.com/en-us/azure/key-vault/secrets/`
`overview-storage-keys`

About Azure Key Vault certificates:

`https://docs.microsoft.com/en-us/azure/key-vault/certificates/`
`about-certificates`

Azure Key Vault recovery management with soft delete and purge protection:

`https://docs.microsoft.com/en-us/azure/key-vault/general/`
`key-vault-recovery`

Authentication in Azure Key Vault:

`https://docs.microsoft.com/en-us/azure/key-vault/general/`
`authentication`

Azure Key Vault security:

`https://docs.microsoft.com/en-us/azure/key-vault/general/`
`security-features`

Azure Dedicated/Managed HSM

Azure Managed HSM and Azure Dedicated HSM are the Azure managed cloud-based **Hardware Security Modules (HSMs)**. They are FIPS 140-2 Level 3 validated HSMs. They are meant to comply with regulated environments such as banks or government agencies.

An HSM device is tamper-resistant and tamper-proof, which means that any attempt to breach the physical device will cause all the keys to be erased.

Federal Information Processing Standards (FIPS) is a US government standard for cryptographic modules (both hardware and software).

Azure Dedicated HSM generates AES256 symmetric encryption keys for encryption at rest, as well as RSA 2,048-bit (up to 4,096-bit) and ECC 256-bit (up to 512-bit) for encryption, digital signing, and signature verification.

The following are some best practices regarding Azure Dedicated/Managed HSM:

- Use Azure Managed HSM to store Azure storage account keys.
- Use Azure Managed HSM to store x509 certificates, such as your organizational PKI CA private key.
- Use Azure RBAC to configure minimal access to Azure Managed HSM.
- Enforce the use of MFA for users with access to the Azure Managed HSM console or through an API.
- Regularly back up your Azure Managed HSM.
- Use virtual network service endpoints to control access from your VNet to Azure Managed HSM.
- Use tagging (that is, labeling) to have a better understanding of which key vault belongs to which Azure resource.
- Enable Azure Managed HSM logging and send the logs to Azure Log Analytics Workspace.
- Forward the logs from Azure Log Analytics Workspace to Azure Sentinel for further analysis.
- Import the encryption keys from your on-premises HSM to Azure Managed HSM (also known as **bring your own keys**).
- Import your on-premises HSM Security Domain into Azure Managed HSM so that you can share an existing security domain.
- Enable soft-delete and purge protection to avoid accidental key deletion.

For more information, please refer to the following resources:

Azure Dedicated HSM documentation:

```
https://docs.microsoft.com/en-us/azure/dedicated-hsm/
```

What is Azure Key Vault Managed HSM?:

```
https://docs.microsoft.com/en-us/azure/key-vault/managed-hsm/
overview
```

Frequently asked questions (FAQs):

```
https://docs.microsoft.com/en-us/azure/dedicated-hsm/faq
```

Managed HSM local RBAC built-in roles:

```
https://docs.microsoft.com/en-us/azure/key-vault/managed-hsm/
built-in-roles
```

General availability: Azure Managed HSM Private Link:

```
https://azure.microsoft.com/en-us/updates/azure-managed-hsm-
private-link-ga-announcement/
```

Managed HSM logging:

```
https://docs.microsoft.com/en-us/azure/key-vault/managed-hsm/
logging
```

Integrate Managed HSM with Azure Private Link:

```
https://docs.microsoft.com/en-us/azure/key-vault/managed-hsm/
private-link
```

Key types, algorithms, and operations:

```
https://docs.microsoft.com/en-us/azure/key-vault/keys/about-
keys-details
```

Import HSM-protected keys to Managed HSM (BYOK):

```
https://docs.microsoft.com/en-us/azure/key-vault/managed-hsm/
hsm-protected-keys-byok
```

Managed HSM soft delete and purge protection:

```
https://docs.microsoft.com/en-us/azure/key-vault/managed-hsm/
recovery
```

About the Managed HSM Security Domain:

```
https://docs.microsoft.com/en-us/azure/key-vault/managed-hsm/
security-domain
```

Google Cloud Key Management Service (KMS)

Google Cloud KMS is GCP's key management service. It allows you to generate and store cryptographic keys in a FIPS 140-2 Level standard as a software-based solution or a FIPS 140-2 Level 3 standard as a hardware-based HSM.

FIPS is a US government standard for cryptographic modules (both hardware and software).

The HSM device is tamper-resistant and tamper-proof, which means that any attempt to breach the physical device will cause all the keys to be erased.

Use Google Cloud HSM to comply with regulated environments such as banks or government agencies – if required, Google also supports **Hosted Private HSMs**.

Google Cloud KMS generates AES256 symmetric encryption keys for encryption at rest, as well as RSA 2,048-bit (up to 4,096-bit) and ECC 256-bit (up to 384-bit) for encryption, digital signing, and signature verification.

The following are some examples of common services that use Google Cloud KMS:

- **Google Cloud Storage** (**object storage**): Protects against unauthorized access to object storage

- **Google Persistent Disk** (**block storage**): Protects against unauthorized access to block storage or snapshots

- **Google Cloud SQL** (**managed relational database**): Protects against unauthorized access to managed databases (usually from within the operating system)

The following are some best practices regarding Google Cloud KMS:

- Use Google Cloud IAM to manage permissions to Google Cloud KMS.

- Ensure your Cloud IAM policy does not allow anonymous or public access to your Cloud KMS keys.

- Use tagging (also known as **labeling**) to have a better understanding of which Cloud KMS keys belong to which GCP resource.

- As a best practice, rotate all your encryption keys every 365 days (a balance between security and administrative overhead).

- Enable Cloud KMS audit logs to monitor Cloud KMS activity.

- Admin activity audit logs are enabled by default and cannot be disabled.

- Explicitly enable **Data access audit** logs to log activities that are performed on Google Cloud KMS.

- Limit the access to audit logs to a minimum number of employees, to avoid possible deletion or changes being made to the audit logs.

- Enable automatic key rotation to avoid possible key compromise.

- If you are not using previous versions of your encryption keys, manually disable them.

- For highly sensitive environments, where you have an HSM on-premises, use **Cloud External Key Manager** (**Cloud EKM**) to store your encryption keys outside Google data centers.

- For large-scale environments with multiple GCP projects, use VPC Service Controls to enforce access restrictions over your Cloud KMS, based on the identity of your IP address.

For more information, please refer to the following resources:

Cloud Key Management Service QuickStart:

```
https://cloud.google.com/kms/docs/quickstart
```

Cloud Key Management Service deep dive:

```
https://cloud.google.com/security/key-management-deep-dive
```

Using IAM with Cloud KMS:

```
https://cloud.google.com/kms/docs/iam
```

Permissions and roles:

```
https://cloud.google.com/kms/docs/reference/permissions-and-roles
```

Cloud KMS audit logging information:

```
https://cloud.google.com/kms/docs/audit-logging
```

Hosted Private HSM:

```
https://cloud.google.com/kms/docs/hosted-private-hsm
```

Cloud External Key Manager:

https://cloud.google.com/kms/docs/ekm

Rotating keys:

https://cloud.google.com/kms/docs/rotating-keys

Enabling and disabling key versions:

https://cloud.google.com/kms/docs/enable-disable

Customer-managed encryption keys (CMEK):

https://cloud.google.com/kms/docs/cmek

VPC Service Controls supported products and limitations:

https://cloud.google.com/vpc-service-controls/docs/supported-products#table_kms

Summary

In this section, we learned how to secure KMSes based on AWS, Azure, and GCP infrastructure (both software-based and hardware-based KMSes) – from authorization and network access control to auditing and monitoring.

Best practices for deploying secrets management services

All major cloud providers have a secrets management service.

The term **secrets** refers to database credentials, API keys, tokens, usernames/passwords, and more. The fundamental concept behind secrets management services is to allow you to store such sensitive information in a secured location, with authorization and audit mechanisms, while allowing users and service accounts to securely retrieve secrets, without having to store the information in cleartext in configuration files.

Since the cloud environment is highly dynamic, it is recommended to have a central and secure repository for storing, generating, and retrieving secrets.

DevOps teams can benefit from secrets management services by redirecting their code to the secrets management services, instead of embedding sensitive information (secrets, credentials, access keys, and more) inside cleartext code.

AWS Secrets Manager

AWS Secrets Manager is Amazon's managed secrets service.

The following are some of the services that support the use of secrets inside AWS services:

- Secrets inside AWS Lambda functions
- Passwords for connecting to Amazon RDS (Aurora, MySQL, PostgreSQL, Oracle, MariaDB, and Microsoft SQL Server)
- Secrets inside Amazon DocumentDB
- Secrets inside Amazon RedShift

AWS Secrets Manager allows you to create, store, rotate, label, and manage the versioning of your secrets. Secrets managed by **AWS Secrets Manager** are encrypted and stored inside AWS KMS.

The following are some best practices regarding AWS Secrets Manager:

- Create an IAM group, add service accounts (or applicative accounts) to the IAM group, and grant the required permissions on AWS Secrets Manager to the target IAM group.
- Use IAM policies to control minimal access to secrets for your users and applications.
- To centrally store secrets from multiple AWS regions, enable Replica Secret and update a Replica Secret encryption key.
- Use tagging (that is, labeling) to have a better understanding of which secret belongs to which AWS resource.
- Make sure **secret rotation** is enabled.
- Store all sensitive information (such as passwords hints) inside secret values that can be retrieved from AWS Secrets Manager.
- Use client-side caching to improve performance when storing secrets inside the AWS Secrets Manager service.
- Avoid storing sensitive information (such as secrets) inside your log files.
- Run all your AWS resources that need access to AWS Secrets Manager inside your VPC.

- For services that operate outside your VPC, use AWS CodeBuild to access secrets from the AWS Secrets Manager service.

- To secure access from your VPC to AWS Secrets Manager, use AWS PrivateLink, which avoids sending network traffic outside your VPC, through a secure channel, using interface VPC endpoints.

- Use AWS CloudTrail to monitor all API activities that are performed through AWS Secrets Manager.

- Use Amazon CloudWatch Logs to monitor for secrets pending deletion or secret rotation.

- Use AWS Config to monitor for changes in your secrets.

- For services that support the use of AWS Secrets Manager, encrypt secrets using an AWS Secrets Manager encryption key inside AWS KMS.

- For highly sensitive environments, encrypt secrets using your CMK inside AWS KMS.

For more information, please refer to the following resources:

Overview of managing access permissions to your Secrets Manager secrets:

https://docs.aws.amazon.com/secretsmanager/latest/userguide/
auth-and-access_overview.html

AWS Secrets Manager best practices:

https://docs.aws.amazon.com/secretsmanager/latest/userguide/
best-practices.html

Using Secrets Manager with VPC endpoints:

https://docs.aws.amazon.com/secretsmanager/latest/userguide/
vpc-endpoint-overview.html

How AWS Secrets Manager uses AWS KMS:

https://docs.aws.amazon.com/kms/latest/developerguide/
services-secrets-manager.html

Monitoring the use of your AWS Secrets Manager secrets:

```
https://docs.aws.amazon.com/secretsmanager/latest/userguide/
monitoring.html
```

Google Secret Manager

Google Secret Manager is the GCP-managed secrets service for managing API keys, passwords, certificates, and more.

This service supports the following types of secrets inside GCP services:

- Environment variables inside Google Cloud Build

- Secrets inside Google Cloud Code

- Secrets inside Google Cloud Functions

- Environment variables inside Google Cloud Run

- Secrets inside Google Compute Engine

- Secrets inside Google Kubernetes Engine

- Secrets inside Google Config Connector

Google Secret Manager allows you to create, store, rotate, label, and manage the versioning of your secrets.

Secrets managed by Google Secret Manager are encrypted and stored inside Google Cloud KMS.

The following are some best practices regarding Google Secret Manager:

- Use Google IAM and IAM roles to configure minimal access to secrets for both IAM users and your applications.

- Use IAM Recommender to identify over-privileged identities.

- Use IAM conditions to limit access to secrets.

- If you have any secrets and you are not using them anymore, disable old secret versions before they are deleted to avoid the possibility that you might need an old version if it is destroyed, and the data becomes inaccessible.

- Enable Cloud Secret Manager audit logs to monitor Cloud Secret Manager activity.

- Admin activity audit logs are enabled by default and cannot be disabled.

- Explicitly enable **data access audit logs** to log activities that are performed on Google Cloud Secret Manager.

- Limit access to audit logs to a minimum number of employees to avoid possible deletion or changes being made to the audit logs.

- Enable automatic key rotation to avoid possible key compromise.

- For highly sensitive environments, encrypt your secrets using **Customer-Managed Encryption Keys** (**CMEKs**).

- For large-scale environments with multiple GCP projects, use **VPC Service Controls** to enforce access restrictions over Cloud Secret Manager based on identity (service account or user) or IP addresses.

For more information, please refer to the following resources:

Access control (IAM):

`https://cloud.google.com/secret-manager/docs/access-control`

Enforce least privilege with role recommendations:

`https://cloud.google.com/iam/docs/recommender-overview`

Overview of VPC Service Controls:

`https://cloud.google.com/vpc-service-controls/docs/overview`

Secret Manager Audit Logging:

`https://cloud.google.com/secret-manager/docs/audit-logging`

Rotation of secrets:

`https://cloud.google.com/secret-manager/docs/rotation-recommendations`

Enabling Customer-Managed Encryption Keys (CMEKs) for Secret Manager:

`https://cloud.google.com/secret-manager/docs/cmek`

Secret Manager Best Practices:

`https://cloud.google.com/secret-manager/docs/best-practices`

Summary

In this section, we learned how to manage secrets using managed services in both AWS and GCP, from authorization to key rotation, encryption, auditing, and monitoring.

Best practices for using encryption in transit

The idea behind *encryption in transit* is to allow two parties to share messages over a publicly exposed network, in a secure way, while retaining message confidentiality and integrity.

IPSec

IPSec is the most commonly used protocol for encryption at transit, mainly for site-to-site VPN and VPN tunnels. IPSec resides on layer 3 of the OSI model.

The following are some best practices regarding IPSec:

- Use the IKEv2 protocol for security association (SA).
- Use AES-GCM for encryption.
- Use HMAC-SHA256 (or higher) for integrity.
- When supported by both the client and the server, use certificate-based authentication instead of a pre-shared key.
- Use an up-to-date VPN client (to avoid known vulnerabilities).

For more information, please refer to the following resources:

Internet Protocol Security (IPSec):

```
https://en.wikipedia.org/wiki/IPsec
```

Guide to IPSec VPNs:

```
https://csrc.nist.gov/publications/detail/sp/800-77/rev-1/
final
```

Transport Layer Security (TLS)

TLS is one of the most used protocols for encryption at transit.

It replaced the old **Secure Sockets Layer** (**SSL**) protocols, which had security flaws, and is now considered the de facto standard for encryption over the public internet.

TLS combines asymmetric encryption for session negotiation between a client and a server (symmetric key generation and copying between the client and the server) with symmetric encryption for securely transferring messages.

Even though TLS relies on TCP (the transport layer of the OSI model), it is considered application layer encryption (the HTTPS of the HTTP protocol) or layer 7 of the OSI model.

Common use cases include web browsers (client) and web servers (server) such as eCommerce sites. In the context of cloud services, almost all cloud service providers' APIs use TLS for encryption in transit.

The following are some best practices regarding TLS:

- Websites, APIs, or applications that reside in a private subnet or serve internal organization employees use certificates signed by a trusted internal CA.

> **Note**
>
> As a best practice, avoid using self-signed certificates since they cannot be verified or trusted.

- For any publicly facing websites, APIs, or applications, use a certificate signed by a well-known public CA.

- Make sure that the certificate is valid (the domain name matches the DNS name) and that the certificate hasn't expired or been revoked.

- Avoid using wildcard certificates – always make sure that the certificate name matches the server's FQDN.

- Avoid using certificates with short validity periods (such as **LetsEncrypt** certificates).

- When using Kubernetes, use mTLS to encrypt traffic between pods and authenticate both the server and client with each other.

- The minimum recommended TLS protocol version is 1.2, and when you have hardware/software to support it, it is recommended to migrate to TLS 1.3 and drop the support for previous versions of TLS and all versions of SSL protocols.

- Disable the use of weak protocols (any version of SSL and TLS that's lower than 1.2).

- Disable the use of weak cipher suites (such as 3DES/DES/RC2/IDEA).

- Use an RSA private key with a minimum size of 2,048-bit.

- Use the signature algorithm of SHA256.

- Enable the use of **Strict Transport Security (HSTS)**.

- Enable the use of **Perfect Forward Secrecy (PFS)**.

- Use `ssllabs.com` to test the score of your TLS protocol.

- If you wish to inspect encrypted traffic in cloud services, use SSL termination (for services that support this capability). SSL termination allows you to open encrypted traffic (for example, on your load balancer or frontend web server) by temporarily decrypting the traffic, inspecting it using devices or software that support traffic inspection (such as IPS, WAF, data leak prevention, and more), and finally encrypt the traffic again, before it reaches the next hop (for example, between the load balancer and the web servers).

For more information, please refer to the following resources:

Transport Layer Security:

https://en.wikipedia.org/wiki/Transport_Layer_Security

SSL and TLS Deployment Best Practices:

https://github.com/ssllabs/research/wiki/SSL-and-TLS-Deployment-Best-Practices

SSL Server Rating Guide:

https://github.com/ssllabs/research/wiki/SSL-Server-Rating-Guide

SSL Server Test:

https://www.ssllabs.com/ssltest

Anthos Service Mesh by example: mTLS:

https://cloud.google.com/service-mesh/docs/by-example/mtls

AWS Elastic Load Balancing: Support for SSL Termination:

https://aws.amazon.com/blogs/aws/elastic-load-balancer-support-for-ssl-termination/

Summary

In this section, we learned about the best practices for encrypting data in transit with the most common protocols – IPSec (for VPN tunnels) and TLS (for applications such as web servers and APIs) – for algorithm selection, as well as how to disable the use of weak and vulnerable ciphers.

Best practices for using encryption at rest

The idea behind *encryption at rest* is to protect data once it has been saved into storage or a database or has been accessed by an untrusted third party.

Object storage encryption

When you're encrypting object storage, each file (or object) is encrypted separately.

Encryption/decryption process

The following workflow explains the process of extracting an encrypted object from object storage:

- The DEK is stored near the object itself, and the object metadata specifies which encryption key version to use.

- The entire DEK is wrapped with a KEK.

- The KEK is stored inside a key-managed service.

- When a request for accessing an object is made, the authorized service (or application) sends a request to the key managed service to locate the KEK and to decrypt the specific DEK.

- The decrypted DEK is sent via a TLS/SSL channel from the KMS to the object storage. The object itself is decrypted using the decrypted DEK.

The following diagram shows the preceding workflow of extracting an encrypted object from object storage:

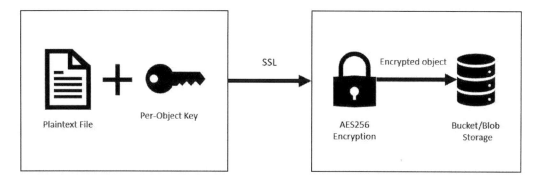

Figure 7.3 – Object storage encryption

In the following sections, we will review the different types of encryption keys that AWS, Azure, and GCP support for object storage.

AWS and object storage encryption

AWS S3 supports the following types of encryption keys:

- Server-side encryption with Amazon S3 Managed Keys (SSE-S3):

  - AES256-based encryption at rest.

  - The encryption keys are generated, rotated, and maintained by AWS.

  - Recommended for all S3 bucket encryption.

- Server-side encryption with CMKs stored in AWS KMS (SSE-KMS):

  - AES256-based encryption at rest.

  - The encryption keys are generated, rotated, and maintained by the customers and stored inside AWS KMS.

  - AWS KMS offers an additional layer of control by configuring access control to the encryption keys.

  - An additional audit trail is enabled using AWS CloudTrail for those who used the CMKs.

  - Recommended for highly sensitive environments that store sensitive data (such as PII, credit card information, healthcare data, and more) inside S3 buckets.

- Server-side encryption with customer-provided keys (SSE-C):

  - When you upload a file, Amazon S3 encrypts it using AES256.

  - Files are encrypted by the customer before the file is uploaded to S3.

  - Amazon does not have any access to the encryption key.

For more information, please refer to the following resource:

Protecting data using server-side encryption:

```
https://docs.aws.amazon.com/AmazonS3/latest/userguide/serv-
side-encryption.html
```

Azure and Blob Storage encryption

Azure Blob Storage supports the following types of encryption keys:

- Microsoft-managed keys:

  - AES256-based encryption at rest.

  - The encryption keys are generated, rotated, and maintained by Azure.

  - Encryption keys are stored inside the Microsoft key store.

  - Recommended for all blob storage encryption.

- Customer-managed keys:

  - AES256-based encryption at rest.

  - The encryption keys are generated, rotated, and maintained by the customers and stored inside Azure Key Vault or Azure Key Vault HSM.

  - Azure Key Vault offers an additional layer of control by configuring access control for the encryption keys.

  - Recommended for highly sensitive environments that store sensitive data (such as PII, credit card information, healthcare data, and more) inside Azure Blob Storage or Azure Files.

For more information, please refer to the following resources:

Azure Storage encryption for data at rest:

```
https://docs.microsoft.com/en-gb/azure/storage/common/storage-
service-encryption
```

Customer-managed keys for Azure Storage encryption:

```
https://docs.microsoft.com/en-us/azure/storage/common/
customer-managed-keys-overview
```

GCP and object storage encryption

Google Cloud Storage supports the following types of encryption keys:

- Google-managed encryption keys:

  - AES256-based encryption at rest.

- The encryption keys are generated, rotated, and maintained by GCP.
- Recommended for all object storage encryption.

- Customer-managed encryption keys:

  - AES256-based encryption at rest.
  - The encryption keys are generated, rotated, and maintained by the customers and stored inside Google Cloud KMS.
  - Google Cloud KMS offers an additional layer of control by configuring access control to the encryption keys.
  - Recommended for highly sensitive environments that store sensitive data (such as PII, credit card information, healthcare data, and more) inside Google Cloud Storage.

- Customer-supplied encryption keys:

  - AES256-based encryption at rest.
  - Files are encrypted by the customer before the files are uploaded to Google Cloud Storage.
  - GCP does not have any access to the encryption key.

For more information, please refer to the following resources:

Google-managed encryption keys:

```
https://cloud.google.com/storage/docs/encryption/default-keys
```

Customer-managed encryption keys:

```
https://cloud.google.com/storage/docs/encryption/customer-
managed-keys
```

Customer-supplied encryption keys:

```
https://cloud.google.com/storage/docs/encryption/customer-
supplied-keys
```

Block storage encryption

When using block storage encryption, a single DEK is used to encrypt the entire block storage (also known as a disk volume). When you're using snapshots, a single encryption key is used to encrypt the entire snapshot.

The DEK is wrapped by a KEK, which is stored inside a secure vault (KMS).

In the following sections, we will review how AWS, Azure, and GCP support different types of encryption keys for block storage.

AWS and block storage encryption

AWS block storage (EBS) supports the following types of encryption keys:

- AWS-managed CMKs:

  - AES256-based encryption at rest.

  - The encryption keys are generated, rotated, and maintained by AWS.

  - Recommended for all types of EBS volume encryption.

- Customer-managed CMKs:

  - AES256-based encryption at rest.

  - The encryption keys are generated, rotated, and maintained by the customers and stored inside AWS KMS.

  - AWS KMS offers an additional layer of control by configuring access control to the encryption keys.

  - Use AWS CloudTrail to check who used the CMKs.

  - Recommended for highly sensitive environments that store sensitive data (such as PII, credit card information, healthcare data, and more) inside EBS volumes.

For more information, please refer to the following resources:

How Amazon Elastic Block Store (Amazon EBS) uses AWS KMS:

https://docs.aws.amazon.com/kms/latest/developerguide/
services-ebs.html

Amazon EBS volume encryption:

https://docs.aws.amazon.com/kms/latest/cryptographic-details/
ebs-volume-encryption.html

Azure Managed Disks encryption

Azure Managed Disks supports the following types of encryption keys:

- Platform-managed keys:

  - AES256-based encryption at rest.

  - The encryption keys are generated, rotated, and maintained by Azure.

  - Recommended for all managed disks, snapshots, and images of VMs.

- Customer-managed keys:

  - AES256-based encryption at rest.

  - The encryption keys are generated, rotated, and maintained by the customers and stored inside Azure Key Vault or Azure Key Vault HSM.

  - Azure Key Vault offers an additional layer of control by configuring access control to the encryption keys.

  - Recommended for highly sensitive environments that store sensitive data (such as PII, credit card information, healthcare data, and more) inside managed disks, snapshots, and images of VMs.

For more information, please refer to the following resources:

Server-side encryption of Azure Disk Storage:

```
https://docs.microsoft.com/en-us/azure/virtual-machines/disk-
encryption#server-side-encryption-versus-azure-disk-encryption
```

Use the Azure portal to enable server-side encryption with customer-managed keys for managed disks:

```
https://docs.microsoft.com/en-us/azure/virtual-machines/disks-
enable-customer-managed-keys-portal
```

GCP Persistent Disks encryption

Google Persistent Disks supports the following types of encryption keys:

- Google-managed encryption keys:

  - AES256-based encryption at rest.

  - The encryption keys are generated, rotated, and maintained by GCP.

  - Recommended for all persistent disks.

- Customer-managed encryption keys:

  - AES256-based encryption at rest.

  - The encryption keys are generated, rotated, and maintained by the customers and stored inside Google Cloud KMS.

  - Google Cloud KMS offers an additional layer of control by configuring access control to the encryption keys.

  - Recommended for new persistent disks in highly sensitive environments that store sensitive data (such as PII, credit card information, healthcare data, and more) inside Google Persistent Disks.

- Customer-supplied encryption keys:

  - AES256-based encryption at rest.

  - Files are encrypted by the customer before the files are uploaded to Google Persistent Disk.

  - GCP does not have any access to the encryption key.

For more information, please refer to the following resources:

Helping to protect resources by using Cloud KMS keys:

```
https://cloud.google.com/compute/docs/disks/customer-managed-
encryption
```

Encrypt disks with customer-supplied encryption keys:

```
https://cloud.google.com/compute/docs/disks/customer-supplied-
encryption
```

Full database encryption

When using full database encryption (sometimes called **Transparent Data Encryption (TDE)**, a single DEK is used to encrypt the entire database, logs, backups, and snapshots.

The DEK is warped by the KEK, which is stored inside a secured vault (KMS).

In the following sections, we will review what types of encryption keys AWS, Azure, and GCP support for managed databases.

Amazon RDS encryption

Amazon RDS supports the following types of encryption keys:

- AWS-managed CMKs:

  - AES256-based encryption at rest.

  - The encryption keys are generated, rotated, and maintained by AWS.

  - Recommended for regular RDS database encryption.

- Customer-managed CMKs:

  - AES256-based encryption at rest.

  - The encryption keys are generated, rotated, and maintained by the customers and stored inside AWS KMS.

  - AWS KMS offers an additional layer of control by configuring access control to the encryption keys.

  - Use AWS CloudTrail to check who used the CMKs.

  - Recommended for highly sensitive environments that store sensitive data (such as PII, credit card information, healthcare data, and more) inside RDS databases.

For more information, please refer to the following resource:

Encrypting Amazon RDS resources:

```
https://docs.aws.amazon.com/AmazonRDS/latest/UserGuide/
Overview.Encryption.html
```

Azure SQL Transparent Data Encryption (TDE)

Azure SQL TDE supports the following types of encryption keys:

- Service-managed transparent data encryption:

  - AES256-based encryption at rest.

  - The encryption keys are generated, rotated, and maintained by Azure.

  - Recommended for all Azure SQL databases.

- Customer-managed transparent data encryption – Bring Your Own Key:

  - AES256-based encryption at rest.

  - The encryption keys are generated, rotated, and maintained by the customers and stored inside Azure Key Vault or Azure Key Vault HSM.

  - Azure Key Vault offers an additional layer of control by configuring access control to the encryption keys.

  - Recommended for highly sensitive environments that store sensitive data (such as PII, credit card information, healthcare data, and more) inside Azure SQL.

For more information, please refer to the following resources:

Transparent data encryption for SQL Database, SQL Managed Instance, and Azure Synapse Analytics:

```
https://docs.microsoft.com/en-us/azure/azure-sql/database/
transparent-data-encryption-tde-overview?tabs=azure-portal
```

Azure SQL Transparent Data Encryption with customer-managed keys:

```
https://docs.microsoft.com/en-us/azure/azure-sql/database/
transparent-data-encryption-byok-overview
```

Google Cloud SQL encryption

Google Cloud SQL supports the following types of encryption keys:

- Google-managed encryption keys:

  - AES256-based encryption at rest.

  - The encryption keys are generated, rotated, and maintained by GCP.

  - Recommended for all Google Cloud SQLs.

- Customer-managed encryption keys:

  - AES256-based encryption at rest.

  - The encryption keys are generated, rotated, and maintained by the customers and stored inside Google Cloud KMS.

  - Google Cloud KMS offers an additional layer of control by configuring access control to the encryption keys.

- Recommended for new persistent disks in highly sensitive environments that store sensitive data (such as PII, credit card information, healthcare data, and more) inside Google Cloud SQL.

For more information, please refer to the following resources:

Overview of customer-managed encryption keys (CMEK):

```
https://cloud.google.com/sql/docs/sqlserver/cmek
```

Using customer-managed encryption keys (CMEK):

```
https://cloud.google.com/sql/docs/sqlserver/configure-cmek
```

Row-level security

Row-level security is a relatively new concept that's meant to resolve access permissions to shared resources, such as databases serving multiple customers in a multi-tenant environment.

It allows you to encrypt data in a more granular way while granting access permissions to the encrypted content based on row, column, or field (depending on the service's capabilities).

For more information on AWS row-level security, please refer to the following resources:

Multi-tenant data isolation with PostgreSQL Row Level Security:

```
https://aws.amazon.com/blogs/database/multi-tenant-data-
isolation-with-postgresql-row-level-security/
```

Using Row-Level Security (RLS) to Restrict Access to a Dataset in Amazon QuickSight:

```
https://docs.aws.amazon.com/quicksight/latest/user/restrict-
access-to-a-data-set-using-row-level-security.html
```

Applying row-level and column-level security on Amazon QuickSight dashboards:

```
https://aws.amazon.com/blogs/big-data/applying-row-level-and-
column-level-security-on-amazon-quicksight-dashboards/
```

Achieve finer-grained data security with column-level access control in Amazon Redshift:

```
https://aws.amazon.com/blogs/big-data/achieve-finer-grained-
data-security-with-column-level-access-control-in-amazon-
redshift/
```

Using field-level encryption to help protect sensitive data in Amazon CloudFront:

```
https://docs.aws.amazon.com/AmazonCloudFront/latest/
DeveloperGuide/field-level-encryption.html
```

For more information on Azure row-level security, please refer to the following resources:

Azure SQL Row-Level Security:

```
https://docs.microsoft.com/en-us/sql/relational-databases/
security/row-level-security?view=azuresqldb-current
```

Azure Data Explorer Row Level Security:

```
https://docs.microsoft.com/en-us/azure/data-explorer/kusto/
management/rowlevelsecuritypolicy
```

For more information on Google row-level security, please refer to the following resources:

Introduction to BigQuery row-level security:

```
https://cloud.google.com/bigquery/docs/row-level-security-
intro
```

Working with row-level security:

```
https://cloud.google.com/bigquery/docs/managing-row-level-
security
```

Summary

In this section, we learned about the best practices for encrypting data at rest using the AWS, Azure, and GCP storage services (through object storage, block storage, full database storage, and row-level security).

Encryption in use

At this point, we understand the concept of protecting data using encryption in transit and encryption at rest. There is still one place we need to protect data – while the data is being used in the server's memory; that is, encryption in use.

AWS Nitro Enclaves

AWS offers its customers a unique architecture that creates an isolated environment for storing sensitive information (such as PII, credit card numbers, and healthcare data), which separates customers' data from the EC2 instance itself while using AWS KMS for data encryption.

For more information, please refer to the following resources:

AWS Nitro Enclaves:

```
https://aws.amazon.com/ec2/nitro/nitro-enclaves/
```

How AWS Nitro Enclaves uses AWS KMS:

```
https://docs.aws.amazon.com/kms/latest/developerguide/
services-nitro-enclaves.html
```

Azure Confidential Computing

Azure Confidential Computing uses hardware to isolate data. Data can be encrypted in use by running it in a **Trusted Execution Environment** (TEE).

Azure Confidential Computing is based on Intel SGX hardware, and it supports both Azure VMs and Azure Kubernetes Service to allow customers to securely store sensitive information (such as PII, credit card numbers, healthcare data, and more).

For more information, please refer to the following resources:

Azure confidential computing:

```
https://docs.microsoft.com/en-us/azure/confidential-computing/
```

Confidential computing nodes on Azure Kubernetes Service:

```
https://docs.microsoft.com/en-us/azure/confidential-computing/
confidential-nodes-aks-overview
```

Google Confidential Computing

Google Confidential Computing uses hardware to isolate data. Data can be encrypted in use by running it in a TEE.

Google Confidential Computing is based on AMD SEV hardware (2nd Gen AMD EPYC CPUs), and it supports both Google confidential VMs and Google confidential GKEs to allow customers to securely store sensitive information (such as PII, credit card numbers, and healthcare data).

For more information, please refer to the following resources:

Google Confidential VM and Compute Engine:

```
https://cloud.google.com/compute/confidential-vm/docs/about-
cvm
```

Using Confidential GKE Nodes:

```
https://cloud.google.com/kubernetes-engine/docs/how-to/
confidential-gke-nodes
```

Summary

In this section, we learned about the various alternatives that AWS, Azure, and GCP offer customers for protecting data in use (from AWS Nitro Enclaves to Azure and Google Confidential Computing).

Summary

In this chapter, we focused on the various encryption alternatives based on AWS, Azure, and GCP.

We began by introducing the concepts of encryption (symmetric and asymmetric algorithms). We continued by introducing the best practices for using KMSes (access control, auditing, and monitoring). Then, we started talking about secrets management services (access control, auditing, and monitoring).

Throughout this chapter, we had a long discussion about encryption in transit and encryption at rest, and we concluded with a short conversation about encryption in use. Following the shared responsibility model, customers can use their own encryption keys, which increases their ability to control the data that's stored in the cloud.

Knowing about the available options for encryption will allow you to choose the most suitable solution for each service you are using in the cloud.

In the next chapter, we will review common security threats to cloud computing (data breaches, misconfiguration, insufficient IAM, account hijacking, insider threats, insecure APIs, and the abuse of cloud services).

Section 3: Threats and Compliance Management

On completion of this part, you will have a solid understanding of the common threats in cloud environments and how to stay compliant with standards and regulations.

This part of the book comprises the following chapters:

- *Chapter 8, Understanding Common Security Threats to Cloud Computing*
- *Chapter 9, Handling Compliance Regulations*
- *Chapter 10, Engaging with Cloud Providers*

8
Understanding Common Security Threats to Cloud Services

In *Chapters 2-7*, we covered the fundamental building blocks of securing cloud services (including services for compute, storage, networking, **identity and access management (IAM)**, auditing, threat management, and incident response), as well as looking at encryption for cloud services.

This chapter will cover the other side of the equation: common security threats to cloud services. We will also consider how to mitigate these threats.

Knowing the threats your organization faces when using cloud services will give you an understanding of what to look for and how to better protect your cloud environments in advance. Getting hacked is more a question of *when* rather than *if*, so the knowledge presented in this chapter should help you to be prepared for such an eventuality.

In this chapter, we will cover the following topics:

- The MITRE ATT&CK framework
- Detecting and mitigating data breaches in cloud services
- Detecting and mitigating misconfigurations in cloud services
- Detecting and mitigating insufficient IAM in cloud services
- Detecting and mitigating account hijacking in cloud services
- Detecting and mitigating insider threats in cloud services
- Detecting and mitigating insecure APIs in cloud services
- Detecting and mitigating the abuse of cloud services

Technical requirements

For this chapter, the reader needs to have a solid understanding of information security concepts. These include (but are not limited to) *threats*, *mitigations*, *data breaches*, *misconfigurations*, *account hijacking*, and others.

The MITRE ATT&CK framework

The **MITRE ATT&CK** framework is a knowledge base of hacking techniques. The cloud matrix of MITRE ATT&CK contains the general flow of cyber attacks:

- Initial access
- Execution
- Persistence
- Privilege escalation
- Defense evasion
- Credential access
- Discovery
- Lateral movement
- Collection
- Exfiltration
- Impact

Understanding attack techniques allows us to understand the results of attacks. For example, using the *abuse of credentials* allows an attacker to gain persistent access to our system.

Another attack example is *cloud object storage discovery*, which may be used by an attacker to gain access to all objects inside a cloud storage instance.

Reviewing all attack techniques will allow us to understand which security controls we can implement to mitigate potential attacks in our cloud environment, whether that's built-in security tools with AWS, Azure, or GCP, or external third-party tools.

For more information, refer to the following resources:

MITRE ATT&CK, Cloud Matrix:

```
https://attack.mitre.org/matrices/enterprise/cloud/
```

MITRE ATT&CK, IaaS Matrix:

```
https://attack.mitre.org/matrices/enterprise/cloud/iaas/
```

MITRE ATT&CK, SaaS Matrix:

```
https://attack.mitre.org/matrices/enterprise/cloud/saas/
```

How to Improve Threat Detection and Hunting in the AWS Cloud Using the MITRE ATT&CK Matrix:

```
https://pages.awscloud.com/rs/112-TZM-766/images/How%20to%20
Improve%20Threat%20Detection%20and%20Hunting%20in%20the%20
AWS%20Cloud%20Using%20the%20MITRE%20ATT%26CK%C2%AE%20Matrix%20
_%20Slides.pdf
```

MITRE ATT&CK mappings released for built-in Azure security controls:

```
https://www.microsoft.com/security/blog/2021/06/29/mitre-
attck-mappings-released-for-built-in-azure-security-controls/
```

Detecting and mitigating data breaches in cloud services

A **data breach**, as its name implies, is the unauthorized access of an organization's data. This can result in the exposure of customer or employee personal data and lead to reputational damage for an organization. Because of the shared responsibility model of cloud computing, we need to think differently about data breaches. For example, we do not control the physical storage of our data. This presents a different threat model when compared to a traditional on-premises data center we manage. Data breaches are more likely when working with public cloud services because in this case, we don't control the physical storage of our data. Does this mean that storing our data in the cloud makes it more prone to data breaches? It depends on the cloud service model and on the maturity of the cloud service provider. According to the *shared responsibility model*, when using an **infrastructure as a service** (**IaaS**) solution, we (customers) are in charge of implementing most of the security controls over the **operating system** (**OS**).

In a **platform as a service** (**PaaS**) context, we rely on the cloud service provider in terms of OS hardening, patch management, and backups, but it is very common in a PaaS that we can review audit logs and set proper permissions for who has application-layer access to the service.

In a **software as a service** (**SaaS**) context, things get tricky. There is no standard for SaaS, meaning anyone who deploys an application on a virtual machine or resides on a public IaaS can declare themselves a SaaS provider.

Depending on the maturity of the SaaS provider, we may have the option to add security controls (such as data encryption at rest), configure strong authentication (such as SAML with **multi-factor authentication** (**MFA**)), connect to audit logs via REST APIs, and others.

Before talking about data breaches, let's try to focus on what data we store in the cloud. The following are a few examples of data we might store in the cloud:

- **Public data**: Data that we can safely store on public websites. If such data is exposed by anonymous users, it will not hurt our organization (this could be news sites, currency rates, the organization's physical address from a *Contact us* web page, and so on).

- **Intellectual property/trade secrets**: This is data that we must keep safe, as exposing it will hurt our business and impact our ability to achieve revenue (examples of intellectual property could be data from a pharmaceutical company developing a cure against COVID-19, data from a start-up developing new technology for allowing secure authentication without using passwords, and so on).

- **Personally identifiable information** (**PII**): This includes any identifiable information about people (for example, contact details, credit card information, healthcare data, and so on).

Common consequences of data breaches

As a result of a data breach, there are a number of things that might happen to our data:

- **Breach of confidentiality**: This could include customer financial or healthcare data being exposed, which could then be used by hackers.

- **Data integrity**: This could include someone accessing a bank's core systems and manipulating customer financial information; as a result, a customer might notice a change in their account balance.

- **Availability**: One of the consequences of a data breach can be the use of ransomware that encrypts the data of the target, making it unavailable.

Let's now look at some of the best practices for detecting and mitigating data breaches.

Best practices for detecting and mitigating data breaches in cloud environments

Here are some of the *controls* that allow us to mitigate data breaches:

- **Networking layer**: Configure access controls (network **Access Control Lists** (**ACLs**), security groups, and more) to control who can access our resources.

- **Encryption**: Implement encryption in transit and at rest. This allows us to keep our data confidential at all times.

- **Auditing**: This allows us to keep track of who accessed (or tried to access) our resources and what actions have been made (for example, through APIs) related to resources.

- **Threat management**: This allows us to review logs and detect potential threats to our services.

- **Recovery strategy**: Prepare a disaster recovery plan. For example, technical backups and snapshots of volumes, databases, and processes. This should also include procedures for the recovery of data (for example, which systems to recover first, how to automate recovery using infrastructure as code, and more).

Here are some of the *best practices* to follow:

- **Use a secure development life cycle**: Embed this as part of your development process – this includes controls such as the following:

  - **Authentication and authorization**: Enforce who can access your application and data.

  - **Input validation**: Check and validate what strings and/or data can be inserted into your application and backend database.

  - **Application-layer attacks**: Detect and mitigate attacks such as code injection attacks, cross-site scripting, and others.

- **Use access control lists**: Set network/firewall rules to configure who can access your resources (for both inbound and outbound network traffic).

- **Use audit trails**: These allow you to monitor the accessing of resources and the actions carried out.

- **Check the integrity of your data**: Make sure stored data hasn't been changed.

- **Use change management**: Check for deviations from preconfigured settings (such as services that have public access or servers that might need hardening, among others).

- **Use data classification**: Combine this with data leakage services to assist the detection of data exfiltration.

- **Use encryption**: Ensure the confidentiality of your data when in transit and at rest.

- **Configure organization-wide policies**: For example, use inherited policies that enforce who can access which resources and what actions can be taken on resources, enforce auditing, enforce encryption, and so on.

- **Use backups**: This allows you to recover your data and applications after a data breach.

In the following section, we will review common services from **Amazon Web Services (AWS)**, **Microsoft Azure**, and **Google Cloud Platform (GCP)** that will allow you to detect and mitigate data breaches.

Common AWS services to assist in the detection and mitigation of data breaches

Here are some of the common AWS services that can be used to mitigate data breaches:

- Use **Amazon VPC** controls (for example, network ACLs and security groups) and **AWS Network Firewall** to configure inbound and outbound network access rules.

- Use **AWS IAM** to configure who can authenticate and access your applications, resources, and data.

- Use **AWS KMS** to encrypt your data, to prevent data breaches.

- Use **AWS Secrets Manager** to keep your secrets (access keys, passwords, credentials, and others) safe from data breaches.

- Use **AWS CloudTrail** to detect API activities (for users, computers, service accounts, and so on) that might indicate a data breach.

- Use **Amazon CloudWatch** to log and alert suspicious activities that pass certain thresholds (such as multiple failed login attempts).

- Use **Amazon GuardDuty** to detect data breaches.

- Use **AWS VPC Flow Logs** to review network activity that might indicate data breaches.

- Use **AWS Config** to detect configuration changes in your environment and cloud resources.

- Use **Amazon Detective** to detect the root cause of a data breach.

- Use **AWS Backup** to recover your environment after a data breach.

Common Azure services to assist in the detection and mitigation of data breaches

Here are some of the common Azure services that can be used to mitigate data breaches:

- Use **Azure network security groups** (**NSGs**) to configure inbound and outbound network access rules.

- Use **Azure Active Directory** (**AD**) to configure who can authenticate and access your applications, resources, and data.

- Use **Azure Key Vault** to encrypt your data to prevent data breaches.

- Use **Azure confidential computing** to protect your data against data breaches.

- Use **Azure Monitor** and **Log Analytics** to detect suspicious activities that might indicate data breaches.

- Use **Azure Defender** (previously known as **Azure Advanced Threat Protection**) to detect misconfigurations that might cause data breaches.

- Use **Azure Network Watcher** to review network activity that might indicate data breaches.

- Use **Azure Security Center** to assist in the detection of data breaches.

- Use **Azure Sentinel** to correlate multiple data sources to assist in the detection of data breaches.

- Use **Azure Backup** to recover your environment after a data breach.

Common GCP services to assist in the detection and mitigation of data breaches

Here are some of the common GCP services that can be used to mitigate data breaches:

- Use **GCP VPC firewall rules** to configure inbound and outbound network access rules.

- Use **Google Cloud IAM** to configure who can authenticate and access your applications, resources, and data.

- Use **Google Cloud KMS** to encrypt your data to prevent data breaches.

- Use **Google Secret Manager** to keep your secrets (access keys, passwords, credentials, and more) safe from data breaches.

- Use **GCP confidential computing** to protect your data against data breaches.

- Use **Google Cloud Logging** to detect suspicious activities that might indicate data breaches.

- Use **GCP VPC Flow Logs** to review network activity that might indicate data breaches.

- Use **Google Cloud Security Command Center** to correlate multiple data sources to assist in the detection of data breaches.

For more information, refer to the following resources:

Beware the top three blind spots that precede cloud data breaches:

```
https://itwire.com/guest-articles/guest-opinion/beware-the-
top-three-blind-spots-that-precede-cloud-data-breaches.html
```

36% of organizations suffered a serious cloud security data leak or a breach in the past year:

```
https://www.helpnetsecurity.com/2021/07/27/cloud-security-
data-leak/
```

Top Cloud Security Breaches and How to Protect Your Organization:

```
https://cloud.netapp.com/blog/cis-blg-top-cloud-security-
breaches-and-how-to-protect-your-organization
```

Nearly 80% of Companies Experienced a Cloud Data Breach in Past 18 Months:

```
https://www.securitymagazine.com/articles/92533-nearly-80-of-
companies-experienced-a-cloud-data-breach-in-past-18-months
```

Detecting and mitigating misconfigurations in cloud services

Misconfigurations are a common threat when using cloud services. Under the *shared responsibility model*, some of the common reasons for misconfigurations in cloud services that fall under the customer's responsibility are as follows:

- Lack of knowledge in operating cloud services
- Human error
- Default settings being left in an unsecured state
- Large and complex environments being deployed in a very short time
- Fast and unmanaged changes to cloud environments

Here are some common examples of misconfigurations in cloud services:

- Having overly broad IAM policies (or role-based access control policies) – for example, default permissions that allow users to conduct actions on sensitive resources, or having more permissions than needed to accomplish their daily tasks
- Object storage being publicly accessible to anyone on the internet

- Snapshots and VM images being publicly accessible to anyone on the internet

- Databases being publicly accessible to anyone on the internet

- Virtual servers being publicly accessible to anyone on the internet using **Secure Shell (SSH)** or **Remote Desktop Protocol (RDP)** ports

- Unpatched servers and databases

Here are some best practices for detecting and mitigating misconfigurations in cloud environments:

- Use organizational configuration policies to enforce the desired configurations, such as encrypted storage, blocking public access to resources, and more (as explained in *Chapter 13, Security in Large-Scale Environments*).

- Use infrastructure as code for automation and standard configurations (as explained in *Chapter 13, Security in Large-Scale Environments*).

- Use **Cloud Security Posture Management (CSPM)** to detect misconfigurations (as explained in *Chapter 12, Managing Multi-Cloud Environments*).

- Scan for misconfigurations (such as the use of vulnerable components) as part of the build process.

- Use **change management** to check for deviations from preconfigured settings (such as services which might have public access or servers which might need hardening, and more)

- Limit access to production environments to the minimum required (both by using minimal permissions and using network access controls) – do not allow developers or end users access to production environments.

- Conduct employee training on the proper use of the various cloud services.

- Review which identities exist in your organization that require access to cloud resources and manage these as required.

In the following section, we will review common services from AWS, Azure, and GCP that will allow you to detect and mitigate misconfigurations.

Common AWS services to assist in the detection and mitigation of misconfigurations

Here are some AWS services that can mitigate misconfigurations:

- Use **AWS IAM** to configure who can authenticate and access your applications, resources, and data.

- Use **AWS IAM Access Analyzer** to detect users who haven't used their accounts for a long time, such as cross-account access on AWS with public access to resources such as **Amazon S3** and AWS KMS.

- Use Amazon GuardDuty to detect misconfigurations, such as **AWS EC2** trying to access **command-and-control** (**C&C**) networks, an S3 bucket being publicly accessible to the internet, and more.

- Use **AWS Config** to detect configuration changes in your environment and cloud resources and compare them against relevant compliance policies.

- Use **AWS Security Hub** to track events from multiple AWS services and detect misconfiguration against policy standards.

- Use **AWS Amazon Inspector** to detect misconfigurations, such as deviations from **Centre for Internet Security** (**CIS**) hardening benchmarks, missing security patches, and so on.

- Use **AWS Audit Manager** to detect misconfigurations against compliance standards.

- Use **AWS Trusted Advisor** to review common security misconfigurations.

- Use **AWS Control Tower** to centrally enforce configurations on entire AWS organization levels (for example, blocking S3 public access, blocking user abilities such as deploying virtual servers, and so on).

- Use **AWS CloudFormation** to deploy new cloud environments in a standardized way.

Let's now look at the detection and mitigation of misconfigurations in Azure cloud services.

Common Azure services to assist in the detection and mitigation of misconfigurations

Here are some Azure services that can mitigate misconfigurations:

- Use **Azure AD** to configure who can authenticate and access your applications, resources, and data.

- Use the **Azure Activity** log, which is a part of Azure Monitor, to detect what actions were made in your Azure environment.

- Use **Microsoft Defender for Cloud** to detect security misconfigurations in various Azure services.

- Use **Azure Advisor** to review common security misconfigurations.

- Use **Azure Policy** and **Azure management groups** to centrally enforce configurations on entire **Azure tenant** levels (for example, blocking blob storage public access, blocking user abilities such as deploying virtual servers, and so on).

- Use **Azure Resource Manager** to deploy new environments in a standard way.

Let's now look at the detection and mitigation of misconfigurations in GCP.

Common GCP services to assist in the detection and mitigation of misconfigurations

Here are some common GCP services that can be used to mitigate misconfigurations:

- Use **Google Cloud IAM** to configure who can authenticate and access your applications, resources, and data.

- Use **Google Cloud Logging** to detect what actions were made in your GCP environment.

- Use **Google Cloud Security Command Center** to detect security misconfigurations in various GCP services.

- Use **GCP Resource Manager** to centrally enforce configurations for entire GCP organization levels (for example, restricting service account creation, restricting resource locations, and more).

- Use **Google Cloud Deployment Manager** to deploy new environments in a standard way.

For more information, please refer to the following resources:

Cloud misconfigurations surge, organizations need continuous controls:

```
https://www.helpnetsecurity.com/2020/02/20/cloud-
misconfigurations/
```

Misconfigurations: A Hidden but Preventable Threat to Cloud Data:

```
https://securityintelligence.com/articles/misconfigurations-
hidden-threat-to-cloud-data/
```

Cloud misconfiguration, a major risk for cloud security:

```
https://securityaffairs.co/wordpress/117305/security/cloud-
misconfiguration-risks.html
```

Detecting and mitigating insufficient IAM and key management in cloud services

Insufficient IAM can happen in a scenario where we have a large number of user identities (such as in an enterprise organization) but we fail to properly manage the identities. Or we might use cryptography to protect sensitive data but fail to follow key rotation best practices, and as a result, increase the chance of data exposure by unauthorized persons.

Here are some common consequences of insufficient IAM and key management:

- Failing to follow *the principle of least privileged*, which leads to excessive permissions being granted
- Failing to configure access controls – for example, allowing unauthorized access to sensitive data (such as PII, credit card data, healthcare data, and so on), which leads to exposed credentials
- Not enforcing the password policy (for example, allowing short passwords, not enforcing password changes, allowing password reuse, and so on), which leads to password brute force attacks
- Encrypting data but keeping the same cryptographic key without key rotation, which can potentially lead to breaches in data confidentiality
- Not enforcing the use of MFA, which can lead to unauthorized access to resources and data

- Embedding credentials or cryptographic keys inside code and scripts, which can lead to exposure of credentials

- Not configuring audit trails, which leads to a lack of visibility of which identities have access to which resources

Here are some best practices for detecting and mitigating insufficient IAM in cloud environments:

- Manage the entire identity life cycle for your employees and any sub-contractors who have access to your systems and data – this should include recruitment, account provisioning, access management to resources, and finally, account deprovisioning when an employee or sub-contractor has left the organization or no longer needs access to systems and data.

- Use a central repository for identities, where you provision and deprovision accounts and set password policies.

- Use federation to allow access from on-premises environments to cloud environments and resources, and between external partners' or customers' IAM systems and your cloud environments.

- Block the use of weak and legacy authentication protocols (such as **New Technology LAN Manager (NTLM)** and clear text **Lightweight Directory Access Protocol (LDAP)**).

- Enforce the use of a password policy (for example, by stipulating a minimum password length, minimum and maximum password age, password history, complex passwords, account lockout and release settings, and more).

- Enforce the use of MFA.

- Audit users' actions and correlate their activities using a **Security Information and Event Management (SIEM)** system that will allow you to detect anomalous behavior (such as user logins after working hours, users trying to access resources for the first time, and so on).

- Review user login activities. If a user hasn't used their account for several weeks, perhaps it is time to lock or disable the account due to inactivity, which is also a part of the *least privilege* principle.

- Implement identity governance – do the right users have the right roles at the right time?

- Review user access privileges, locate accounts with default or increased permissions that are not needed, and fine-tune the accounts' privileges.

- Follow the principle of *least privilege* when granting permissions to resources.

- Follow the concept of *segregation of duties* to avoid single users having privileges to conduct sensitive actions (such as a user with the permissions both to generate encryption keys and use encryption keys).

- Use a secure and central repository for generating, storing, retrieving, and rotating encryption keys.

- Use a secrets management service to generate, store, retrieve, and rotate secrets, passwords, API keys, and access keys inside code to access resources, while keeping secrets secured and encrypted.

- Encrypt all sensitive information (such as PII, credit card numbers, healthcare data, and so on).

In the following section, we will review common services from AWS, Azure, and GCP that will allow you to detect and mitigate insufficient IAM in your cloud services.

Common AWS services to assist in the detection and mitigation of insufficient IAM and key management

Here are some common AWS services that can be used to mitigate insufficient IAM and key management:

- Use **AWS IAM** to configure who can authenticate and access your applications, resources, and data and to enforce password policies.

- Use **AWS IAM Access Analyzer** to detect users who haven't used their accounts for a long time.

- Use **AWS Directory Service** to configure who can authenticate and access your legacy (based on **Kerberos** authentication) servers and applications and to enforce password policies.

- Enforce the use of MFA to avoid the successful use of your users' credentials to access your applications and systems.

- Use **AWS KMS** to generate, store, and rotate encryption keys.

- Use **AWS Secrets Manager** to generate, store, and rotate secrets (for example, credentials, access keys, passwords, and more).

- Use **AWS CloudTrail** to detect API activities, such as failed login attempts.

Common Azure services to assist in the detection and mitigation of insufficient IAM and key management

Here are some common Azure services that can be used to mitigate insufficient IAM and key management:

- Use **Azure AD** to configure who can authenticate and access your applications, resources, and data and to enforce password policies.

- Use **Azure AD Domain Services** to configure who can authenticate and access your legacy (Kerberos-based) servers, applications, resources, and data, and use it to enforce password policies.

- Enforce the use of MFA to avoid the successful use of your users' credentials to access your applications and systems.

- Use **Azure AD Conditional Access** to enforce different access and authentication methods when users are connecting from the corporate network versus an unknown IP address.

- Use **Azure Privileged Identity Management** (**PIM**) to restrict users' permissions to your Azure resources.

- Use **Azure Key Vault** to generate, store, and rotate encryption keys and secrets (for example, credentials, access keys, passwords, and more).

- Enable **Azure AD audit logs** and use **Azure Log Analytics** to detect activities such as failed login attempts.

- Use **Azure Information Protection** to detect authentication failure events.

- Use **Azure Sentinel** to correlate logs from multiple log sources to detect failed login attempts.

- Use **Azure Customer Lockbox** to detect login attempts by **Microsoft** support engineers.

Common GCP services to assist in the detection and mitigation of insufficient IAM and key management

Here are some common GCP services that can be used to mitigate insufficient identity and access management:

- Use **Google Cloud IAM** to configure who can authenticate and access your applications, resources, and data and to enforce password policies.

- Use the **Google Managed Service** for Microsoft **Active Directory** to configure who can authenticate and access your legacy (Kerberos-based) servers and applications, resources, and data, and use it to enforce password policies.

- Enforce the use of MFA to avoid successful but unauthorized use of your users' credentials to access your applications and systems.

- Use **Google Cloud KMS** to generate, store, and rotate encryption keys.

- Use **Google Secret Manager** to generate, store, and rotate secrets (for example, credentials, access keys, passwords, and more).

- Use **Google Cloud Logging** to detect activities such as failed login attempts.

- Use **Google Cloud Security Command Center** to correlate logs from multiple log sources to detect failed login attempts.

- Use **Google Access Transparency** and **Access Approval** to detect login attempts by Google support engineers.

For more information, refer to the following resources:

Are Your Cloud Environments Protected from Identity-Based Attacks?:

```
https://www.eweek.com/cloud/are-your-cloud-environments-
protected-from-identity-based-attacks/
```

Top 9 Identity & Access Management Challenges with Your Hybrid IT Environment:

```
https://www.okta.com/resources/whitepaper/top-9-iam-
challenges-with-your-hybrid-it-environment/
```

Major threats to cloud infrastructure security include a lack of visibility and inadequate IAM:

```
https://www.helpnetsecurity.com/2021/06/30/cloud-
infrastructure-security/
```

7 Best Practices for Identity Access Management:

```
https://www.sailpoint.com/identity-library/7-best-practices-
for-identity-access-management/
```

Detecting and mitigating account hijacking in cloud services

Account hijacking happens when an account (either belonging to a human or a system/application/service account) is compromised and an unauthorized person gains access to use resources and data on behalf of the (usually high-privileged) compromised account.

Here are some common consequences of account hijacking:

- Unauthorized access to resources
- Data exposure and leakage
- Data deletion
- System compromise
- Identity theft
- Ransomware or malicious code infection
- Account lock-out
- Denial of services
- Denial of wallet (there could be a huge cloud spend due to resource misuses such as Bitcoin mining)
- Website defacement

Some common methods of account hijacking are as follows:

- **Phishing attacks** against a system administrator's account, allowing an attacker to gain access to databases with customer data
- Access keys for a privileged account stored on an S3 bucket that was publicly accessible and as a result, hackers being able to use the access keys to deploy multiple expensive virtual machines for bitcoin mining
- Weak administrator passwords allowing attackers to gain control over the administrator privileges and change permissions to allow public access to backups containing customer financial details

Here are some best practices for detecting and mitigating account hijacking:

- Enforce the use of strong passwords (for example, by stipulating a minimum password length, minimum and maximum password age, password history, complex passwords, account lockout and release settings, and more)

- Enforce the use of MFA.

- Audit user actions and correlate their activities using an SIEM system that will allow you to detect anomalous behavior (such as user logins after working hours, users trying to access resources for the first time, and so on).

- Follow the principle of *least privilege* when granting permissions to resources.

- Follow the concept of *segregation of duties* to avoid single user having the privilege to conduct sensitive actions (such as a user with the permissions both to generate encryption keys and use encryption keys).

- Invest in employee awareness to allow all your employees to detect phishing attempts, avoid opening emails from unknown sources, avoid running unknown executables, and avoid plugging in removable media from unknown sources.

- Invest in business continuity planning to prepare for recovery after a system is compromised (for example, rebuilding systems, recovering data from backups, changing credentials, and so on).

In the following section, we will review common services from AWS, Azure, and GCP that will allow you to detect and mitigate account hijacking.

Common AWS services to assist in the detection and mitigation of account hijacking

Some common AWS services to protect against account hijacking are as follows:

- Use **AWS IAM** to configure who can authenticate and access your applications, resources, and data and to enforce password policies.

- Use **AWS IAM Access Analyzer** to detect users who haven't used their accounts for a long time.

- Use **AWS Directory Service** to configure who can authenticate and access your legacy (Kerberos-based) servers and applications and to enforce password policies.

- Enforce the use of MFA to avoid the successful use of your users' credentials to access your applications and systems.

- Use **Amazon GuardDuty** to detect account compromise.

- Use **AWS CloudTrail** to detect API activities such as failed login attempts.

- Use **AWS Backup** to recover your cloud environment after an account is hijacked.

Common Azure services to assist in the detection and mitigation of account hijacking

Some common Azure services to protect against account hijacking are as follows:

- Use **Azure AD** to configure who can authenticate and access your applications, resources, and data and to enforce password policies.

- Use **Azure AD Domain Services** to configure who can authenticate and access your legacy (Kerberos-based) servers and applications, resources, and data, and use it to enforce password policies.

- Enforce the use of MFA to avoid the successful use of your users' credentials to access your applications and systems.

- Use **Azure AD Conditional Access** to enforce different levels of access and different authentication methods when users are connecting from the corporate network versus an unknown IP address.

- Use **Azure PIM** to restrict users' permissions to your Azure resources.

- Enable Azure AD audit logs and use Azure Log Analytics to detect activities such as failed login attempts.

- Use **Azure Information Protection** to detect authentication failure events.

- Use **Azure Sentinel** to correlate logs from multiple log sources to detect failed login attempts.

- Use **Azure Backup** to recover your cloud environment after an account is hijacked.

Common GCP services to assist in the detection and mitigation of account hijacking

Here are some GCP services that can protect against account hijacking:

- Use **Google Cloud IAM** to configure who can authenticate and access your applications, resources, and data and to enforce password policies.

- Use the **Google Managed Service** for Microsoft Active Directory to configure who can authenticate and access your legacy (Kerberos-based) servers and applications, resources, and data, and use it to enforce password policies.

- Enforce the use of MFA to avoid the successful use of your users' credentials to access your applications and systems.

- Use **Google Cloud Logging** to detect activities such as failed login attempts.

- Use **Google Cloud Security Command Center** to correlate logs from multiple log sources to detect failed login attempts.

For more information, refer to the following resources:

CLOUD-JACKING: AN EVOLVING AND DANGEROUS CYBERSECURITY THREAT:

```
https://techgenix.com/cloud-jacking/
```

Prevent cloud account hijacking with 3 key strategies:

```
https://searchcloudsecurity.techtarget.com/tip/Prevent-cloud-
account-hijacking-with-3-key-strategies
```

What Is Cloud Jacking? How to Keep Your Cloud-Stored Data Safe:

```
https://www.magnify247.com/cloud-jacking-keep-safe/
```

Detecting and mitigating insider threats in cloud services

Insider threat is a concept where an authorized employee (that is, an *insider*) performs an action (either maliciously or accidentally) that they are not supposed to. Some common consequences of insider threats are as follows:

- Loss of data
- Data leakage
- System downtime
- Loss of company reputation
- Monetary loss due to lawsuits

Some common examples of insider threats are as follows:

- An administrator clicks on a phishing email from an unknown source, and as a result, a file server gets infected by ransomware, and all the files are encrypted.
- An employee with the privilege to access an accounting system leaves their laptop unattended and an unauthorized person takes over his laptop and steals customer data.
- A sub-contractor with access to databases with customer email addresses exports customer data and sells it on the dark web.

- An administrator with access to backup files decides to delete all backup files before leaving the organization out of spite.

Some best practices for detecting and mitigating insider threats in cloud environments are as follows:

- Invest in background screening before hiring employees or sub-contractors.

- Enforce the use of strong passwords (for example, by stipulating a minimum password length, minimum and maximum password age, password history, complex passwords, account lockout and release settings, and more).

- Audit user actions and correlate their activities using an SIEM system that will allow you to detect anomalous behavior (such as user logins after working hours, users trying to access resources for the first time, and so on).

- Follow the principle of *least privilege* when granting permissions to resources.

- Follow the concept of *segregation of duties* to avoid single users having the privilege to conduct sensitive actions (such as a user with the permissions both to generate encryption keys and use encryption keys).

- Enforce the use of MFA to minimize the risk of attackers taking control of an internal employee's account without the employee's knowledge to access internal systems and data.

- Invest in employee awareness to allow all your employees to detect phishing attempts, avoid opening emails from unknown sources, avoid running unknown executables, and avoid plugging in removable media from unknown sources.

- Invest in business continuity planning to prepare for recovery after a system is compromised (for example, rebuilding systems, recovering data from backups, changing credentials, and so on).

- Encrypt sensitive customer data and make sure access to encryption keys is limited to authorized personnel only, with audits for the entire key encryption/decryption process.

- Store backups off-site and audit all access to backups.

In the following section, we will review common services from AWS, Azure, and GCP that will allow you to detect and mitigate insider threats.

Common AWS services to assist in the detection and mitigation of insider threats

Here are some AWS services that can protect against insider threats:

- Use **Amazon GuardDuty** to detect anomalous behavior across your accounts.

- Use **AWS CloudTrail** to detect API activities such as authorized users accessing a system after working hours or performing excessive actions, such as multiple file downloads, large select actions from databases, and so on.

- Use **AWS KMS** to encrypt your data and control who has access to the encryption keys.

- Use **AWS Secrets Manager** to store secrets (for example, credentials, access keys, passwords, and so on) and control who has access to the secrets.

- Once an account compromise is detected, be sure to replace credentials, secrets, and encryption keys as appropriate.

Common Azure services to assist in the detection and mitigation of insider threats

Here are some Azure services that can protect against insider threats:

- Use **Azure AD Conditional Access** to enforce different access and authentication methods when users are connecting from the corporate network versus an unknown IP address.

- Use **Azure PIM** to restrict users' permissions to your Azure resources.

- Enable **Azure AD** audit logs and use Azure Log Analytics to detect activities such as failed login attempts.

- Use **Azure Sentinel** to correlate logs from multiple log sources to detect activities such as authorized users accessing a system after working hours or performing excessive actions, such as multiple file downloads, large select actions from databases, and so on.

- Use **Azure Key Vault** to encrypt your data and control who has access to the encryption keys.

- Use **Azure Key Vault** to store secrets (for example, credentials, access keys, passwords, and so on) and control who has access to the secrets.

- Once an account compromise is detected, replace credentials, secrets, and encryption keys as appropriate.

Common GCP services to assist in the detection and mitigation of insider threats

Here are some GCP services that can protect against insider threats:

- Use **Google Cloud Logging** to detect activities such as failed login attempts.

- Use **Google Cloud Security Command Center** to correlate logs from multiple log sources to detect failed login attempts.

- Use **GCP Cloud KMS** to encrypt your data and control who has access to the encryption keys.

- Use **Google Secret Manager** to store secrets (for example, credentials, access keys, passwords, and more) and control who has access to the secrets.

- Once an account compromise is detected, replace credentials, secrets, and encryption keys as appropriate.

For more information, refer to the following resources:

Five Tips for Protecting Cloud Resources from Internal Threats:

```
https://morpheusdata.com/cloud-blog/five-tips-for-protecting-
cloud-resources-from-internal-threats
```

Don't let insider threats rain on your cloud deployment:

```
https://www.synopsys.com/blogs/software-security/insider-
threats-cloud/
```

6 Insider Cloud Security Threats to Look Out for in 2021:

```
https://n.gatlabs.com/blogpost/insider-cloud-security-threats-
watch-out-for/
```

What is an Insider Threat?:

```
https://www.code42.com/glossary/what-is-insider-threat/
```

Detecting and mitigating insecure APIs in cloud services

In today's world, all modern developments are based on **Application Programming Interfaces (APIs)** to communicate between system components, mostly based on web services (using **Simple Object Access Protocol (SOAP)**) or REST APIs. The fact that APIs are publicly exposed makes them an easy target for attackers trying to access a system and cause damage. Some common consequences of insecure APIs are as follows:

- Data breaches
- Data leakage
- Damage to data integrity
- Denial of service

Some common examples of attacks exploiting insecure APIs are as follows:

- Due to a lack of input validation, an attacker can misuse an exposed API and inject malicious code through the API into a backend database.
- Due to a lack of input validation, an attacker can perform an SQL injection through an exposed API and exfiltrate customer data from a retail site.
- Due to a lack of application access control mechanisms, an attacker can use an API to penetrate a cloud service by using a low-privilege account.
- An attacker located an API key stored in an open source code repository and was able to run remote commands against an internal system, using the permissions that the API key had.

Here are some best practices for detecting and mitigating against insecure APIs in cloud environments:

- **Use a secure development life cycle**: Embed this as part of your development process – this includes controls such as the following:

  - **Authentication and authorization**: Enforce who can access the API.
  - **Input validation**: Check and validate what strings and/or data can be inserted into the API.
  - **Application layer attacks**: Detect and mitigate attacks such as injection attacks, cross-site scripting, and so on.
  - Conduct code reviews for all your APIs.

- Encrypt data in transit by default for all APIs.

- Sign each message through the API using a cryptographic key to avoid data tampering or changes to data integrity.

- Use a **web application firewall (WAF)** to protect against well-known application-layer attacks.

- Use **distributed denial of service (DDoS)** protection services to protect the API service from denial-of-service attacks.

- Use an XML gateway to protect the service against SOAP or REST API-based attacks.

- Enforce a rate limit on the API to decrease the chance of automated attacks.

- Limit the type of HTTP methods to the minimum required (for example, GET without POST or DELETE).

- Audit the use of exposed APIs and the backend systems to detect anomalous behavior (such as brute force attacks or data exfiltration).

- Perform schema validation at the server side to make sure only well-known field sizes, characters, or regular expressions can pass through the API.

In the following section, we will review common services from AWS, Azure, and GCP that will allow you to detect and mitigate insecure APIs.

Common AWS services to assist in the detection and mitigation of insecure APIs

Here are some AWS services that can provide protection against insecure APIs:

- Use **Amazon API Gateway** to allow inbound access to APIs in your cloud environment.

- Use **AWS WAF** to detect and protect against application-layer attacks.

- Use **AWS Shield** to detect and protect against DDoS attacks.

- Use **AWS IAM** to authorize access to APIs.

- Use **Amazon CloudWatch** to detect spikes in API requests.

- Use **AWS CloudTrail** to detect who can conduct API activity through the API gateway.

- Use **Amazon GuardDuty** to detect potential hacking activities using your APIs.

- Use **AWS Secrets Manager** to generate, store, and rotate API keys.

Common Azure services to assist in the detection and mitigation of insecure APIs

Here are some Azure services that can provide protection against insecure APIs:

- Use **Azure API Management** to allow inbound access to APIs in your cloud environment.

- Use **Azure WAF** to detect and protect against application-layer attacks.

- Use **Azure DDoS Protection** to detect and protect against DDoS attacks.

- Use **Azure Active Directory** to authorize access to APIs.

- Use **Azure Monitor** to detect spikes in API requests.

- Use **Azure Key Vault** to generate, store, and rotate API keys.

- Use **Azure Sentinel** to correlate multiple data sources to assist in detecting potential attacks against APIs.

Common GCP services to assist in the detection and mitigation of insecure APIs

Here are some GCP services that can provide protection against insecure APIs:

- Use **Google API Gateway** to allow inbound access to APIs in your cloud environment.

- Use **Google Cloud Armor** to detect and protect against both application-layer attacks and DDoS attacks.

- Use **Google Cloud IAM** to authorize access to APIs.

- Use **Google Cloud Audit Logs** to monitor API Gateway activities.

For more information, refer to the following resources:

Insecure API Cloud Computing: The Causes and Solutions:

```
https://cybersecurityasean.com/expert-opinions-opinion-byline/
insecure-api-cloud-computing-causes-and-solutions
```

API Security Top 10 2019:

```
https://owasp.org/www-project-api-security/
```

As API Threats Multiply, Cybersecurity Lags:

```
https://containerjournal.com/features/as-api-threats-multiply-
cybersecurity-lags/
```

Detecting and mitigating the abuse of cloud services

The abuse of cloud services is about using the scale of the cloud provider's resources and the multi-tenancy architecture to conduct malicious activities. Some common consequences of the abuse of cloud services are as follows:

- Loss of service availability due to DDoS attacks
- Monetary loss due to the use of cloud resources being exploited for bitcoin mining without the customer's awareness

Some common examples of the abuse of cloud services are as follows:

- Using the cloud to deploy multiple servers and conducting DDoS attacks
- Using the cloud to deploy multiple expensive servers for bitcoin mining
- Using the cloud to spread email spam and phishing attacks
- Using the cloud for brute force attacks on passwords

Some best practices for detecting and mitigating against the abuse of cloud services are as follows:

- Configure billing alerts to get notified in advance about any increase in resource consumption.
- Follow the concept of *segregation of duties* to avoid single users having the privileges to conduct damaging actions (such as a user with the permissions both to deploy an expensive virtual machine and to log in to the machine for ongoing maintenance).
- Use access control lists and set network/firewall rules to configure who can access your resources (for both inbound and outbound network traffic).
- Use IAM to control who has access to your cloud environments.
- Rotate credentials to avoid misuse.
- Use audit trails to allow you to monitor the access of resources and the actions carried out.

- Use DDoS protection services to protect your cloud environment from denial-of-service attacks.

- Use WAF services to detect and protect against application-layer attacks.

- Invest in employee awareness regarding the cloud provider's terms of acceptable use.

Common AWS services to assist in the detection and mitigation of the abuse of cloud services

Here are some common AWS services that can protect against the abuse of cloud services:

- Use **Amazon CloudWatch** to configure billing alerts and get notifications when certain thresholds have been passed.

- Use **AWS IAM** to configure who can authenticate and access your applications, resources, and data.

- Use **AWS Config** to detect configuration changes in your environment and cloud resources.

- Use **AWS WAF** to detect and protect against application-layer attacks.

- Use **AWS Shield** to detect and protect against DDoS attacks.

- Use **AWS CloudTrail** to detect API activities (for users, computers, service accounts, and others) that might indicate the misuse of resources in your cloud environment.

- Use **Amazon GuardDuty** to detect any anomalous behavior across your cloud resources (such as bitcoin mining).

- Use **Amazon VPC controls** (for example, network ACLs and security groups) and AWS Network Firewall to configure inbound and outbound network access rules.

- Use **AWS Systems Manager Patch Manager** to automatically deploy security patches for servers in your cloud environment.

Common Azure services to assist in the detection and mitigation of the abuse of cloud services

Here are some common Azure services that can protect against the abuse of cloud services:

- Use Azure budgets to configure billing alerts and get notifications when certain thresholds have been passed.

- Use **Azure AD** to configure who can authenticate and access your applications, resources, and data.

- Use **Azure Monitor** to detect activities (for users, computers, service accounts, and others) that might indicate the misuse of resources in your cloud environment.

- Use **Microsoft Defender for Cloud** to detect and send alerts about possible misuse of resources in your cloud environment.

- Use **Azure WAF** to detect and protect against application-layer attacks.

- Use **Azure DDoS Protection** to detect and protect against DDoS attacks.

- Use **Azure NSGs** to configure inbound and outbound network access rules.

- Use **Azure Customer Lockbox** to detect login attempts by Microsoft support engineers.

- Use **Azure Update Management** to automatically deploy security patches for servers in your cloud environment.

Common GCP services to assist in the detection and mitigation of the abuse of cloud services

Here are some common GCP services that can protect against the abuse of cloud services:

- Use GCP Billing budgets to configure billing alerts and get notifications when certain thresholds have been passed.

- Use **Google Cloud IAM** to configure who can authenticate and access your applications, resources, and data.

- Use **Google Cloud Logging** to detect suspicious activities that might indicate the misuse of resources in your cloud environment.

- Use **Google Cloud Armor** to detect and protect against both application layer and DDoS attacks.

- Use **Google Cloud Security Command Center** to correlate multiple data sources to assist in detecting the misuse of resources in your cloud environment.

- Use GCP VPC firewall rules to configure inbound and outbound network access rules.

- Use **Google Access Transparency** and **Access Approval** to detect login attempts by Google support engineers.

- Use **Google OS patch management** to automatically deploy security patches for servers in your cloud environment.

For more information, refer to the following resources:

Abuse in the Cloud:

```
https://cloudsecurityalliance.org/blog/2021/02/12/abuse-in-
the-cloud/
```

Abusing cloud services to fly under the radar:

```
https://research.nccgroup.com/2021/01/12/abusing-cloud-
services-to-fly-under-the-radar/
```

Summary

In this chapter, we focused on common security threats to cloud services.

For each of the identified threats, we reviewed potential consequences of the threat, a common example of the threat, and the best practices to detect and mitigate the threat, and after that, we reviewed the built-in services from AWS, Azure, and GCP that allow you to protect your cloud environment.

Knowing the most common threats you face when using cloud services and the various built-in cloud service capabilities will allow you to better protect your cloud environment.

In the next chapter, we will review compliance standards for cloud security (such as ISO 27001, **Security Operations Centre** (**SOC**), **Cloud Security Alliance** (**CSA**) Star, and more) and the European GDPR privacy regulation, the PCI DSS, and the HIPAA laws.

9
Handling Compliance and Regulation

In previous chapters, we covered cloud infrastructure fundamentals and common threats in cloud environments. This chapter will cover security standards related to cloud services and compliance with some of the common regulations.

Standards ensure that we follow best practices in the same way as most organizations around the world in various fields, such as information security, privacy and data protection, health, finance, and more.

Compliance in cloud services is the act of complying with regulatory requirements and industry standards. Complying with laws, regulations, and standards enables organizations to conduct their business in a secure manner, by ensuring that customer data remains protected.

In this chapter, we will cover the following topics:

- Compliance and the shared responsibility model
- Introduction to compliance with regulatory requirements and industry best practices

- What are the common **International Organization for Standardization (ISO)** standards related to cloud computing?

- What is a **System and Organization Controls (SOC)** report?

- What is the **Cloud Security Alliance (CSA) Security, Trust, Assurance, and Risk (STAR)** program?

- What is the **Payment Card Industry Data Security Standard (PCI DSS)**?

- What is the **General Data Protection Regulation (GDPR)**?

- What is the **Health Insurance Portability and Accountability Act (HIPAA)**?

Technical requirements

For this chapter, the reader needs to have a solid understanding of information security concepts such as standards, compliance programs, data protection, and others.

Compliance and the shared responsibility model

According to the shared responsibility model (as explained in *Chapter 1, Introduction to Cloud Security*), the cloud provider in **infrastructure as a service/platform as a service (IaaS/PaaS)** is responsible for the physical aspects of the cloud (from physical data centers, hardware, storage, network equipment, host servers, to virtualization).

Software as a service (SaaS) providers are also responsible for application layers (guest **operating system (OS)**, managed databases, managed storage, application tier, and more). As customers, we expect our cloud providers to be both compliant with regulatory requirements (such as protecting credit card information in PCI DSS, protecting **personally identifiable information (PII)** in GDPR, and more) and to work according to the highest security standards (such as ISO *27001*, SOC, and more).

When we as organizations serve customers, we need to be compliant with regulations (when dealing with financial, healthcare, or personal data), whether we build our infrastructure above IaaS/PaaS or serve customers as SaaS providers. When we serve customers as SaaS providers, our customers expect us to work according to the highest security standards and we need to prove to our customers that our security controls are effective.

To prove that a cloud provider is compliant with security best practices, the cloud providers pass an assessment by third-party assessors—neutral security vendors (such as major accountant firms). The reason for using third-party assessors is because we, as customers, have no way of checking either the physical, logical, or procedural effectiveness of cloud vendors who make their own self-assessments.

Introduction to compliance with regulatory requirements and industry best practices

Law and regulations are mandatory for any organization conducting business, storing and processing sensitive data (such as PII, credit card information, healthcare information, and more), and serving customers in either private or public environments, and the cloud environment is no different.

Standards are optionally considered as a best practice and, in many cases, provide an organization leverage for conducting business—for example, compliance with ISO *27001* shows customers and business partners that an organization has achieved a certain level of maturity in **information security management** (**ISM**).

The best way to manage compliance in cloud services as an automated and ongoing process is to constantly review your entire cloud environment, present the information, dashboards, and reports, and fix settings and resources that are in a non-compliant status.

How to maintain compliance in AWS

Amazon Web Services (**AWS**) offers its customers a service called **AWS Config** that allows customers to continuously check their entire AWS organization's compliance status against regulatory requirements and industry best practices. To review an up-to-date list of compliance reports that AWS is compliant against, you can use **AWS Artifact**.

For more information, refer to the following resources:

AWS Artifact

```
https://aws.amazon.com/artifact
```

AWS Config

```
https://docs.aws.amazon.com/config/latest/developerguide/
conformancepack-sample-templates.html
```

How to maintain compliance in Azure

Azure offers its customers a service called **Microsoft Defender for Cloud** that allows them to continuously check their entire Azure tenant's compliance status against regulatory requirements and industry best practices. Through Azure, customers can review an up-to-date list of compliance reports that Azure is compliant against, as appears in the **Azure Trust Center**.

For more information, refer to the following resources:

Azure Security Center—Improve your regulatory compliance

```
https://docs.microsoft.com/en-us/azure/security-center/
security-center-compliance-dashboard
```

Azure Trust Center

```
https://www.microsoft.com/en-ww/trust-center/compliance/
compliance-overview
```

Microsoft Azure Compliance Offerings

```
https://azure.microsoft.com/mediahandler/files/resourcefiles/
microsoft-azure-compliance-offerings/Microsoft%20Azure%20
Compliance%20Offerings.pdf
```

How to maintain compliance in GCP

Google Cloud Platform (**GCP**) offers its customers a service called **Google Security Command Center**, which allows customers to continuously check their entire GCP organization's compliance status against regulatory requirements and industry best practices.

GCP also allows its customers the ability to review an up-to-date list of compliance reports that GCP is compliant with, as appears in the **Google Compliance Reports Manager**.

For more information, refer to the following resources:

Google Security Command Center compliance dashboard:

```
https://cloud.google.com/security-command-center/docs/how-to-
use-security-command-center#compliance
```

Google Compliance Reports Manager:

```
https://cloud.google.com/security/compliance/compliance-
reports-manager
```

Summary

In this section we reviewed the industry best practices to maintain compliance in AWS, Azure, and GCP.

What are the common ISO standards related to cloud computing?

ISO is a non-governmental international organization that publishes documents and raises awareness for standards in various topics and, in the context of this book, standards related to information security and cloud services.

ISO/IEC 27001 standard

The ISO/**International Electrotechnical Commission (IEC)** *27000* standard is the most widely used standard for ISM. Though it is not cloud-specific, it is considered the most fundamental standard for **cloud service providers (CSPs)**, and it sets a solid foundation for any cloud provider, from a hyper-scale cloud provider to a small SaaS provider.

The ISO *2700x* is split into the following sections:

- ISO/IEC *27000:2018* provides an overview of **ISM systems (ISMS)**.
- ISO/IEC *27001:2013* is a standard for ISM.
- ISO/IEC *27002:2013* specifies best practices for ISM.

The ISO *27001* is made of the following domains:

- Information Security Policies
- Organization of Information Security
- Human Resources Security
- Asset Management
- Access Control
- Cryptographic
- Physical and Environmental Security
- Operations Security
- Communications Security
- System Acquisition, Development, and Maintenance

- Supplier Relationship
- Information Security Incident Management
- Information Security Business Continuity Management
- Compliance

For more information, refer to the following resources:

ISO/IEC 27001 INFORMATION SECURITY MANAGEMENT

```
https://www.iso.org/isoiec-27001-information-security.html
```

AWS—ISO/IEC 27001:2013

```
https://aws.amazon.com/compliance/iso-27001-faqs/
```

Azure—ISO/IEC 27001:2013

```
https://docs.microsoft.com/en-us/azure/compliance/offerings/
offering-iso-27001
```

GCP—ISO/IEC 27001

```
https://cloud.google.com/security/compliance/iso-27001
```

ISO 27017 standard

The ISO/IEC *27017* is a set of guidelines for information security controls applicable to cloud services, based on ISO/IEC *27002*. Since ISO *27017* is based on ISO *27002*, most of the controls are the same.

Any organization that provides cloud services should consider complying with the ISO *27017* standard. ISO *27017* adds the following controls:

- Shared roles and responsibilities within a cloud computing environment
- Removal of cloud service customer assets
- Segregation in virtual computing environments
- **Virtual machine (VM)** hardening
- Administrator's operational security
- Monitoring of cloud services
- Alignment of security management for virtual and physical networks

For more information, refer to the following resources:

ISO/IEC 27017:2015

`https://www.iso.org/standard/43757.html`

AWS—ISO/IEC 27017:2015 Compliance

`https://aws.amazon.com/compliance/iso-27017-faqs/`

Azure—ISO/IEC 27017:2015

`https://docs.microsoft.com/en-us/azure/compliance/offerings/offering-iso-27017`

GCP—ISO/IEC 27017

`https://cloud.google.com/security/compliance/iso-27017`

ISO 27018 standard

ISO/IEC *27018* is a set of guidelines for implementing measures to protect PII for cloud services, based on ISO/IEC *27002*. As ISO *27018* is based on ISO *27002*, most of the controls are the same.

Any organization that provides cloud services and stores or processes PII should consider complying with the ISO *27018* standard. ISO *27018* adds the following controls:

- **Customers' rights:**

  - Ability to access their data

  - Ability to erase their data

  - Know the purpose of processing their data

- **Service provider (SP) obligations:**

  - Process data disclosure requests from customers

  - Document all data disclosure requests

  - Audit all access attempts to customers' data

  - Notify customers about sub-contractors with access to customers' personal data

  - Notify customers about data breaches relating to their personal data

  - Document all policies and procedures relating to customers' personal data

  - Encrypt all customers' personal data at rest (including backups)

- Data deletion procedures

- Notify customers about countries where their data is been stored and processed

For more information, refer to the following resources:

ISO/IEC 27018:2019

```
https://www.iso.org/standard/76559.html
```

AWS—ISO/IEC 27018:2019 Compliance

```
https://aws.amazon.com/compliance/iso-27018-faqs/
```

Azure—ISO/IEC 27018:2019

```
https://docs.microsoft.com/en-us/azure/compliance/offerings/
offering-iso-27018
```

GCP—ISO/IEC 27018

```
https://cloud.google.com/security/compliance/iso-27018
```

Summary

In this section, we have reviewed the ISO standards and the controls required by cloud providers to be compliant with the ISO standards mentioned previously.

ISO *27001* is recommended for any organization maintaining environments in the public cloud, whether you are a cloud provider or whether you maintain your own IaaS environment.

ISO *27017* is recommended for any cloud provider who offers services to customers over the public cloud; this standard is complementary to ISO *27001*.

From a customer's point of view (organizations that consume cloud services), it is recommended to increase your compliance requirements from cloud providers and demand compliance with both ISO *27001* and ISO *27017*.

ISO *27018* is recommended for any cloud provider that stores or processes customers' PII.

From a customer's point of view (organizations that consume cloud services), it is recommended to increase your compliance requirements from cloud providers and demand compliance with ISO *27001*, ISO *27017*, and ISO *27018*, for any service you consume that stores or processes your PII.

What is a SOC report?

SOC is a reporting framework that allows cloud providers to communicate the effectiveness of their cybersecurity risk management program to **certified public accountants (CPAs)** and broad-range stakeholders—customers, among others.

Any organization that provides cloud services should consider complying with the SOC standard. A SOC is made up of the following type of reports:

- **SOC 1**—A financial statement:

  - **SOC 1 Type 1**—An attestation of controls for a CSP at a specific point in time

  - **SOC 1 Type 2**—An attestation of controls for a CSP and their effectiveness over a minimum 6-month period

- **SOC 2**—A report of controls relevant to security, availability, integrity, and confidentiality or privacy

  - **SOC 2 Type 1**—A description of cloud providers' systems and suitability of the design of controls

  - **SOC 2 Type 2**—A description of cloud providers' systems and suitability of the design of controls and the effectiveness of controls

> **Note**
> From a customer's point of view, SOC 2 Type 2 is the most relevant report since it presents the actual effectiveness of the cloud provider's security controls.

- **SOC 3**—A management report that contains an assurance about the controls of the cloud provider, relevant to security, availability, integrity, and confidentiality or privacy

> **Note**
> SOC 3 reports are high-level reports and, as a result, they are publicly shared with customers.

For more information, refer to the following resources:

System and Organization Controls: SOC Suite of Services

```
https://www.aicpa.org/interestareas/frc/
assuranceadvisoryservices/sorhome.html
```

AWS System and Organization Controls (SOC)

`https://aws.amazon.com/compliance/soc-faqs/`

Azure—System and Organization Controls (SOC) 1 Type 2

`https://docs.microsoft.com/en-us/compliance/regulatory/`
`offering-soc-1`

GCP—SOC 2

`https://cloud.google.com/security/compliance/soc-2`

Summary

In this section, we have reviewed SOC reports, their levels, and the importance of reviewing SOC 2 Type 2 reports by customers to get a better understanding of cloud providers' effectiveness in terms of security controls.

From a customer's point of view (organizations that consume cloud services), it is recommended to increase your compliance requirements from cloud providers and demand a copy of SOC 2 Type II reports from any public cloud provider.

What is the CSA STAR program?

The CSA is an organization that publishes documents, best practices, and raises awareness for cloud security.

Any organization that provides cloud services should consider being compliant with the CSA STAR program. The CSA has created two documents related to cloud security, as follows:

- **Cloud Control Matrix (CCM)**—A cybersecurity control framework for cloud computing
- **Consensus Assessment Initiative Questionnaire (CAIQ)**—A set of industry-accepted security controls for IaaS/PaaS/SaaS services

The CSA has created a program called STAR that is an open registry of cloud providers who publicly share their security controls for the various service models and allow customers to download and review the vendor's compliance against industry best practices.

STAR Level 1

STAR Level 1 is a self-assessment questionnaire where cloud providers transparently share their security controls.

Customers should use a self-assessment questionnaire as a good starting point for low-risk environments since the questionnaire was not reviewed for the effectiveness of the controls by an independent third-party auditor.

STAR Level 2

STAR Level 2 offers cloud providers who already have compliance with ISO *27001*, SOC 2 reports, and more the ability to have their security controls be reviewed by a third-party auditor and adds a level of comfort for the cloud provider's self-assessment questionnaire to the customer by evaluating the actual effectiveness of controls declared by the cloud provider. Customers should use STAR Level 2 compliance for medium-to-high-risk environments, and to increase assurance for cloud security and privacy.

For more information, refer to the following resources:

Cloud Controls Matrix (CCM)

```
https://cloudsecurityalliance.org/research/cloud-controls-
matrix/
```

CSA Star

```
https://cloudsecurityalliance.org/star/
```

AWS and Cloud Security Alliance (CSA)

```
https://aws.amazon.com/compliance/csa/
```

Azure—Cloud Security Alliance (CSA) STAR Certification

```
https://docs.microsoft.com/en-us/azure/compliance/offerings/
offering-csa-star-certification
```

GCP and Cloud Security Alliance (CSA)

```
https://cloud.google.com/security/compliance/csa
```

Summary

In this section, we have reviewed the CSA STAR program, based on the CCM. For medium-to high-risk environments, customers should look for cloud providers who have received CSA STAR Level 2 certification.

What is PCI DSS?

PCI DSS is an information security standard for storing, transferring, and processing credit card information, created by MasterCard, American Express, Visa, JCB International, and Discover Financial Services.

Any organization storing or processing credit card information should comply with PCI DSS. The PCI has the following requirements:

- Use a firewall to protect the PCI environment
- Set password policies
- Protect stored credit card data
- Encrypt credit card data at transit
- Use anti-virus software
- Conduct patch management
- Restrict access to credit card data
- Assign a unique identity to each person with access to credit card data
- Restrict physical access to credit card data
- Conduct log management
- Conduct vulnerability assessments and penetration tests
- Conduct risk assessments and document the process

Any provider or organization that stores, transfers, or processes credit card information should follow the PCI DSS standard. As a best practice, follow your cloud provider's documentation regarding which services and controls to use to be compliant with the PCI standard and keep credit card information safe.

For more information, refer to the following resources:

PCI Security Standards

```
https://www.pcisecuritystandards.org/
```

Information Supplement: PCI SSC Cloud Computing Guidelines

```
https://www.pcisecuritystandards.org/pdfs/PCI_SSC_Cloud_
Guidelines_v3.pdf
```

Payment Card Industry Data Security Standard (PCI DSS) 3.2.1 on AWS

```
https://d1.awsstatic.com/whitepapers/compliance/pci-dss-
compliance-on-aws.pdf
```

Azure—Control mapping of the PCI-DSS v3.2.1 blueprint sample

```
https://docs.microsoft.com/en-us/azure/governance/blueprints/
samples/pci-dss-3.2.1/control-mapping
```

GCP—PCI Data Security Standard compliance

```
https://cloud.google.com/architecture/pci-dss-compliance-in-
gcp
```

Summary

In this section, we have reviewed the PCI DSS standard, as it relates to cloud services. If your organization is storing, transferring, or processing credit card information, you should separate your PCI environment from the rest of your cloud environments, and follow both PCI guidelines and your cloud provider's documentation and best practices.

What is the GDPR?

The GDPR is a European data protection regulation, aimed to protect the personal data of **European Union** (**EU**) citizens.

Any organization storing or processing information about EU citizens must comply with the GDPR. It defines personal data as any information that is related to an identified or identifiable natural person. GDPR applies to any organization that processes or collects personal data of EU citizens, either within data centers in Europe or to/from outside Europe.

These are the main GDPR chapters dealing with technical measures that might be related to cloud services:

- *Chapter 2—Principles*
- *Chapter 3—Rights of the data subject*
- *Chapter 4—Controller and processor*
- *Chapter 5—Transfer of personal data to third countries or international organizations*
- *Chapter 9 —Provisions relating to specific processing situations*

Here are some practices for protecting personal data:

- Encrypt all personal data while at transit (use **Transport Layer Security (TLS)** 1.2) or at rest (use the **Advanced Encryption Standard (AES)** 256 algorithm).

- Make sure the cloud provider offers you the ability to control the encryption keys (**customer-managed keys**).

- Enforce the use of **multi-factor authentication (MFA)** for any user who has access to personal data.

- Follow the principle of *need to know*.

- Make sure EU citizens' personal data is kept in data centers inside the EU, or within data centers of countries that receive an adequate level of data protection from the EU.

- Make sure you sign a *data processing agreement* with your cloud provider.

- Make sure the cloud provider has performed security audits by a third-party auditor before processing personal data.

- Collect only the minimal required personal data.

- Make sure you can locate personal data and erase it, following the customer's request.

For more information, refer to the following resources:

General Data Protection Regulation

```
https://gdpr-info.eu/
```

Code of Conduct for GDPR

```
https://cloudsecurityalliance.org/artifacts/pla-code-of-
conduct-coc-statement-of-adherence-self-assessment/
```

Navigating GDPR Compliance on AWS

```
https://docs.aws.amazon.com/whitepapers/latest/navigating-
gdpr-compliance/welcome.html
```

Azure—General Data Protection Regulation Summary

```
https://docs.microsoft.com/en-us/compliance/regulatory/gdpr
```

Azure—European Union Model Clauses

```
https://docs.microsoft.com/en-us/compliance/regulatory/
offering-eu-model-clauses
```

Google Cloud & the General Data Protection Regulation (GDPR)

`https://cloud.google.com/security/gdpr`

GCP—EU Model Contract Clauses

`https://cloud.google.com/security/compliance/eu-mcc`

Summary

In this section, we have reviewed the GDPR—a European data protection regulation, related to any organization worldwide that collects or processes personal data of EU citizens. As a best practice, follow your cloud provider's documentation regarding which services or controls to use while designing new systems or to be compliant with the GDPR.

What is HIPAA?

HIPAA is a United States Act for organizations dealing with electronic healthcare transactions and PIIs in the healthcare and healthcare insurance industries.

These are the main HIPAA security rules:

- Administrative Safeguards
- Physical Safeguards
- Technical Safeguards
- Organizational, Policies and Procedures and Documentation Requirements
- Basics of Risk Analysis and Risk Management

Here are some best practices to implement:

- Encrypt all healthcare information, while in transit (using TLS 1.2) or at rest (using the AES 256 algorithm).
- Enable an audit log for any information related to healthcare data.
- Authenticate and authorize any request to access healthcare data.
- Follow the *principle of least privilege* (**POLP**) when accessing healthcare data.
- Conduct penetration testing for systems that contain healthcare data.
- Keep all systems up to date (enforce patch management).
- Enable backups for any system that contains healthcare data.

For more information, refer to the following resources:

Summary of the HIPAA Privacy Rule

```
https://www.hhs.gov/hipaa/for-professionals/privacy/laws-
regulations/index.html
```

Guidance on HIPAA & Cloud Computing

```
https://www.hhs.gov/hipaa/for-professionals/special-topics/
health-information-technology/cloud-computing/index.html
```

Architecting for HIPAA Security and Compliance on Amazon Web Services

```
https://d1.awsstatic.com/whitepapers/compliance/AWS_HIPAA_
Compliance_Whitepaper.pdf
```

Azure—HIPAA

```
https://docs.microsoft.com/en-us/azure/compliance/offerings/
offering-hipaa-us
```

A Practical Guide to Designing Secure Health Solutions Using Microsoft Azure

```
https://azure.microsoft.com/mediahandler/files/resourcefiles/
a-practical-guide-to-designing-secure-health-solutions-using-
microsoft-azure/A_Practical_Guide_to_Designing_Secure_Health_
Solutions_using_Microsoft_Azure.pdf
```

GCP—HIPAA

```
https://cloud.google.com/security/compliance/hipaa-compliance
```

Google Cloud Platform HIPAA overview guide

```
https://services.google.com/fh/files/misc/google-cloud-
platform-hipaa-overview-guide.pdf
```

Summary

In this section, we have reviewed the HIPAA Act, which relates to any organization dealing with US healthcare information. As a best practice, follow your cloud provider's documentation regarding how to protect healthcare data.

Summary

In this chapter, we have focused on compliance with common regulations and standards while using cloud services. For each of the mentioned regulations or standards, we have reviewed its highlights and some best practices for either cloud providers or customers (organizations consuming cloud services). The mentioned regulations or standards might be relevant when dealing with certain types of data or certain types of cloud environments.

For each of the mentioned regulations or standards, we have supplied references on how to be compliant while working with AWS, Azure, and GCP. From a customer point of view, knowing which security standards exist will allow you to set the security prerequisites from your cloud providers. Knowing which law or regulation applies to your industry will allow you to know which security controls to set for your cloud environments.

In the next chapter, we will review how to engage with cloud providers—how to choose a cloud provider, cloud provider questionnaires, important topics regarding contracts with cloud providers, and, finally, tips for conducting penetration tests in cloud environments.

10
Engaging with Cloud Providers

In previous chapters, we have covered cloud infrastructure fundamentals, common threats in cloud environments, and how to handle compliance and regulation. This chapter will cover fundamental steps prior to working with cloud services, such as engaging with cloud providers.

In the traditional data center, we control everything – from physical to logical security controls. To get assurance when working with cloud providers, there are several options, such as the following:

- Conduct a risk assessment prior to engaging with a cloud provider – one good option is to review SOC2 Type 2 reports (what controls the cloud provider has set and how effective they are).

- Have a good contract that clearly sets the obligations of the cloud provider (such as an **Service Level Agreement (SLA)** for handling security incidents and an SLA to notify us as customers).

- Conduct a penetration test at least once every 12 months on the system that stores or processes our data.

In this chapter, we will cover the following topics:

- Choosing a cloud provider
- What is a cloud provider?
- Tips for contracts with cloud providers
- Conducting penetration testing in cloud environments

Technical requirements

For this chapter, the reader needs to have a fundamental understanding of concepts such as cloud service models, business requirements, vendor evaluation, and penetration testing.

Choosing a cloud provider

Prior to choosing a cloud provider, we need to ask ourselves – *what are we trying to achieve from migrating to the cloud or from using the cloud?*

There are a few steps that we need to take before we begin working with a cloud provider:

- Decide on our business goals that the cloud provider will assist us to achieve.
- Get ourselves familiar with a potential cloud provider and try to understand its maturity level.
- Sign a contract with a cloud provider that will protect us as customers.
- Conduct an assessment of the cloud environment to make sure their security controls are effective.

The following diagram illustrates the steps involved while choosing a cloud provider:

Choosing a cloud provider

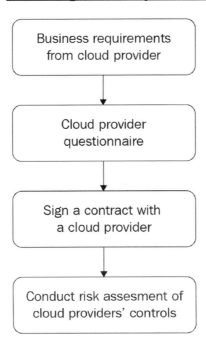

Figure 10.1 – Choosing a cloud provider

What is the most suitable cloud service model for our needs?

This is the first question we need to ask ourselves. If we are still taking the first steps in the cloud, have legacy systems that we wish to migrate to the cloud, and don't have dependencies on specific vendors hardware (such as IBM AIX, Oracle SPARC, and so on), then **Infrastructure as a Service (IaaS)** is the most suitable model.

As long as our on-premises servers are based on x86 architecture and can be virtualized, we should be able to migrate or rebuild our systems based on any of the major IaaS providers.

One of the topics we should consider is our ability to connect to a cloud provider in a hybrid model and to extend our on-premises data center – what are the potential cloud providers' hybrid cloud capabilities?

Perhaps we have already chosen a cloud provider, but now we have a business or technical requirement to work with a specific service (such as **Internet of Things** (**IoT**), machine learning, and data analytics) that is considered superior, and it exists on another cloud provider. In this case, we need to consider multi-cloud architecture and review both cloud providers' multi-cloud capabilities.

We must remember that according to the shared responsibility model, we are responsible for the entire operating system maintenance, such as patch management, software upgrades, backup, hardening, and availability.

If we are planning to build new applications, based on serverless (or function-as-a-service) architecture, or if we prefer to use managed services (such as database services, machine learning, and data analytics), then **Platform as a Service** (**PaaS**) should be our preferred service model.

If we choose the PaaS model, we need to consider how are we planning to connect our development (or **Continuous Integration/Continuous Delivery** (**CI/CD**)) infrastructure to the cloud environment and how are we planning to connect our applications (whether they are located on-premises or in our IaaS environment) to the PaaS services.

Perhaps the easiest service model for organizations who wish to consume cloud services or replace a legacy on-premises system, such as **Customer Relationship Management** (**CRM**), **Enterprise Resource Planning** (**ERP**), and messaging, with a fully managed service is to choose the SaaS model.

When choosing a mature SaaS provider (as explained later in this chapter, from the answers we received from the service provider to the questionnaire mentioned in the *What is a cloud provider?* section), we have the benefits of consuming a service, without the burden of ongoing maintenance, adding security controls, taking care of availability, and so on.

If we do decide to use a SaaS model, we need to understand that not all SaaS providers offer us the same level of security. Not all SaaS providers follow security best practices such as multi-tenancy (complete separation between customers of the service), protection against infrastructure-based or application-based attacks, audit reports, and security certifications.

Data privacy and data sovereignty

Prior to choosing a public cloud provider (from any of the service models), we need to consult with our data protection officer, our legal department, or an expert on data privacy to check what laws and regulations are required by our organization regarding our industry, our country, and the data we are planning to store or process in the cloud.

Since the data stored in the cloud can (potentially) be replicated around the world, we need to understand whether there are laws that require us to keep our data locally in a specific country.

Whether we serve customers in a specific country or multiple locations (or perhaps globally), we need to know whether a cloud provider has a data center presence in specific countries.

There are scenarios where we have regulation requirements (such as **Payment Card Industry** (**PCI**) and FedRAMP), and we need to build an entire cloud environment to be compliant with such regulations – in this case, we need to check whether the cloud provider has environments compliant with those regulations in specific regions.

One good example is AWS GovCloud and Azure for US Government, which are dedicated cloud environments just for government agencies. Another example is AWS China and Microsoft Azure in China, which are completely separated cloud environments for storing and processing data in China.

For the IaaS and PaaS models, it should not be an issue, since most IaaS or even PaaS services are regional – once we choose a target region, our data will not leave the region (unless we chose a global service or we decided to replicate data between regions to get closer to our customers).

One of the alternatives for making sure our data will not be copied outside a specific region is to encrypt our data, since encryption keys are regional resources, making sure that our data will not be replicated or be available outside a specific region.

For SaaS services, there is no one answer to whether we can keep data sovereignty. Some SaaS providers replicate our data across regions to allow better service availability, or they might store our backups in a different region to better protect our data. The best solution for the IaaS and PaaS services is to read the vendor's documentation.

For SaaS services, other than reading the vendor's documentation, it is strongly recommend consulting with the SaaS vendor and asking specific questions regarding data privacy or data sovereignty prior to signing a contract with SaaS vendors.

Auditing and monitoring

As we previously talked about in *Chapter 6, Monitoring and Auditing of Your Cloud Environments*, auditing is crucial to protect cloud environments, to gain insights about what is going on in your cloud environment, and as part of incident response and forensics if the cloud environment has been breached.

Mature cloud providers will offer you documented APIs to pull activity audit logs to your **Security Information and Event Management (SIEM)** systems for further analysis of who logged into the service and what actions were taken (both successes and failures).

Another type of log is a service log (such as object storage, load balancers, and managed databases). Most mature cloud providers offer us documented APIs to pull those logs.

Another type of audit log is a host log (such as an **Operating System (OS)**, security, and application logs). Look for a cloud provider that offers you a way to pull host logs and store them in a centralized logging service that exposes an API. This will allow us to connect to the API and pull the logs to our SIEM systems for further analysis.

From an infrastructure point of view, look for cloud providers who offer you documented APIs to pull performance data and allow you to anticipate performance issues before you get complaints from your customers.

From an application point of view, look for cloud providers who offer you documented APIs to pull application insights, error logs, and statistics about the number of failed actions inside the system that enable you to ingest data into an **Application Performance Management (APM)** tool.

From a financial point of view, look for cloud providers who offer you documented APIs to pull billing information that enable you to ingest data into cost management tools, generate billing alerts, and so on.

An important thing to consider regarding logs is cost. Some of the services offer us a free tier (such as lasting for 30 days), and if we wish to store logs for a long period of time (for example, due to a regulation requirement), we need to consider the cost.

Another important thing to consider is log retention. Cloud providers (such as SaaS providers) might keep logs for 60–90 days. If we are required to keep logs for a longer period, we need a way to pull those logs and copy them to an external log repository.

Migration capabilities

When evaluating a cloud provider, it is important to review what your migration capabilities are in an on-premises environment or even from hosting on another cloud provider.

Consider topics such as the following:

- **Secure data transfer**: A mechanism for transferring files into cloud storage
- **Database migration**: Managed services to allow transfer of an entire database (including database schema) into a managed service in the cloud, or migration between one database engine to another
- **Virtual machine migration**: The ability to transfer (in either real time or offline) an entire server stack from on-premises to the cloud
- **Lift and shift capabilities**: The ability to migrate existing workloads, as is, assuming the cloud provider supports the same OS or database engine and versions

Authentication

Before using a cloud service, we must consider how are we going to authenticate our internal users or our external customers. We have discussed authentication in *Chapter 5, Effective Strategies to Implement IAM Solutions.*

When evaluating a cloud service, we need to check what authentication mechanisms are available. Some cloud providers offer us internal authentication and authorization capabilities that come built in as part of the cloud solution.

As best practice, we should avoid using cloud services that do not support standard authentication mechanisms, such as Azure **Active Directory** (**AD**) or any of the known SAML-based or OAuth 2.0 protocols, which allows us to federate our existing directory service into the cloud service without having to provision new accounts for our end users.

For external customers, choose solutions that support the OpenID Connect protocol, which allows your customers to authenticate using their personal Facebook, Apple, LinkedIn, Twitter, and other identity providers.

Summary

In this section, we discussed the methods and best practices to consider before choosing a suitable cloud provider.

What is a cloud provider questionnaire?

To evaluate a cloud provider, prior to engagement, it is very common to send the cloud provider a questionnaire, with all the topics your team believes need to be asked, to get familiar with the cloud provider.

Mature cloud providers have, most likely, shared information about their compliance and security controls.

For more information, please refer to the following resources:

AWS CSA Consensus Assessments Initiative Questionnaire (CAIQ):

```
https://d1.awsstatic.com/whitepapers/compliance/CSA_Consensus_
Assessments_Initiative_Questionnaire.pdf
```

Microsoft Azure Responses to Cloud Security Alliance Consensus Assessments Initiative Questionnaire v3.0.1:

```
https://azure.microsoft.com/en-us/resources/microsoft-azure-
responses-to-cloud-security-alliance-consensus-assessments-
initiative-questionnaire-v301/
```

GCP CSA Consensus Assessments Initiative Questionnaire (CAIQ):

```
https://services.google.com/fh/files/misc/sep_2021_caiq_self_
assessment.pdf
```

When reviewing a potential cloud provider, consider the shared responsibility model. The answers of the cloud provider will allow us a clear understanding of what the cloud provider's responsibilities are (for protecting our data) versus our responsibilities (and capabilities) as customers for protecting our data.

Questions are a part of a risk assessment process and they can come from various domains.

I'm open for suggestions, perhaps, we should ask other cloud providers, the following questions:

- **Cloud infrastructure-related**:
  - What is the cloud service model (IaaS, PaaS, and SaaS)?
  - What is the cloud infrastructure provider's name?
  - Where are the cloud provider's data center locations?

- **Architecture-related**:

  - Does the cloud provider offer full multi-tenant separation between customers (compute, storage, database, and networking)?

  - Does the cloud provider offer separation between production and development or test environments (compute, storage, database, and networking)?

- **Network-related**:

  - Does the cloud provider offer site-to-site (or point-to-site) **Virtual Private Network** (**VPN**) connectivity from on-premises (or from anywhere on the internet) to the cloud environment?

  - Does the cloud provider offer a dedicated network connection (such as AWS Direct Connect, Azure ExpressRoute, and Google Cloud Interconnect) from on-premises to the cloud environment?

- **Data-related**:

  - Does the cloud provider have an official privacy policy?

  - Does the cloud provider have a full-time **Data Protection Officer** (**DPO**)?

  - Is the cloud infrastructure service provider compliant with data privacy laws and regulations (such as the **General Data Protection Regulation** (**GDPR**) in Europe and the **California Consumer Privacy Act** (**CCPA**) in California)?

  - Does the cloud provider offer a built-in mechanism for data classification (such as PII, credit card information, or healthcare data)?

  - Does the cloud provider offer documentation on how to deploy and protect PCI environments (such as containing, storing, or processing credit card information)?

  - Does the cloud provider offer documentation on how to deploy and protect environments containing personal information (such as European citizens' information as defined by the GDPR)?

  - Does the cloud provider offer documentation on how to deploy and protect environments containing healthcare information (such as US healthcare information as defined by the **Health Insurance Portability and Accountability Act** (**HIPAA**)?

- **API-related** (the ability to pull logs from the cloud provider):

  - Does the cloud offer documented APIs for pulling audit logs to a SIEM system?

  - Does the cloud offer documented APIs for pulling performance data?

  - Does the cloud offer documented APIs for pulling application insights?

  - Does the cloud offer documented APIs for deploying new environments in an automated way (such as infrastructure as code)?

- **Authentication and authorization-related**:

  - Does the cloud provider support standard authentication and authorization protocols for connecting from on-premises or any type of external environment to the cloud (protocols such as SAML and OAuth 2.0)?

  - Does the cloud provider support authentication protocols (such as OpenID Connect) for authenticating external identities (such as Facebook, Apple, LinkedIn, and Twitter)?

  - Does the cloud provider support **Role-Based Access Control** (**RBAC**)?

  - Does the cloud provider allow managing permissions to cloud resources based on **Identity Provider** (**IdP**) groups (such as Azure AD groups) and match groups to roles?

  - Does the cloud provider support **Multi-Factor Authentication** (**MFA**)?

  - Does the cloud contain default passwords? If so, can we disable or replace all default passwords?

  - Does the cloud contain default accounts (such as administrator and root)? If so, can we disable or remove those accounts?

- **Session management**:

  - Does the cloud provider support automatic session disconnection after 15 minutes of inactivity?

  - Does the cloud provider generate random and time-restricted session IDs for each identity authenticated to the service?

  - Does the cloud provider enforce session disconnection at the end of each session?

  - Does the cloud provider enforce a single session for each authenticated identity?

- **Encryption at transit**:

  - Does the cloud provider enforce encryption at rest using secured protocols (such as TLS 1.2 or above) for each of the supported services?

  - If the cloud provider is exposing HTTPS services to the internet, do all services (or URLs) achieve a score of A+ in an SSL Labs test (`https://www.ssllabs.com/ssltest`)?

- **Encryption at rest**:

  - Does the cloud provider offer encryption at rest for databases?

  - Does the cloud provider offer encryption at rest for object storage?

  - Does the cloud provider offer encryption at rest for file-sharing protocols (such as **Network File Transfer (NFS)** or **Common Internet File Transfer (CIFS)/Server Message Block (SMB)**)?

  - For each of the supported mechanisms for encryption at rest, does the cloud provider offer a key rotation mechanism?

  - For each of the supported mechanisms for encryption at rest, does the cloud provider support customer-managed keys?

- **Incident response**:

  - Does the cloud provider have built-in mechanisms to detect security incidents on its infrastructure or the infrastructure serving its customers?

  - Does the cloud provider have a documented incident response process?

  - Does the cloud provider have a dedicated incident response team?

  - What is the cloud provider's SLA for handling security incidents?

  - What is the cloud provider's SLA for handling critical vulnerabilities?

- **Penetration testing and security assessment**:

  - Has the cloud provider conducted a security assessment by an external auditor in the past 12 months?

  - If the cloud provider conducted security assessments in the past, were all the vulnerabilities fixed?

  - Has the cloud provider conducted penetration testing by an external auditor in the past 12 months?

- If the cloud provider conducted penetration testing in the past, were all the vulnerabilities fixed?

- Will the cloud provider allow its customers to schedule penetration testing?

- **Secure development life cycle**:

  - Does the cloud provider conduct ongoing training for its employees (and its third-party suppliers) regarding secure development?

  - Does the cloud provider follow known secure development life cycle methodology (such as the Microsoft Security Development Lifecycle, NIST Secure Software Development Framework, or some other methodology)?

  - Does the cloud provider implement **Static Application Security Testing** (**SAST**) as part of its secure development life cycle?

  - Does the cloud provider implement **Dynamic Application Security Testing** (**DAST**) as part of its secure development life cycle?

  - Does the cloud provider implement **Interactive Application Security Testing** (**IAST**) as part of its secure development life cycle?

  - Does the cloud provider implement **Software Composition Analysis (SCA)** as part of its secure development life cycle?

  - How does the cloud provider store secrets (such as API keys, privileged credentials, and SSH keys) as part of its infrastructure and code?

  - What security controls are been implemented by the cloud provider for handling file uploads?

- **Audit and monitoring**:

  - Does the cloud provider keep an audit trail of every login attempt to its services (both successes and failures)?

  - Does the cloud provider keep an audit trail of actions done on its services (both successes and failures)?

  - What records are saved by the cloud provider as part of its logging process?

  - Does the cloud provider keep a record of actions done by its own system administrators (including third-party suppliers), with access to customers' infrastructure and data?

- **Business continuity**:

  - Does the cloud provider share information about service outages and historical information about past outages?

  - Does the cloud provider have documented business continuity and disaster recovery processes?

  - What is the cloud provider's **Recovery Time Objective (RTO)**?

  - What is the cloud provider's **Recovery Point Objective (RPO)**?

  - Does the cloud provider have documented change management processes?

  - Does the cloud provider have documented backup processes?

- **Compliance-related**:

  - What cloud and cloud security-related ISO standard does the cloud provider have from the past 12 months?

  - Has the cloud provider published a CSA **Security, Trust, Assurance and Risk (STAR)** report?

  - Has the cloud provider published a SOC 2 report in the past 12 months?

  - Does the cloud provider have a documented information security policy?

  - Does the cloud provider have a dedicated **Chief Information Security Officer (CISO)/Chief Strategy Officer (CSO)**?

  - What logical controls are implemented by the cloud provider to protect its infrastructure?

  - What logical controls are offered by the cloud provider to protect customers' data?

  - What logical controls have been enforced on cloud providers employees with access to customers' infrastructure and data (such as anti-malware, device control, full disk encryption, MFA, and a VPN client)?

  - What physical controls are implemented by the cloud provider to protect its data centers?

  - Does the cloud provider perform an ongoing vulnerability assessment?

  - Does the cloud provider perform ongoing patch management?

  - Does the cloud provider's infrastructure (compute, storage, and network) comply with known hardening standards (such as CIS benchmarks, NIST, and more)?

  - Does the cloud provider conduct ongoing training for its employees (and its third-party suppliers) regarding information security and data privacy?

The CSA **Cloud Controls Matrix (CCM)** is a cybersecurity control framework for cloud computing. For more information, please refer to the following resources:

`https://cloudsecurityalliance.org/research/cloud-controls-matrix/`

The What, Why, and How on Answering Security Questionnaires:

`https://learn.g2.com/security-questionnaire`

7 Cloud Service Evaluation Criteria to Help You Choose the Right Cloud Service Provider:

`https://www.threatstack.com/blog/7-cloud-service-evaluation-criteria-to-help-you-choose-the-right-cloud-service-provider`

8 criteria to ensure you select the right cloud service provider:

`https://www.cloudindustryforum.org/content/8-criteria-ensure-you-select-right-cloud-service-provider`

Summary

In this section, we have suggested many questions to assist organizations in the reviewing process of cloud providers. Most of the topics can be answered by reviewing mature cloud providers' SOC2 Type 2 reports or the CSA Cloud Control Matrix (as explained in detail in *Chapter 9, Handling Compliance and Regulation*). I strongly recommend conducting a cloud provider assessment – a questionnaire is one of the effective ways to find out the maturity level and transparency of cloud providers.

Tips for contracts with cloud providers

A good contract protects your organization when engaging with cloud providers, since you do not have physical control over your data. You do not always have the ability to influence contracts with cloud providers.

To consume IaaS services, all you need is a credit card number. As a small organization, you will get the same contract as all other customers receive, and once you agree with the contractual terms, you cannot make any changes.

If you are able to commit to a large consumption of cloud services, you may contact your IaaS provider and sign an agreement, such as the AWS **Enterprise Discount Program (EDP)** or Azure EA agreements, to be able to negotiate pricing terms.

To use SaaS services, you sign a contract with your chosen SaaS provider, where you have the ability to influence the contract terms – much more than just pricing topics.

In this section, we will review common topics that should be negotiated and be embedded in contracts with cloud providers:

- **Exit terms**:
  - What are the customers' options for terminating a contract?
  - Are there any penalties from the customers' side for terminating a contract?

- **Data location**:
  - Does the contract specify what the exact data location is (that is, the country)?
  - Does the contract contain a **data processing agreement** for setting where customers' data is located and whether data can be processed outside a specific country?
  - Does the contract specify how the cloud provider will protect customers' data?

- **Data deletion**:
  - Is the cloud provider obligated to erase customers' data when terminating a contract?
  - What data erase standards does the cloud provider use when terminating a contract with its customers?
  - How long will the cloud provider keep customers' data after terminating a contract?

- **Data export**:
  - Is there an obligation from the cloud provider's side to return customers' data after contract termination?
  - What options does the cloud provider offer its customers to export backups of their data after terminating a contract?

- **Incident response**:
  - Does the contract specify what the cloud provider's obligations are regarding handling security incidents for the systems that store or process customers' data?
  - What is the cloud provider's SLA for fixing security vulnerabilities on the systems that store or process customers' data?
  - What is the cloud provider's SLA for notifying its customers about security incidents that affect the systems that store or process customers' data?
  - Does the contract specify what the cloud provider's third-party suppliers' obligations are regarding systems that store or process customers' data?

- Does the contract contain information about security awareness, privacy, and secure development for the cloud provider's employees and third-party providers?

For more information, please refer to the following resources:

Custom terms and pricing in AWS Marketplace:

```
https://aws.amazon.com/marketplace/features/custom-terms-
pricing/
```

Azure EA agreements and amendments:

```
https://docs.microsoft.com/en-us/azure/cost-management-
billing/manage/ea-portal-agreements
```

Summary

In this section, we have reviewed the important topics that should appear in any contract with cloud providers in order to protect customers' data while being stored or processed by them.

Conducting penetration testing in cloud environments

One of the ways to raise our assurance with a cloud provider is to conduct a penetration test to measure the effectiveness of their security controls.

In the SaaS model, a penetration test allows us to measure how the SaaS provider protects our data. In the IaaS model, a penetration test allows us to measure the effectiveness of the security controls we have implemented. In IaaS environments, we are in charge of the OS layer and the network environment around the virtual machines or containers.

In PaaS environments, specifically in serverless (or **Function as a Service (FaaS)**), we are not in charge of the lower layer of the OS; however, since we import our code, we are in charge of making sure we follow a secure development life cycle.

In SaaS environments, we are only in charge of inserting data and controlling access to the service.

If we expose a service to the internet or use a SaaS service, we need to evaluate topics such as the following:

- Is the service allowing only the minimum number of ports/protocols to the public internet?

- Is the service enforcing proper authentication controls to make sure only authenticated identities can access it?

- Is the service enforcing proper authorization controls to make sure authenticated identities have the minimum amount of access required to achieve their tasks?

- Is the service performing proper input validation to make sure all data inserted into the system is sanitized and the system is protected from injection attacks, cross-site scripting, and any other attacks originating from improper input validation?

- Is the service performing an escape before inserting data into a backend database – data that potentially can return to the end customer and impact them?

- Is the service keeping an audit log of any access attempt and request performed by its end customer?

A penetration test, together with a vulnerability assessment, allow us to measure the service security controls; however, we must always remember that cloud environments are different than on-premises.

By design, cloud environments are public and shared with many customers.

We must follow the cloud provider's terms of use. Unless we are using a SaaS service from one of the hyper-scale cloud providers, the chances are that the SaaS service is deployed above one of the hyper-scale IaaS providers, meaning we must follow the entire supply chain – both the lower layer IaaS and upper layer SaaS providers' terms of use.

Mature cloud providers build their services in a fully multi-tenant model, meaning that each customer will have its own dedicated infrastructure (such as servers, database, storage, and network separation).

It is not that rare to come across a SaaS provider that offers us their services while sharing resources between their customers (such as sharing virtual servers and databases).

In scenarios where the SaaS provider hasn't embraced modern cloud architecture (that is, multi-tenancy), one customer being targeted by an attacker will increase the chances of our organization being impacted while working with the same SaaS provider.

Most IaaS providers will allow you to run security tools against virtual servers in your IaaS environment, port scanning, or application layer tests (such as injection attacks) against virtual servers in your IaaS environment.

SaaS providers will allow you to conduct security tests against your environment, assuming the SaaS was originally built in a multi-tenant environment.

It is likely that no cloud provider will allow you to run denial-of-service-type attacks against the cloud infrastructure or any type of attempt to breach or impact other customers' environments or resources.

For more information, please refer to the following resources:

AWS – *Penetration Testing*:

`https://aws.amazon.com/security/penetration-testing/`

Azure – *Penetration Testing Rules of Engagement*:

`https://www.microsoft.com/en-us/msrc/pentest-rules-of-engagement`

Google – *Cloud Security FAQ*:

`https://support.google.com/cloud/answer/6262505`

Cloud Penetration Testing Playbook:

`https://cloudsecurityalliance.org/artifacts/cloud-penetration-testing-playbook`

Summary

In this section, we have reviewed the concept of penetration testing, which allows you to test the effectiveness of the cloud service security controls.

The most important thing to remember is to always follow the cloud provider's terms of use.

Summary

In this chapter, we focused on engagement with cloud providers. We reviewed topics that will assist an organization to choose a cloud provider (always focusing on business goals).

We then reviewed the cloud provider questionnaire, which allows organizations to get familiar with and select mature cloud providers once they have decided to sign up with one.

We reviewed important topics that should appear in any contract with a cloud provider, ensuring that both the legal and purchase departments have a solid understanding of what to look out for in the contractual phase.

Finally, we reviewed our ability as customers to measure the effectiveness of cloud environments (whether they are IaaS environments that we deploy and control, or SaaS offerings that we use) by conducting penetration testing on cloud environments, and the importance of following the cloud vendor's terms of use.

Understanding the topics discussed in this chapter will give customers confidence in using cloud services that store or process data outside their data centers.

In the next chapter, we will review hybrid clouds (such as the hybrid cloud strategy, identity management, network connectivity, storage and compute-related services in hybrid cloud environments, and monitoring and security-related topics).

Section 4: Advanced Use of Cloud Services

On completion of this part, you will have a solid understanding of the advanced use of cloud services.

This part of the book comprises the following chapters:

- *Chapter 11, Managing Hybrid Clouds*
- *Chapter 12, Managing Multi-Cloud Environments*
- *Chapter 13, Security in Large-Scale Environments*

11
Managing Hybrid Clouds

In the previous chapters, we covered cloud infrastructure fundamentals, common threats in cloud environments, how to handle compliance and regulation, and how to engage with cloud providers. In this chapter, we will discuss hybrid clouds.

A hybrid cloud is a combination of an on-premises data center or private cloud and a public cloud environment.

Hybrid cloud is considered an extension of our local data center and, as such, helps us in minimizing the efforts required to control, maintain, and secure our infrastructure and services across the entire hybrid solution.

We are not only extending our local data center infrastructure to the cloud, but we are also extending our security boundaries to the cloud, so we wish to have a central way to control security operations in a hybrid architecture.

In this chapter, we will cover the following topics:

- Hybrid cloud strategy
- Identity management over hybrid cloud environments
- Network architecture for hybrid cloud environments
- Storage services for hybrid cloud environments

- Compute services for hybrid cloud environments
- Securing hybrid cloud environments

Technical requirements

For this chapter, you will need to have a solid understanding of concepts such as identity management, network, storage, compute, and how to secure cloud environments.

Hybrid cloud strategy

Before using the hybrid cloud architecture, we need to ask ourselves, what are we trying to achieve through a hybrid cloud solution?

Cloud-native solutions for hybrid environments have the following benefits:

- Integration of both on-premises resources with cloud resources
- Built-in integration with cloud services
- Virtually unlimited capacity (compute and storage) for storing logs and running correlations between events
- Virtually unlimited storage capacity for storing data (for backups, regulation compliance, disaster recovery, and more)
- Support for federated identity management (allows a single identity to access resources in hybrid environments)

Let's look at some of the most common use cases for choosing hybrid cloud solutions.

Cloud bursting

The idea behind cloud bursting is to allow applications that run on-premises to burst into the cloud when there is a need for extra resource capacity – both planned and unplanned.

Some examples of cloud bursting are as follows:

- A large demand for cloud resources for a short period during the Black Friday weekend until Cyber Monday
- A campaign where a phone company ships a new product to the market
- Large batch processing, such as genetic research

Backup and disaster recovery

The cloud is an excellent solution for backup and/or disaster recovery for your on-premises environments. It has (almost) no limitations for storing long-term backups, and it is highly suitable for building entire environments (when using **Infrastructure as Code (IaC)**, as explained in *Chapter 13, Security in Large-Scale Environments*) within minutes to serve as disaster recovery.

Archive and data retention

Regulation might require us to archive logs and retain them for a long period (years).

The cloud offers us a cheap solution for archiving storage tiers.

Distributed data processing

If there is a need for processing huge amounts of data (such as *Apache Hadoop*), high-performance computing (such as weather forecasting), or machine learning (such as video analysis), the cloud can be a perfect solution.

Whenever we do not have the necessary resources in our local data center, we can deploy clusters in the cloud, perform our data analysis process, and, by the end of the process, erase all the unneeded resources to save money.

Application modernization

To avoid the on-premises and legacy infrastructure constraints, the cloud allows us to re-architect our applications and switch to modern architectures such as microservices or even become serverless.

Some workloads can be migrated to the cloud (such as modern developments), while other workloads must remain on-premises (due to regulations that force us to keep data on-premises) – such a mixed environment creates a hybrid architecture.

The cloud strategy helps organizations decide what to do with their existing applications and systems:

- **Retire**: Decide which applications are no longer needed.
- **Retain**: Decide which applications are needed but the migration to the cloud will be too complex and should remain on-premises.
- **Replace**: Decide which applications can be replaced with managed services or SaaS solutions.

- **Rehost**: Decide which applications can be *lift and shift* with minimal effort to the cloud

- **Re-platform**: Decide which applications need minimal changes to migrate to the cloud (for example, an OS upgrade).

- **Refactor**: Decide which application requires significant modifications to migrate to the cloud (for example, switch from a monolith to a microservice architecture).

- **Reimagine**: Decide which applications need to be rebuilt from scratch to benefit from cloud advantages (such as elasticity, multi-region, and more).

For more information, please refer to the following resources:

AWS database migration strategy: `https://docs.aws.amazon.com/prescriptive-guidance/latest/strategy-database-migration/planning-phase.html`

What is a hybrid cloud strategy?: `https://www.vmware.com/topics/glossary/content/hybrid-cloud-strategy`

Hybrid cloud: Enabling the rotation to the New: `https://www.accenture.com/us-en/insights/cloud/hybrid-cloud-strategy`

Summary

A hybrid cloud strategy helps organizations decide what to do with existing applications and set security policies for storing data in the cloud. Hybrid cloud strategies help organizations leverage cloud advantages (such as scale and short purchase processes), while still keeping legacy applications on-premises.

Identity management over hybrid cloud environments

One of the first things to decide on, before using the hybrid cloud, is identity management. Organizations would like to keep their existing identity provider, have a single identity for each of their end users (while preserving existing credentials), and still be able to access resources in the cloud.

Identity management in hybrid cloud environments can be split into the following areas:

- **Directory replication**: Extending the on-premises directory into the cloud with either one-way replication or synchronization between the two.

- **Federated authentication**: An on-premises component brokers the user authentication to the cloud using SAML, OIDC, or some other protocol.

Some of the benefits of using centralized identity management are as follows:

- A single place to provision or de-provision identities

- Reusing strong credentials and authentication capabilities

- Centralization of access audits

- Avoid supporting every cloud identity mechanism

How to manage identity over hybrid AWS environments

On-premises environments can have various types of identity providers – from **Active Directory** (**AD**) (for Windows-based applications) to LDAP-based identity directories (mostly for Linux-based applications). An organization may also consider **Security Assertion Markup Language** (**SAML**)-based authentication for cloud-native services.

Amazon supports the following identity management solutions for hybrid environments:

- **AWS IAM with AD Federation Services** (**ADFS**): Gives you the ability to use AWS IAM SAML-based directory service to manage your on-premises identities (from the on-premises AD).

- **AWS Managed Microsoft AD**: A fully managed AD allows you to manage user identities from on-premises AD or a local LDAP provider (usually for Linux-based applications).

- **AD Connector**: A proxy service that allows you to manage AWS services such as Amazon WorkSpaces, Amazon EC2, and more using the on-premises AD.

- **AWS SSO**: This allows you to centrally create identities across AWS organizations or bring identities from Microsoft AD or other identity providers (such as Okta, OneLogin, and more).

For more information, please refer to the following resources:

What is AWS Directory Service?: https://docs.aws.amazon.com/directoryservice/latest/admin-guide/what_is.html

AWS Federated Authentication with Active Directory Federation Services (AD FS): https://aws.amazon.com/blogs/security/aws-federated-authentication-with-active-directory-federation-services-ad-fs/

AWS Single Sign-On FAQs https://aws.amazon.com/single-sign-on/faqs/

How to manage identity over hybrid Azure environments

Azure supports the following identity management solutions for hybrid environments:

- **Azure AD**: SAML-based authentication. When synced with on-premises AD (using Azure AD Connect), you can have a single identity with access (according to business needs) to both on-premises resources and cloud-based resources (such as Azure resources and any SAML-based cloud service).

- **Azure AD Domain Services**: A role that allows legacy protocols such as Kerberos (for Windows-based applications) or LDAP (for Linux-based applications) to be integrated.

For more information, please refer to the following resources:

Azure Active Directory integrations with authentication and synchronization protocols: https://docs.microsoft.com/en-us/azure/active-directory/fundamentals/auth-sync-overview

What authentication and verification methods are available in Azure Active Directory?: https://docs.microsoft.com/en-us/azure/active-directory/authentication/concept-authentication-methods

How to manage identity over GCP hybrid environments

Google supports the following identity management solutions for hybrid environments:

- **Google Cloud Identity with AD Federation Services (AD FS)**: Gives you the ability to use SAML-based directory services to manage your on-premises identities (from the on-premises AD) or LDAP (for Linux-based applications).

- **Google Managed Service for Microsoft AD**: A fully managed AD that allows you to manage user identities from on-premises AD.

For more information, please refer to the following resources:

Authenticating corporate users in a hybrid environment: `https://cloud.google.com/architecture/authenticating-corporate-users-in-a-hybrid-environment`

Federating Google Cloud with Active Directory: `https://cloud.google.com/architecture/identity/federating-gcp-with-active-directory-introduction`

Deploying Active Directory Federation Services: `https://cloud.google.com/managed-microsoft-ad/docs/deploy-adfs`

Best practices for managing identities in hybrid environments

Since identity management follows the same concepts over different hybrid cloud scenarios, it is recommended to follow these best practices:

- Always pass authentication information through secured protocols – from TLS for SAML-based authentication, through Kerberos inside site-to-site VPN tunnels (over IPsec), to LDAP over SSL (LDAPS).

- Enable **Multi-Factor Authentication (MFA)** for any account with privileges to access the cloud environment.

- When you're granting access to resources, always follow the concept of *least privilege*.

- Enable auditing for all login events (both success and fail) and send the logs to your preferred SIEM system.

- Create rules on your SIEM system to alert you of anomalous behavior (such as root or administrator login, multiple failed logins, and more).

- Use dedicated services such as **Amazon GuardDuty**, **Microsoft Defender for Cloud**, **Google Security Command Center**, and more to detect identity-based attacks.

- When possible, use **Identity Management** (**IDM**) systems for provisioning, de-provisioning, and access (permissions) management over your entire hybrid environment.

Summary

Selecting authentication and authorization methods allows organizations to reuse their existing identity providers and keep a single identity for each of their end users in a central repository.

Network architecture for hybrid cloud environments

The second important thing to consider when building a hybrid architecture is how to connect from the on-premises environment to the cloud.

The recommended way to connect to cloud environments, considering the cloud as an extension of the local data center, is to use a secure and permanent network connection – either site-to-site VPN or a dedicated connection.

A secured and permanent connection will allow you to set access control (layer 4 firewall rules) between on-premises segments and cloud segments and retain access to resources in the cloud (or allow access from cloud resources to the on-premises environment) in terms of business needs. The following are some of the solutions that you can choose depending upon the specific situation you are dealing with:

- You should choose a VPN solution in the following situations:

  - You need a fast deployment time.

  - You are OK passing an IPsec tunnel over the internet.

  - You do not have bandwidth requirements.

  - You are looking for a low-cost solution.

- You should choose to interconnect (**AWS Direct Connect (DX)**, **Azure ExpressRoute**, **Google Cloud Interconnect**) in the following situations:

  - You have bandwidth requirements (you need a solution with a fixed bandwidth).

  - You would like to have **Service-Level Agreements (SLAs)** on the network connectivity.

  - You would like to have private connectivity between your on-premises environment and the cloud environment.

How to connect the on-premises environment to AWS

Amazon offers the following services to allow hybrid connectivity:

- **AWS Managed Site-to-Site VPN**: A fully managed VPN service that provides connectivity from the customer gateway (customer side of the VPN) over an IPsec tunnel.

- **AWS VPN CloudHub**: A hub and spoke model that uses AWS-managed VPNs to connect Amazon VPC to multiple customer data centers, each with its own IPsec tunnels.

- **AWS Transit Gateway and VPN**: A service that allows single-network connectivity (hub) over a VPN tunnel between the on-premises environment and multiple VPCs in the same region.

- **AWS DX**: A dedicated connection from the on-premises environment to one or more VPCs in the same region in a pre-defined network bandwidth.

- **AWS DX and AWS Transit Gateway**: A dedicated connection from the on-premises environment to one or more VPCs in up to three regions in a pre-defined network bandwidth.

The following are some best practices to keep in mind:

- Always think about **Classless Inter-Domain Routing (CIDR)** before configuring network segments in the cloud to avoid IP conflicts between the on-premises environment and the cloud.

- Use **network ACLs**, **security groups**, and **route tables** to configure network access rules between the on-premises environment and the resources inside your VPCs.

- For redundancy, plan for failover connectivity – from multiple VPN connections or redundant interconnects – using different network providers or a combination of interconnect and VPN connectivity.

- Use a dual site-to-site VPN connection, along with an AWS transit gateway, for connection redundancy between your on-premises environment and the cloud.

- Use multiple **DX** connections with the DX gateway so that you have connection redundancy between your on-premises environment and the cloud.

For more information, please refer to the following resources:

Hybrid network connection: `https://docs.aws.amazon.com/whitepapers/latest/hybrid-connectivity/hybrid-network-connection.html`

AWS Transit Gateway and VPN: `https://docs.aws.amazon.com/whitepapers/latest/aws-vpc-connectivity-options/aws-transit-gateway-vpn.html`

AWS Direct Connect and AWS Transit Gateway: `https://docs.aws.amazon.com/whitepapers/latest/aws-vpc-connectivity-options/aws-direct-connect-aws-transit-gateway.html`

AWS VPN CloudHub: `https://docs.aws.amazon.com/whitepapers/latest/aws-vpc-connectivity-options/aws-vpn-cloudhub.html`

How to connect the on-premises environment to Azure

Azure offers the following services to allow hybrid connectivity:

- **Azure VPN Gateway**: A fully managed VPN service that provides connectivity from the on-premises environment to the cloud over IPsec tunnels.

- **Azure ExpressRoute**: A dedicated connection from the on-premises environment to one or more Azure VNets in a pre-defined network bandwidth.

- **Hub and spoke network connectivity**: A hub and spoke model that uses Azure VPN Gateway to connect the on-premises environment to multiple VNets using a single IPsec tunnel.

The following are some best practices to consider:

- Always think about CIDR before configuring network segments in the cloud to avoid IP conflicts between the on-premises environment and the cloud.

- Use **Network Security Groups (NSGs)** to configure network access rules between the on-premises environment and the resources inside your VNets.

- For redundancy, plan for failover connectivity – from multiple VPN connections or a redundant ExpressRoute using different network providers, or a combination of ExpressRoute and VPN connectivity.

- Use multiple site-to-site VPN connections for connection redundancy between your on-premises environment and the cloud.

- Configure multiple connections from your on-premises environment (through your service provider's network) to the Azure ExpressRoute circuit for connection redundancy between your on-premises environment and the cloud.

For more information, please refer to the following resource:

Connect an on-premises network to Azure: `https://docs.microsoft.com/en-us/azure/architecture/reference-architectures/hybrid-networking/`

How to connect the on-premises environment to GCP

GCP offers the following services to allow hybrid connectivity:

- **Google Cloud VPN**: A fully managed VPN service that provides connectivity from the on-premises environment to the cloud over an IPsec tunnel.

- **Google Cloud Interconnect**: A dedicated connection from the on-premises environment to one or more VPCs in a pre-defined network bandwidth.

The following are some best practices to consider:

- Always think about CIDR before configuring network segments in the cloud to avoid IP conflicts between the on-premises environment and the cloud.

- Use **firewall rules** to configure network access rules between the on-premises environment and the resources inside your VPCs.

- For redundancy, plan for failover connectivity – from multiple VPN connections or redundant Cloud Interconnect using different network providers, or a combination of Cloud Interconnect and VPN connectivity.

- Use a **High-Availability (HA)** VPN for connection redundancy between your on-premises environment and the cloud.

- Use **Dedicated Interconnect** for connection redundancy between your on-premises environment and the cloud.

For more information, please refer to the following resource:

Hybrid and multi-cloud network topologies: `https://cloud.google.com/architecture/hybrid-and-multi-cloud-network-topologies`

Summary

According to your business requirements, you can have a secured and redundant connection between your on-premises environment and the cloud.

Storage services for hybrid cloud environments

Now that we have decided on an identity management and network topology, the next thing we need to consider is how to use hybrid clouds for data transfer and storage.

In this section, we will review the various options for data transfer.

When considering hybrid storage connectivity, consider the following:

- Bandwidth/latency/time to transfer
- Use of public versus private connectivity
- Moving files versus file synchronization
- Encryption requirements (in transit and at rest)
- Access control for a hybrid solution
- Supported protocols (NFS, CIFS, and more)

How to connect to storage services over AWS hybrid environments

Amazon offers the following services to transfer data to the cloud in a hybrid architecture:

- **AWS Storage Gateway**: A virtual appliance for installing on-premises environments that allows access from the on-premises environments to an object storage service (Amazon S3/Glacier), file storage (**Amazon FSx for Windows**), block storage (**Amazon EBS**), and the backup service (**AWS Backup**)

- **AWS DataSync**: A data transfer service between the on-premises environment and object storage (**Amazon S3**), NFS file storage (**Amazon EFS**), and SMB file storage (**Amazon FSx for Windows**)

- **AWS Transfer Family**: A file transfer service between the on-premises environment and the object storage (**Amazon S3**) or NFS file storage (**Amazon EFS**), above the SFTP, FTPS, and FTP protocols

The following are some best practices to consider:

- Use **AWS Storage Gateway** when you need constant connectivity between the on-premises environment and your AWS storage services.

- Use **AWS DataSync** when you need to copy files to/from the cloud.

- Use **AWS Transfer Family** when you would like to copy files to the cloud over SFTP or FTPS protocols.

- Always choose secured protocols (such as TLS, SFTP, or FTPS) when transferring files to the cloud.

- Always configure IAM permissions on cloud resources, according to your business needs.

- Enable auditing on any access to cloud resources.

- Encrypt data at rest when it's stored in the cloud.

For more information, please refer to the following resources:

AWS Storage Gateway FAQs: `https://aws.amazon.com/storagegateway/faqs/`

Back up your on-premises applications to the cloud using AWS Storage Gateway: `https://aws.amazon.com/blogs/storage/back-up-your-on-premises-applications-to-the-cloud-using-aws-storage-gateway/`

How AWS DataSync works: `https://docs.aws.amazon.com/datasync/latest/userguide/how-datasync-works.html`

How to connect to storage services over Azure hybrid environments

Azure offers the following services to transfer data to the cloud in a hybrid architecture:

- **Azure Data Box Gateway**: A device for installing on-premises environments that allows you to copy data from the on-premises environment to Azure Storage using the NFS or SMB protocol.

- **Azure Data Factory**: An **Extract-Transform-Load** (**ETL**) solution for copying files to services such as Azure Storage, Azure SQL, Azure HDInsight, and more.

- **Azure File Sync**: A data copy service that's installed as an agent on Windows machines and allows you to copy files over the SMB or NFS protocol to Azure Storage.

The following are some best practices to consider:

- Use **Azure Data Box Gateway** when you need a long-term archive of your data or for bulk data transfer.

- Use **Azure Data Factory** when you need to create a process for moving data to/from the cloud to services such as Azure Storage, Azure SQL, Azure Data Lake Storage, and more.

- Use **Azure File Sync** when you need to copy (or sync) files to Azure Storage.

- Always choose secured protocols (such as TLS) when you're transferring files to the cloud.

- Always configure permissions on cloud resources, according to your business needs.

- Enable auditing on any access to cloud resources.

- Encrypt data at rest when it's stored in the cloud.

For more information, please refer to the following resources:

Use cases for Azure Data Box Gateway: `https://docs.microsoft.com/en-us/azure/databox-gateway/data-box-gateway-use-cases`

What is Azure Data Factory?: `https://docs.microsoft.com/en-us/azure/data-factory/introduction`

What is Azure File Sync?: `https://docs.microsoft.com/en-us/azure/storage/file-sync/file-sync-introduction`

How to connect to storage services over GCP hybrid environments

GCP offers a transfer service for on-premises data – a software service that allows you to transfer large amounts of data from an on-premises environment to Google Cloud Storage.

The following are some best practices to consider:

- Always choose secured protocols (such as TLS) when transferring files to the cloud.
- Always configure permissions on cloud resources according to your business needs.
- Enable auditing on any access to cloud resources.
- Encrypt **data at rest** when it's stored in the cloud.

For more information, please refer to the following resource:

Transfer service for on-premises data overview: `https://cloud.google.com/storage-transfer/docs/on-prem-overview`

Summary

In this section, we reviewed the various options that AWS, Azure, and GCP offer for transferring data from on-premises environments to the cloud in a hybrid cloud scenario.

Compute services for hybrid cloud environments

The hybrid cloud architecture is not just limited to connecting on-premises environments to the cloud for resource consumption. It can also be used in scenarios where an organization would like to keep its data locally (due to regulatory restrictions or network latency) while still benefitting from cloud capabilities and, perhaps sometime in the future, be able to migrate data and resources to the cloud.

Using compute services over AWS hybrid environments

Amazon offers the following services in a local deployment topology:

- **AWS Outposts**: A fully managed service that contains the same type of compute, storage, database, and networking capabilities that are deployed on-premises in the shape of a physical rack

- **Amazon ECS Anywhere**: Gives you the ability to deploy Amazon ECS on-premises (same capabilities and APIs as the cloud version)

- **Amazon EKS Anywhere**: Gives you the ability to deploy **Amazon Kubernetes Service** (**EKS**) on-premises (same capabilities as the cloud version)

The following are some best practices to consider:

- Connect the local service (AWS Outposts, ECS Anywhere, or EKS Anywhere) to an AWS Region close to your physical location.

- Make sure there is network connectivity between your local data center (where you deployed the preceding services locally) and the AWS Region.

- Use **AWS Outposts** when you would like to have AWS services (EC2, EBS, RDS, and more) deployed locally to make sure your data does not leave your data center (or your country).

- Use **VPC**, **security groups**, and **Local Gateway** (**LGW**) to restrict access between your on-premises data center resources and the resources that have been deployed inside AWS Outposts.

- Use **encrypted protocols** (such as TLS) between your local data center and the AWS services you've deployed locally (AWS Outposts, ECS Anywhere, and EKS Anywhere).

- Encrypt **data at rest** for resources that are deployed inside AWS Outposts (the same way you would do in the cloud).

- Use **Amazon ECS Anywhere** to deploy development environments or small-scale production ECS environments locally based on your ECS capabilities and APIs, and then burst to the cloud to have the full scale of the Amazon ECS service.

- Use **Amazon EKS** Anywhere to deploy development environments or small-scale production Kubernetes environments locally based on your EKS capabilities and then burst to the cloud to have the full scale of the Amazon EKS service.

- Use minimal **IAM permissions** for all AWS resources that are deployed locally (the same way you would do in the cloud).

- Use **AWS CloudTrail** to monitor the activity of all AWS resources that are deployed locally (the same way you would do in the cloud).

For more information, please refer to the following resources:

AWS Outposts User Guide: `https://docs.aws.amazon.com/outposts/latest/userguide/outposts.pdf`

Amazon ECS Anywhere FAQs: `https://aws.amazon.com/ecs/anywhere/faqs/`

Amazon EKS Anywhere FAQs: `https://aws.amazon.com/eks/eks-anywhere/faqs/`

Using compute services over Azure hybrid environments

Azure offers the following services in a local deployment topology:

- **Azure Stack Hub**: A fully managed service containing the same type of compute, storage, database, and networking capabilities that are deployed on-premises in the shape of a physical rack

- **Azure Arc**: A service that allows unified management of your resources – both on Azure and on-premises (configuring Azure Policy and managing VMs, Kubernetes clusters, and databases from a single console)

The following are some best practices to consider:

- Use **Azure Stack Hub** when you would like to have Azure services (VM, Azure Managed Disks, Azure Blob Storage, and more) deployed locally to make sure your data does not leave your data center (or your country).

- Use Azure Stack Hub's built-in network ACLs to restrict access between your on-premises data center resources and resources that are deployed inside Azure Stack Hub.

- Encrypt all data in transit using the **TLS protocol** when you're passing traffic between Azure Stack Hub and your local data center.

- Connect **Azure Stack Hub** to Azure AD or AD FS to configure minimal role-based access control to resources inside Azure Stack Hub.

- Use **Microsoft Defender for Endpoint** to protect VMs that are deployed inside Azure Stack Hub and make sure that you keep the antivirus up to date.

- Use Azure Arc for the following scenarios:

  - Asset management for all your resources (VMs, Kubernetes, and databases)

  - Centrally configuring role-based access controls for both Azure resources and on-premises resources

  - Centrally configuring policies using **Azure Policy**, both on VMs and Kubernetes clusters

  - Updating security patches on servers, both on Azure and on-premises

  - Protecting your servers using **Microsoft Defender for Cloud**, both on Azure and on-premises

  - Connecting all your servers to the **Azure Sentinel SIEM service**, both on Azure and on-premises

  - Monitoring your servers using **Azure Monitor**, both on Azure and on-premises

  - Protecting Kubernetes clusters using **Microsoft Defender for Containers**, both on Azure and on-premises

For more information, please refer to the following resources:

What is Azure Stack Hub?: https://docs.microsoft.com/en-us/azure-stack/user/user-overview

Azure Arc overview: https://docs.microsoft.com/en-us/azure/azure-arc/overview

Using compute services over GCP hybrid environments

GCP offers a service called **Anthos clusters** that allows you to manage and deploy Kubernetes clusters in the cloud and on-premises (based on the virtualization platform or bare metal).

The following are some best practices to consider:

- Use Anthos clusters when you wish to run a GKE cluster on-premises using the same capabilities, version, and APIs as the fully managed GKE in the cloud.

- Use a private package repository server to make sure your packages are kept secure and never leave your local data center. Make sure all the packages are using the most recent libraries and binaries.

- Use a **Container Storage Interface** (**CSI**) driver to connect the local Kubernetes cluster to storage.

- Use **Google Cloud IAM** to grant minimal permissions for the Kubernetes cluster to access resources.

- When you're using RHEL or CentOS, enforce the use of SELinux.

For more information, please refer to the following resource:

Anthos clusters: `https://cloud.google.com/anthos/clusters/docs`

Summary

In this section, we reviewed some of the alternatives to using cloud resources locally based on AWS, Azure, and GCP services. Each cloud provider takes a different approach for hybrid cloud.

AWS and Azure offer a physical rack to be deployed on-premises and can run VMs, storage, and databases. Both AWS and GCP offer solutions to allow you to deploy Kubernetes clusters on-premises with the same APIs and capabilities as the cloud version.

Securing hybrid cloud environments

When it comes to talking about securing hybrid cloud environments, we are looking for solutions that can manage your entire environment (both on-premises and in the cloud) in a centralized way.

How to secure AWS hybrid environments

AWS offers the following services for managing security in hybrid environments:

- **AWS Systems Manager**: This allows you to manage VMs from a compliance, patch management, and hardening perspective (central location for running scripts over hybrid environments).

- **AWS Secrets Manager**: A central and secured location for managing secrets (credentials, API keys, and more) over hybrid environments.

- **AWS Elastic Disaster Recovery**: Provides secure data replication for disaster recovery between on-premises environments and the cloud.

- **Amazon CloudWatch agent**: This allows you to collect OS logs from VMs in hybrid environments.

The following are some best practices to consider:

- Deploy **AWS Systems Manager Agent** on both EC2 instances in the cloud and on your on-premises servers (Windows or Linux).

- Use **AWS Systems Manager** to set a patch baseline and get notified about VMs missing security patches (afterward, you can push security patches using Systems Manager).

- Use **AWS Systems Manager Agent** to push audit logs from your local VMs to AWS CloudTrail. Once all the logs have been stored inside CloudTrail, you can use AWS GuardDuty to get notified about a possible breach in your hybrid environment.

- Use **AWS IAM** to grant minimal permissions to allow your local VMs to communicate with AWS services.

- Encrypt all traffic between your local Systems Manager agents and the AWS Systems Manager service using TLS.

- Use **AWS Systems Manager Change Manager** to check for configuration changes on all your VMs (both in the cloud and on-premises).

- Use **AWS Secrets Manager** to generate, revoke, store, and retrieve sensitive information (such as database credentials, API keys, and more) instead of storing secrets hardcoded on your VMs.

- Use **CloudTrail** to audit API activities of AWS Secrets Manager (such as who generates secrets, who accesses secrets, and more).

- Use **AWS Elastic Disaster Recovery** to build a disaster recovery solution for your on-premises VMs by replicating entire VMs to the cloud.

- Deploy **Amazon CloudWatch Agent** on both EC2 instances in the cloud and on your on-premises servers (Windows or Linux).

- Use **Amazon CloudWatch Logs** as a central log repository where you can create alerts on activities such as failed logins, security-related events from the OS security event logs, and more.

For more information, please refer to the following resources:

Setting up AWS Systems Manager for hybrid environments: `https://docs.aws.amazon.com/systems-manager/latest/userguide/systems-manager-managedinstances.html`

AWS Secrets Manager Features: `https://aws.amazon.com/secrets-manager/features/`

AWS Elastic Disaster Recovery: `https://aws.amazon.com/disaster-recovery/`

Installing the CloudWatch agent on on-premises servers: `https://docs.aws.amazon.com/AmazonCloudWatch/latest/monitoring/install-CloudWatch-Agent-on-premise.html`

What is Amazon CloudWatch Logs?: `https://docs.aws.amazon.com/AmazonCloudWatch/latest/logs/WhatIsCloudWatchLogs.html`

How to secure Azure hybrid environments

Azure offers the following services for managing security in hybrid environments:

- **Microsoft Defender for Cloud**: A service for protecting servers and clients (Windows and Linux) and SQL databases. It is also a centralized service for managing security in the cloud and on-premises.

- **Azure Sentinel**: A cloud-based SIEM service.

The following are some best practices to consider:

- Deploy **Azure Arc** and enable **Microsoft Defender** on all your VM that are on-premises and in the cloud.

- Deploy a **Log Analytics** agent on your on-premises servers to allow security information to be received inside the **Microsoft Defender for Cloud console**.

- Deploy Microsoft Defender for SQL on your local SQL databases.

- Use the built-in vulnerability assessment that comes with Microsoft Defender for Cloud to detect vulnerabilities in your on-premises environment and the cloud.

- Use Microsoft Defender for SQL to scan for vulnerabilities on all your SQL databases – both on-premises and in the cloud.

- Use Microsoft Defender for Containers clusters to defend all your Kubernetes clusters – both on-premises and in the cloud.

- Connect Microsoft Defender for Containers to Azure Sentinel to be able to correlate between security incidents and response to security alerts – both on-premises and in the cloud.

For more information, please refer to the following resources:

What is Microsoft Defender for Cloud?: `https://docs.microsoft.com/en-us/azure/security-center/azure-defender`

What is Azure Sentinel?: `https://docs.microsoft.com/en-us/azure/sentinel/overview`

How to secure GCP hybrid environments

GCP offers the following services for managing security in hybrid environments:

- **Google Cloud Endpoints**: A service for securing, monitoring, analyzing, and setting quotas for APIs – both in the cloud and on-premises

- **Private Google Access**: Allows private access from on-premises environments to Google APIs and services

The following are some best practices to consider:

- When you're using Google Cloud Endpoints, remember the following:

  - Encrypt traffic using SSL with **Extensible Service Proxy** (**ESP**) to keep the confidentiality of sensitive information (such as credentials, PII, and more).

  - Use ESP to validate authentication requests to the API backend (such as Firebase authentication, Auth0, Google ID token authentication, and more).

  - If you're using API keys, restrict access to those API keys using the Service Control API.

  - Use Google Cloud IAM to restrict access to APIs.

- When you need to access Google APIs or services from the on-premises environments, remember the following:

  - Connect to your VPC using Cloud VPN or Cloud Interconnect.

  - Redirect traffic through `private.googleapis.com` for APIs that do not support VPC service controls.

- Redirect traffic through `restricted.googleapis.com` for APIs that support VPC service controls.
- Use firewall rules to allow access from the on-premises environment to your VPC.

For more information, please refer to the following resources:

Cloud Endpoints documentation: `https://cloud.google.com/endpoints/docs`

Configuring Private Google Access for on-premises hosts: `https://cloud.google.com/vpc/docs/configure-private-google-access-hybrid`

Summary

In this section, we reviewed several services from AWS, Azure, and GCP that allows you to have central management over your hybrid environments – both on-premises and cloud resources.

Summary

In this chapter, we focused on hybrid clouds. We reviewed the importance of having a hybrid cloud strategy to allow organizations to adopt cloud services and hybrid solutions. We also discussed the various IAM solutions from AWS, Azure, and GCP, which allow organizations to have a central directory service so that they can keep a single identity for each end user.

We looked at the various methods that AWS, Azure, and GCP use to help organizations connect their on-premises environment to the cloud in a hybrid architecture. We also discussed the various storage services that allow organizations to transfer data to the cloud. Then, we dived into various compute services that allow organizations to control all their compute needs using the same technology and capabilities – both on-premises and in the cloud.

Finally, we reviewed several services from AWS, Azure, and GCP that allow organizations to achieve a single pane of glass for managing security both on-premises and in the cloud.

Understanding the topics mentioned in this chapter will provide organizations with the necessary tools for when they build a hybrid cloud architecture.

In the next chapter, we will review multi-clouds (including identity management, vulnerability and patch management, configuration management, monitoring, and network security-related topics).

12
Managing Multi-Cloud Environments

In previous chapters, we covered hybrid cloud and how to connect your on-premises data centers to **Amazon Web Services** (**AWS**), Azure, and **Google Cloud Platform** (**GCP**), and how to create a hybrid cloud architecture. In this chapter, we will cover one of the most complex scenarios in the cloud – managing multi-cloud environments. Multi-cloud is about using more than one cloud or cloud provider to setup a common environment, infrastructure, or even an application layer.

Organizations taking their first steps using cloud services consider a multi-cloud approach as a solution for protecting themselves against a *vendor lock-in* scenario – a scenario where our entire infrastructure or applications rely on a single cloud provider's ecosystem.

One of the questions organizations ask themselves is, what do we do if the cloud provider goes out of business? How do we migrate our assets to another cloud provider? In theory, a multi-cloud approach might resolve the vendor lock-in risk; however, organizations need to be aware of the complexities that come with multi-cloud environments.

Business continuity is another major concern. A multi-cloud architecture allows us to deploy workloads on more than one cloud provider, which reduces the impact on a business that might happen with a single cloud provider (for example, an outage to an authentication service that blocks us from working with services deployed on the cloud).

A multi-cloud architecture allows us to create disaster recovery solutions, where one cloud provider is configured as a failover for another cloud provider. These architectures, based on containers, allow us portability between cloud providers while decreasing the dependencies on a specific cloud ecosystem (from **Virtual Machines (VMs)**, storage services, managed databases, and so on). Multi-cloud allows us to have the benefits of each cloud provider's ecosystem, including the latest versions of Kubernetes, the most scalable NoSQL database, and the latest GPU processors.

In this chapter, we will cover the following topics:

- Multi-cloud strategy
- Identity management over multi-cloud environments
- Network architecture for multi-cloud environments
- Data security in multi-cloud environments
- Cost management in multi-cloud environments
- **Cloud Security Posture Management (CSPM)**
- **Cloud Infrastructure Entitlement Management (CIEM)**
- Patch and configuration management in multi-cloud environments
- Monitoring and auditing of multi-cloud environments

Technical requirements

For this chapter, you need to have a solid understanding of concepts such as identity management, network, compute, and how to secure cloud environments.

Multi-cloud strategy

Prior to using a multi-cloud architecture, we need to ask ourselves, what are we trying to achieve through a multi-cloud strategy? Some of the most common use cases for choosing a multi-cloud strategy are discussed in the following sections.

Freedom to select a cloud provider

Most cloud providers offer us the same fundamental services (such as compute, storage, and database). Having the freedom to select a cloud provider allows us to decide for each workload where we wish to deploy our resources (VMs, containers, database, and so on), in case one of the cloud providers changes its **Service Level Agreement (SLA)** or pricing model.

Freedom to select your services

This freedom means that if one of the cloud providers offers a certain service that is not available on other cloud providers, such as data analytics for large datasets, or a Function-as-a-Service offering that supports a certain development language that is not supported by other cloud providers, you are free to select a multi-cloud strategy.

Reduced cost

In most cases, spreading your workloads over several cloud providers will increase the cost, due to outbound (or egress) traffic costs over the internet and between cloud providers, and the knowledge required to train your staff to work with multiple cloud providers.

There are scenarios where you are able to consume the same service from multiple cloud providers, while the cost of using the service is cheaper with one of the cloud providers, in a region close to your customers.

Organizations need to take into consideration that spreading their workloads over multiple cloud providers will impact volume-based discounts, where they may not achieve economies of scale. In the context of this section, an organization must consider what capabilities it must establish in all cloud providers.

Data sovereignty

Even though most major cloud providers have data centers in central locations in US and Europe, there are cases where your organization is required by local laws or regulations to keep customer data locally in a specific country. There might be scenarios where a specific cloud provider has no local presence in one of your customer's origins, making a multi-cloud approach a suitable solution.

Backup and disaster recovery

Storing data in multiple locations, with multiple cloud providers, will decrease the risk of your organization losing data or overcoming cloud provider service availability in a certain region or even overcoming global service availability issues.

Improving reliability

Even though most major cloud providers offer **Distributed Denial of Service (DDoS)** protection services, there might be scenarios where one of the cloud providers is currently under a DDoS attack themselves, cloud providers might suffer from service outages, internet providers may encounter latency, or workloads may fail for various reasons.

To improve reliability, consider topics such as the following:

- Data replication between cloud providers, which impacts cost (redundant storage, data transfer cost, and so on).

- Failover scenarios – where do you manage your DNS records and update them in case of failover between providers?

- Automation – what tools or services will you use for failover between providers?

- Knowledge – does your IT or development staff have enough knowledge to switch between cloud providers?

Having the ability to switch your workloads to another cloud provider (assuming you have already built an entire production environment on another cloud provider and synched data) will allow you to mitigate the risk of having your services unavailable.

Identity management

A multi-cloud strategy must address identity management. Each cloud provider has its own **Identity and Access Management (IAM)** solution, which causes challenges and opportunities for a centralized identity life cycle (onboarding, access management, and offboarding) and credential management.

The aforementioned challenges increase the motivation to centralize on a single **IAM** solution that must be integrated with each cloud provider.

Data security

A multi-cloud strategy must address data security issues. Common examples of data security in a multi-cloud environment are as follows:

- Keeping data residency, while working with multiple cloud providers

- Data replication between cloud providers and within a single cloud provider over multiple regions

- Access control of your data over multiple cloud providers

- Encryption and key management over multiple cloud providers

- Audit access to data over decentralized audit solutions

- Misconfigurations when working with multiple cloud providers, each with its own services and capabilities

Asset management

A multi-cloud strategy makes asset management a challenge for any organization. An organization must have visibility or a real-time, centralized inventory of its entire cloud environment – what assets it has, where its assets are located (which cloud provider and which account), who owns its assets, and who has access to its assets.

Skills gap

A multi-cloud strategy must address the fact that working with multiple cloud providers requires hands-on experience in architecture, development, and operations, working with multiple cloud solutions. An organization must invest in employee training as an ongoing process to allow employees the necessary knowledge to maintain multiple cloud platforms. An important topic to invest in is automation, to scale the impact of employees and to reduce the operational burden.

For more information, refer to the following resources:

How computing has evolved, and why you need a multi-cloud strategy:

```
https://cloud.google.com/blog/topics/hybrid-cloud/future-isnt-just-cloud-its-multi-cloud
```

The Multi-Cloud & How To Create A Multi-Cloud Strategy:

```
https://www.bmc.com/blogs/multi-cloud-strategy
```

Summary

A multi-cloud strategy helps organizations decide in which scenario to select a different cloud provider or different cloud service. Such a strategy must address data security topics (including data residency, availability, and protection mechanisms).

One important topic that organizations should consider is the fact that a multi-cloud approach demands highly experienced and trained employees, and as such, organizations must invest in employee training.

Identity management over multi-cloud environments

One of the first things to decide on, prior to using a multi-cloud strategy, is identity management. Organizations would like to keep their existing Identity Provider (IdP), have a single identity for each of their end users (while preserving existing credentials), and still be able to access resources in the cloud. If an organization is already using Office 365 for managing mailboxes and collaboration, consider using **Azure Active Directory** (**AAD**) and its central identity management service.

Azure AD is considered the most used IdP. It supports identity federation to most major cloud providers and is able to integrate with most **Software as a Service** (**SaaS**) solutions. Other popular identity management providers that are outside the scope of this book are Okta, Ping Identity, and OneLogin, which allow you a universal directory service for managing your users, groups, and devices, enforcement of **Multi-Factor Authentication** (**MFA**), and single sign-on for multiple cloud providers and SaaS applications.

How to manage identity in AWS over multi-cloud environments

AWS provides the following services to manage identity over multi-cloud environments:

- **AWS Single Sign-On** (**SSO**) – a service that allows single sign-on across AWS organizations or connection to identities in external cloud identity services based on the SAML protocol, such as Azure AD or Google G Suite.

- **Amazon Cognito** – a service that allows single sign-on for web or mobile applications while allowing customers to connect using external IdPs, such as Apple, Facebook, or Google, or SAML-based authentication, such as Azure AD.

Best practices are as follows:

- Use **AWS SSO** as an **IdP** to federate and manage access to cloud applications (such as Salesforce, Box, and Office 365). AWS SSO can also provide federated access by accepting inbound SAML for services such as Okta.

- Use **Amazon Cognito** to manage access to customer-facing web or mobile applications, using external IdPs such as Azure AD, Apple, Facebook, or Google.

- Use **AWS CloudTrail** to log all AWS SSO API calls.

- Use **AWS CloudTrail** to log all Amazon Cognito API calls.

- Use **Amazon GuardDuty** to generate security events (based on AWS CloudTrail) about suspicious activities (such as a brute-force attempt using an external identity) and send notifications using as **AWS Simple Notification Service (SNS)**, to services such as SMS, mobile, email notifications, or trigger a Lambda function to take some action (such as blocking network access using a security group). The best use of Amazon GuardDuty is to aggregate events into **AWS Security Hub** or to a centralized **Security Information and Event Management (SIEM)**.

- Use **TLS 1.2** when sending API calls to Amazon Cognito.

- When working with AWS SSO, if you need to configure fine-grain access to resources, based on external identity attributes (such as title and location), use **Attribute-Based Access Control (ABAC)** in conjunction with an IAM policy (such as conditions in the IAM policy).

- When working with AWS SSO with an external IdP, or AWS SSO as an IdP that supports **MFA**, enforce the use of MFA in your external IdP settings to allow strong authentication.

- When working with **Amazon Cognito** to allow access to web or mobile applications, enforce the use of MFA to a user pool to allow strong authentication.

- Use **Amazon CloudWatch** or any other SIEM or analytics tools to monitor Amazon Cognito user pools and raise an alarm when a certain threshold is passed (such as a high number of unsuccessful federation login attempts from an external IdP).

- Use **Amazon Cognito** compromised credentials protection features to detect whether a user's credentials were compromised and block access attempts from that user.

For more information, refer to the following resources:

Automate SAML 2.0 federation for AWS multi-account environments that use Azure AD:

```
https://docs.aws.amazon.com/prescriptive-guidance/latest/
patterns/automate-saml-2-0-federation-for-aws-multi-account-
environments-that-use-azure-ad.html
```

Adding SAML identity providers to a user pool:

```
https://docs.aws.amazon.com/cognito/latest/developerguide/
cognito-user-pools-saml-idp.html
```

Adding multi-factor authentication (MFA) to a user pool:

```
https://docs.aws.amazon.com/cognito/latest/developerguide/
user-pool-settings-mfa.html
```

How to use G Suite as an external identity provider for AWS SSO:

```
https://aws.amazon.com/blogs/security/how-to-use-g-suite-as-
external-identity-provider-aws-sso/
```

How to manage identity in Azure over multi-cloud environments

Azure provides the following services to manage identity over multi-cloud environments:

- **Azure AD** – an Azure IdP that allows access to Azure resources or SaaS applications using external SAML-based IdPs such as AWS SSO or Google Identity.

- **Azure AD B2C** – an Azure IdP that allows access to customer-facing applications or non-Microsoft SaaS services, using external identities such as Gmail and Facebook.

Best practices are as follows:

- Use Azure AD, combined with **AWS SSO**, to allow central identity management for both Azure and AWS resources.

- Use Azure AD, combined with Google Identity or Google IAM to allow central identity management for both Azure and GCP resources.

- Use Azure AD B2C to allow access to customer-facing applications or third-party SaaS services.

- Use Conditional Access to enforce the use of MFA when connecting using external IdPs.

- When using **AWS SSO** as an IdP, integrated with Azure AD, configure Azure **Privileged Identity Management** (**PIM**) to configure just-in-time access to the Azure portal and Azure resources.

- Use **Microsoft Defender for Cloud Apps** to monitor protected services (using a combined identity).

- Use **Microsoft Defender for Cloud Apps** to protect your combined environment from risky users or data exfiltration.

- Use TLS 1.2 when sending API calls to Azure AD B2C.

- When using Azure AD B2C to authenticate web applications, create separate environments – split between development, testing, and production.

- Audit each of the web applications that are using Azure AD B2C using audit log events stored in Azure Monitor and send the logs to a SIEM service (such as Azure Sentinel).

For more information, refer to the following resources:

Multi-cloud security and identity with Azure and Amazon Web Services (AWS):

```
https://docs.microsoft.com/en-us/azure/architecture/
aws-professional/security-identity
```

Azure Active Directory integration with Amazon Web Services:

```
https://docs.microsoft.com/en-us/azure/active-directory/saas-
apps/aws-multi-accounts-tutorial
```

Recommendations and best practices for Azure Active Directory B2C:

```
https://docs.microsoft.com/en-us/azure/active-directory-b2c/
best-practices
```

How to manage identity in GCP over multi-cloud environments

Google provides Cloud IAM as a service that allows integration with other IdPs such as AWS or Azure AD.

Best practices are as follows:

- When integrating Google Cloud with external IdPs (such as AWS or Azure AD), use short-lived Google access tokens such as **AWS Security Token Service** to impersonate a service account.

- When integrating Google Cloud with Azure AD, enforce the use of MFA on Azure AD.

- When integrating between Google Cloud and Azure AD, sync groups from Azure AD instead of managing groups in Google Cloud.

- Avoid automatic user provisioning for identities with consumer accounts to avoid creating duplicate accounts.

- When connecting Google identities to Azure AD, the user identities become guest accounts on Azure AD. As best practice, do the following:

  - Provision guest users on Google Cloud inside a dedicated organizational unit.

  - Apply policy to restrict the maximum session duration for guests' users to 8 hours.

  - Set the re-authentication method to using a password to force the user to re-authenticate using their Azure AD credentials.

For more information, refer to the following resources:

Configuring workload identity federation:

```
https://cloud.google.com/iam/docs/configuring-workload-
identity-federation
```

Federating Google Cloud with Azure Active Directory:

```
https://cloud.google.com/architecture/identity/federating-gcp-
with-azure-active-directory
```

Azure AD user provisioning and single sign-on:

```
https://cloud.google.com/architecture/identity/federating-gcp-
with-azure-ad-configuring-provisioning-and-single-sign-on
```

Summary

Selecting an authentication and authorization method allows an organization to reuse its existing IdPs and to keep a single identity for each of its end users in a central repository.

When possible, it is recommended to manage user identities using a central **Identity Management** (**IDM**) system for provisioning and de-provisioning on your chosen cloud IdP.

Network architecture for multi-cloud environments

The second important thing to consider when building a multi-cloud architecture is how to set up network connectivity between the various cloud providers, and between on-premises software and cloud providers.

The recommended way to connect to cloud environments is a secure and permanent network connection using dedicated interconnect (such as **AWS Direct Connect** or **Azure ExpressRoute**) for connecting from the on-premises to the cloud or using a site-to-site **Virtual Private Network** (**VPN**) (either from on-premises to the cloud or between cloud providers).

A secured and permanent connection will allow access control (layer 4 firewall rules) to be set between cloud providers and cloud segments, and keep access to resources in the cloud (or allowing access to cloud resources) according to business needs.

When considering network architecture, you need to consider the following:

- Which resources should be kept private (such as data transfer and backend service-to-service communication)?

- Which resources can be public (such as public API calls, frontend services, and VPN endpoints)?

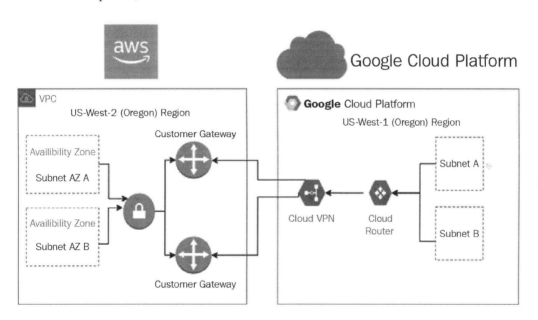

Figure 12.1 – Network connectivity from GCP to AWS

Let's now proceed to look at how to create connectivity between AWS and GCP in the next section.

How to create network connectivity between AWS and GCP

To create an IPsec VPN tunnel between AWS and GCP, follow these high-level guidelines:

- Create a dedicated AWS **Virtual Private Cloud** (**VPC**) with a new subnet for the VPN tunnel.

- Create a dedicated GCP VPC with a new subnet for the VPN tunnel.

- If network redundancy is not required, create a connection between an AWS **virtual private gateway** (using an AWS-managed VPN) and Google Cloud VPN.

- If network redundancy is required, create a connection between an AWS **transit gateway** and Google **High Availability** (**HA**) VPN.

Best practices are as follows:

- Always think about **Classless Inter-Domain Routing** (**CIDR**) prior to configuring network segments in the cloud to avoid IP conflict between the cloud providers.

- On the AWS side, use network **Access Control Lists** (**ACLs**) and security groups to protect resources inside your AWS VPC.

- On the GCP side, use firewall rules to protect resources inside your GCP VPC.

For more information, refer to the following resources:

Connecting an AWS and GCP VPC using an IPSec VPN Tunnel with BGP:

```
https://medium.com/peek-travel/connecting-an-aws-and-gcp-vpc-
using-an-ipsec-vpn-tunnel-with-bgp-f332c2885975
```

Build HA VPN connections between Google Cloud and AWS:

```
https://cloud.google.com/architecture/build-ha-vpn-
connections-google-cloud-aws
```

Multi-Cloud Architecture using VPN between GCP and AWS:

```
https://blog.searce.com/multi-cloud-architecture-using-vpn-
between-gcp-and-aws-167a5e739079
```

How to create network connectivity between AWS and Azure

To create an IPsec VPN tunnel between AWS and Azure, follow these high-level guidelines:

- Create a dedicated AWS VPC with a new subnet for the VPN tunnel.
- Create a dedicated Azure VNet with a new subnet for the VPN tunnel.
- Create a connection between an AWS virtual private gateway (using an AWS-managed VPN) and Azure VPN Gateway.

> **Important Note**
> For network redundancy, create two VPN tunnels.

Best practices are as follows:

- Always think about CIDR prior to configuring network segments in the cloud to avoid IP conflict between the cloud providers.
- On the AWS side, use network ACLs and security groups to protect resources inside your AWS VPC.
- On the Azure side, use network security groups to protect resources inside your Azure VNet.

For more information, refer to the following resource:

How to create a VPN between Azure and AWS using only managed solutions:

```
https://techcommunity.microsoft.com/t5/fasttrack-for-azure/
how-to-create-a-vpn-between-azure-and-aws-using-only-managed/
ba-p/2281900
```

How to create network connectivity between Azure and GCP

To create an IPsec VPN tunnel between Azure and GCP, follow these high-level guidelines:

- Create a dedicated Azure VNet with a new subnet for the VPN tunnel.
- Create a dedicated GCP VPC with a new subnet for the VPN tunnel.
- If network redundancy is not required, create a connection between Azure VPN Gateway and Google Cloud VPN.

- If network redundancy is required, create a connection between Azure VPN Gateway and Google HA VPN.

> **Important Note**
>
> For network redundancy, create two VPN tunnels.

Best practices are as follows:

- Always think about CIDR prior to configuring network segments in the cloud to avoid IP conflict between the cloud providers.

- On the Azure side, use network security groups to protect resources inside your Azure VNet.

- On the GCP side, use firewall rules to protect resources inside your GCP VPC.

For more information, refer to the following resource:

Creating a Site to Site VPN Connection Between GCP and Azure with Google Private Access:

```
https://cloudywithachanceofbigdata.com/creating-a-site-to-
site-vpn-connection-between-gcp-and-azure-with-google-private-
access
```

Summary

According to your business requirements, you can have a secured and redundant connection between cloud providers using a site-to-site VPN connection.

Data security in multi-cloud environments

Data security in the cloud relates to protecting data as it transfers over the network, at rest, and in use.

Encryption in transit

To secure your cloud environment, make sure that all data traverses through secured protocols. Some alternatives to secured protocols are as follows:

- Enforce the use of TLS 1.2 for accessing resources over your entire multi-cloud environment.

- Configure IPsec VPN tunnels between your on-premises and cloud environments, and between cloud providers.

Encryption at rest

All major cloud providers have their own **Key Management Services** (**KMSes**), for managing keys, secrets, credentials, and so on. Although the built-in KMSes can store, manage, retrieve, and rotate keys and secrets, they are integrated into their own cloud provider's ecosystem. When selecting a solution for handing encryption at rest, look for the following capabilities:

- The ability to encrypt data at rest over multiple cloud providers – each cloud provider has its own KMS. If you need to share encryption keys across multiple cloud providers, you need to deploy a third-party solution to achieve this goal.

- The ability to handle the scale of your cloud environment (generating thousands of keys from multiple cloud providers).

> **Important Note**
> Consider a **Hardware Security Module** (**HSM**)-based solution when you need to comply with regulations (such as PCI DDS), since HSM devices are tamper-resistant and tamper-proof.

- The ability to create, store, retrieve, and rotate both keys and secrets from multiple cloud provider services.

- The ability to configure role-based access control – who can generate keys/secrets on which cloud account or cloud provider.

- The ability to generate a full audit log for the KMS solution for further investigation.

Encryption in use

The concept of encryption in use is to be able to protect data while running in memory on a **VM** or a container. The best-known concept for encryption in use is **confidential computing**. Common confidential computing alternatives are as follows:

- AWS Nitro Enclaves
- Azure confidential computing
- Google Confidential Computing

To protect data in multi-cloud environments, combined with central provisioning solutions, aim to deploy VMs or containers that support one of the aforementioned confidential computing solutions.

Summary

In this section, we have reviewed various ways to protect data in cloud environments. Enforcing the use of encryption in all layers (at transit, at rest, and in use) will allow you to protect your cloud environment, even when working in multi-cloud environments.

Cost management in multi-cloud environments

Although cost management (also known as **financial management** or **FinOps**) may not seem directly related to security, it has implications on a multi-cloud environment.

Cost management is part of having visibility over your entire multi-cloud environment, from a cost point of view. All major cloud providers have their own built-in cost management services that allow you the necessary visibility of your cloud accounts, subscriptions, or projects.

When organizations are moving from a single cloud provider (in many cases, with multiple accounts at the same cloud provider, for different environments or business needs) to a multi-cloud setup, they begin to realize that they lack the necessary visibility regarding cloud cost.

Some of the concerns organizations often have are as follows:

- Data transfer cost (also known as egress data)
- Redundant resources being spent (such as multiple log systems, backup services, and anti-malware solutions)

The possible risks of not having cost visibility are as follows:

- High payments from multiple cloud providers, without knowing what resources are been consumed and whether we need those resources.
- Identifying anomalous spend, such as charges in unexpected regions, unexpected services, or anomalous volumes, which may be indicators of compromise, specifically when working in a multi-cloud environment.
- A potential denial-of-wallet scenario, where a hacker gains access to one of our cloud accounts, consuming expensive compute resources for bitcoin mining. Without proper visibility or an alerting mechanism, by the time we become aware that someone is using our resources, we will have to pay thousands of dollars to the cloud providers.

Best practices are as follows:

- Deploy a cost management solution that supports multiple cloud providers.

- Tag all resources in all your cloud accounts, in all your cloud providers.

- Create billing alerts for each of your cloud accounts when a certain threshold is passed (for example, when the total monthly consumption of a test environment account passes $500 or when the total monthly consumption of a production environment account passes $1,500).

- Configure a budget for each of your cloud accounts. Once the budget has been configured, generate an automatic budget alert once a certain threshold of the budget (such as 75%) has been passed.

- Deploy automation capabilities to remove unused resources (such as VMs, containers, and managed databases). Automation will allow you to deploy development or testing environments when resources are needed.

- Review cost recommendation reports and follow the recommendations, such as the following:

  - Rightsizing a VM to a smaller VM type (with less CPU or memory).

  - Shut down underutilized VMs.

  - Change the purchase options of VMs from on-demand (or pay as you go) to a reserved instance (a commit for 1 or 3 years in advance) or even spot (or pre-emptible), according to the expected VM runtime.

  - Switch to cheaper block storage (disk volumes) according to the actual usage (disk utilization).

  - Migrate objects on object storage services to a cheaper tier (from hot or real-time storage to cool or near real-time, or even to cold or archive storage).

  - Delete unneeded backups or snapshots.

For more information, refer to the following resources:

The 2021 Guide to Multi-Cloud Billing and Cost Management:

```
https://www.meshcloud.io/2020/12/23/the-2021-guide-to-multi-
cloud-billing-and-cost-management/
```

How to take control of your multi-cloud costs:

```
https://www.cio.com/native/be-ready/collection/cloud-
operations-and-management/article/how-to-take-control-of-your-
multi-cloud-costs
```

Summary

In this section, we have reviewed the importance of having visibility of your cloud costs over multi-cloud environments, as part of multi-cloud governance. Having visibility over costs in a multi-cloud environment will allow you to mitigate the risk of high payments or potential hidden bitcoin mining in one of your cloud accounts.

Cloud Security Posture Management (CSPM)

As part of having visibility in your multi-cloud environments, over the past couple of years, a new concept has emerged.

There are multiple offers from many third-party **CSPM** vendors, but the fundamental idea behind all CSPM solutions is to have visibility of misconfigurations – a crucial topic when working in a multi-cloud environment and managing multiple cloud accounts. When selecting a CSPM solution, look for the following capabilities:

- Support for multiple cloud providers.
- Visibility of misconfigurations (such as an opened port and publicly accessible object storage).
- Visibility of IAM (such as API keys located in publicly accessible object storage, access keys or passwords that were not rotated in the past 90 days, users' permissions, and accounts missing MFA).
- Visibility of your entire cloud assets across a multi-cloud environment.
- The ability to assess risks over your entire multi-cloud environment.
- The ability to prioritize risk mitigations – your staff needs to know what risks need to be handled immediately.
- Contextualized visibility – a publicly accessible web server must be patched first, while servers that reside in a private subnet, protected with strict access network controls, can be patched later.
- The ability to remediate misconfigurations automatically.

- Get insights into attack vectors – understand how a potential attacker can take advantage of misconfiguration to breach your cloud environment.

- Visibility in vulnerable components (such as missing security patches on a VM or an old open source library inside a container).

- Get insights into mitigation actions – your staff needs to know what actions to take in order to resolve a misconfiguration or potential risk.

- Check for compliance in your entire multi-cloud environment against well-known security frameworks (such as ISO 27001) and regulations (such as **General Data Protection Regulation (GDPR)** and **Health Insurance Portability and Accountability Act (HIPAA)**).

- Continuous monitoring of your entire multi-cloud environment – detecting threats and misconfiguration must be an ongoing process.

- Integration with SIEM systems for further investigation.

- Integration with a ticketing system for submitting tasks to allow your staff to handle alerts from the CSPM solution.

For more information, refer to the following resources:

Cloud Security Posture Management (CSPM):

```
https://searchcloudsecurity.techtarget.com/definition/Cloud-
Security-Posture-Management-CSPM
```

The Past, Present And Future Of Cloud Security And CSPM Solutions:

```
https://www.forbes.com/sites/forbestechcouncil/2021/07/05/
the-past-present-and-future-of-cloud-security-and-cspm-
solutions/?sh=56380a13a7e8
```

Summary

In this section, we have reviewed the concept of CSPM solutions to have visibility of our entire cloud environments. We have also reviewed the CSPM capabilities when selecting a CSPM solution.

Cloud Infrastructure Entitlement Management (CIEM)

A new concept developed in the past couple of years is CIEM. Some vendors offer a combined solution of both CSPM and CIEM into a single product, which factors in a multi-cloud partner strategy.

CIEM solutions allow us to monitor and manage identities (both human and machine) and access privileges in a multi-cloud environment, from a central console, while applying the principle of least privilege access to our cloud infrastructure. When selecting a CIEM solution, look for the following capabilities:

- Support for multiple cloud providers
- An inventory of existing entitlements
- Detecting and remediating IAM misconfigurations
- The ability to control access to resources, services, and administrative accounts
- Identifying risks associated with configuration errors
- Identifying shadow admin accounts in a multi-cloud environment
- Suggestions for policy correction
- Auto-generation of access policies according to actual identity needs
- Detecting excessive permissions to identities
- Detecting external and cross-account access permissions

For more information, refer to the following resource:

What is CIEM and why should CISOs care?

```
https://searchcloudsecurity.techtarget.com/post/What-is-CIEM-
and-why-should-CISOs-care
```

Summary

In this section, we have reviewed the concept of CIEM solutions for detecting and remediating misconfiguration regarding IAM. We have also reviewed the CIEM capabilities when selecting a CIEM solution.

Patch and configuration management in multi-cloud environments

One of the challenges in multi-cloud environments is controlling software updates and configuration changes from a central place. When selecting a patch management solution, look for the following capabilities:

- The ability to centrally manage patch deployment from a central place
- Support for deploying security patches on both Windows and Linux platforms
- Support for asset inventories
- Support for patch rollback in case of a problematic security patch
- Support for deploying security patches over secured protocols (such as the TLS tunnel between the central patch server and the remote VM)
- The ability to deploy security patches to a group of servers (such as different environments and a different patch cycle to avoid breaking availability in case of server clustering)
- The ability to deploy third-party security patches (such as patches to self-managed database servers, web servers, and client tools)
- The ability to configure minimal credentials to access remote VMs over your entire multi-cloud environment for patch deployment
- The ability to configure a maintenance window for patch deployment (to avoid deploying patches during working hours)
- The ability to generate compliance reports (such as what percentage of your servers were already deployed with a patch and which servers are still missing a patch)
- The ability to integrate a patch management solution with a ticketing system to allow your staff to take care of vulnerable VMs

Another topic that needs to be addressed when working with development teams is taking care of open source libraries, also known as **Software Composition Analysis (SCA)**. When selecting an SCA solution, look for the following capabilities:

- The ability to centrally manage your entire multi-cloud environment from a central location
- The ability to integrate with multiple source code repositories
- The ability to integrate with multiple container registries in multi-cloud environments

- The ability to search for outdated open source library repositories

- The ability to detect both a vulnerable or outdated open source library and all of its dependencies

- The ability to configure minimal credentials to access a remote source code or container registries

- The ability to integrate the SCA solution with **Continuous Integration/Continuous Delivery (CI/CD)** processes (in multi-cloud and multi-account environments, it is common to have multiple CI/CD pipelines)

- The ability to generate reports to allow you to see which vulnerable components exist in your development or production environments

- The ability to break a build process if you are using vulnerable components

- The ability to set the vulnerability severity that is allowed in your environments before breaking a build process (for example, do not allow the completion of a build process if critical vulnerabilities exist in one of the open source libraries or dependencies)

- The ability to integrate an SCA solution with a ticketing system to allow your staff to take care of vulnerable components as part of the build process

Configuration and change management are also crucial topics to take care of in multi-cloud environments. When selecting configuration and change management solutions, look for the following capabilities:

- The ability to manage your entire multi-cloud environment from a central place

- The ability to configure minimal credentials to access assets in multiple cloud providers and multiple cloud accounts

- The ability to detect compliance against well-known standards, such as a **Centre of Internet Security (CIS)** benchmark or **National Institute of Standard and Technology (NIST)**

- The ability to detect a configuration change in a multi-cloud environment

- The ability to automate a configuration change in multiple cloud accounts

- The ability to integrate a configuration or change management solution with a ticketing system to allow your staff to take care of the changes

- The ability to integrate with a SIEM system to raise alerts when a configuration change is detected in one of your systems

Summary

In this section, we have reviewed patch management and configuration/change management in a multi-cloud environment. Since multi-cloud environments face many challenges in these areas, we have reviewed important capabilities to look out for when searching for a solution to manage security patches and configuration management.

The monitoring and auditing of multi-cloud environments

Monitoring is a crucial part of multi-cloud visibility. It can have multiple layers, such as the following:

- Resource utilization (performance logging)
- Monitoring running applications for errors (application logging)
- Security auditing and logging to detect security incidents

In this section, we will focus on security monitoring. When selecting a security monitoring solution for multi-cloud environments, look for the following capabilities:

- The ability to connect to multiple cloud providers, using the native cloud provider APIs
- The ability to connect to remote APIs using secured protocols (such as TLS 1.2)
- Built-in connectors for multiple cloud solutions (both common **Infrastrucure as a Service (IaaS)/Platform as a Service (PaaS)** and **SaaS**)
- The ability to receive feeds from threat detection services such as **Amazon GuardDuty**, **Microsoft Defender for Cloud**, and **Google Security Command Center**
- The ability to receive feeds from third-party vulnerability management solutions
- The ability to receive feeds from configuration management solutions to detect a misconfiguration or deviation from standards
- The ability to detect anomalous user behavior (such as a user trying to access a resource for the first time or outside the normal working hours) and raise an alert
- The ability to store all logs encrypted at rest

- The ability to configure role-based access control of the monitoring solution to various employees in various roles (such as IT staff, security analysts, and auditors) and in different places in your organization (for example, not all teams need access to view information about your entire cloud environment)

- The ability to receive real-time and continuous monitoring from your entire multi-cloud environment

- The ability to create correlation rules between various log sources (such as audit logs, endpoint detection solutions, and network traffic flow logs)

- The ability to run automated remediation actions (such as closing an open port and disabling a compromised account)

- The ability to create alerts based on logs and send them to a central SIEM system

- The ability to integrate with a ticketing system to allow your staff to take care of discovered security incidents

Summary

In this section, we have reviewed security monitoring and auditing in a multi-cloud environment. We have also reviewed the important capabilities to look for when searching for a solution for security monitoring in multi-cloud environments.

Summary

In this chapter, we have focused on multi-cloud environments. We have reviewed the importance of having a multi-cloud strategy to allow organizations to adopt multi-cloud environments. We have also discussed the various IAM solutions from AWS, Azure, and GCP that allow organizations to have a central directory service that can keep a single identity for each end user.

We looked at the various methods that AWS, Azure, and GCP allow organizations to connect between different cloud environments on different cloud providers using a site-to-site VPN tunnel. We also discussed the various data security mechanisms (encryption at transit, encryption at rest, and confidential computing). Then, we reviewed the importance of cost management in multi-cloud environments. We reviewed the concepts of CSPM and CIEM. Finally, we looked at patch management, configuration management, and monitoring in multi-cloud environments.

Understanding the topics mentioned in this chapter will provide organizations with the necessary tools when they build multi-cloud architectures.

In the final chapter of the book, we will review security in large-scale cloud environments (such as configuring governance and policies using infrastructure as code for automation, patch management, compliance, and vulnerability management).

13
Security in Large-Scale Environments

In the previous chapters, we covered cloud services, right from the basic building blocks (such as compute, network, storage, and security) to hybrid and multi-cloud architectures.

In the final chapter of this book, we will cover security in large-scale environments. Previously, we looked at managing an account based on a single cloud provider while having all the resources located in a single place. In this chapter, we will zoom out of this picture and look at large-scale cloud environments – having multiple accounts, for different departments or different business needs, often in multiple regions around the world.

The following are some of the questions organizations often ask themselves:

- How do I enforce governance over multiple accounts?
- How do I get visibility into my entire cloud environment?
- How do I manage a multi-region environment?
- What automation capabilities do I have?

In this chapter, we will cover the following topics:

- Managing governance and policies at a large scale
- Automation using infrastructure as code
- Security in large-scale cloud environments

Technical requirements

For this chapter, you need to have a solid understanding of concepts such as landing zones, policies, guardrails, **infrastructure as code (IaC)**, and security-related concepts such as patch management, configuration management, and compliance and vulnerability management.

Managing governance and policies at a large scale

When organizations begin to adopt cloud services, it is highly recommended to plan and consider cloud governance (asset deployment, data security, risk management, and more), even before they find themselves managing multiple cloud environments and multiple accounts.

Failing to plan makes it challenging to fix configuration that was done ad hoc as lack of uniformity results in heterogeneous assets that need to be protected, lack of repeatability, redundancy, large attack surface, and self-imposed constraints from technical debt that are a challenge to recover from (such as overlapping CIDR blocks).

Some of the important terminology related to governance is as follows:

- **Landing Zones**: These are pre-configured environments that are provisioned through code (policies, best practices, guidelines, and centrally managed services), as explained in the following section.

- **Compliance Policies**: These are specific rules for evaluating or enforcing resource configuration to comply with best practices or regulatory requirements (for example, any newly created object storage must be encrypted at rest using a customer-managed key).

- **Guardrails**: An automated way to detect or enforce the desired configuration (for example, make sure that no public S3 bucket is configured or encrypt a database at rest when it's created) before changes reach the production environment (allowing employees to do their job with minimum restrictions imposed on them).

Landing zones offer the following benefits:

- An automated way to create the structure of accounts according to best practices
- A common type of shared or pre-configured accounts baseline:

  - **Network**: A placeholder for network-related services (such as a VPN gateway).
  - **Identity and Access Management**: A placeholder for services such as directory or IAM services, password policies, and more.
  - **Management and Monitoring**: A placeholder for services such as central log management, monitoring and alerting, and more.
  - **Pre-configured Account Baselines**: An example is a vending machine with automated integration, along with other shared services (compliance, security controls, networking, monitoring, and more).

- Central billing configuration
- Account quota settings (such as how many VMs can be created by users in a specific account)
- **Tagging**: Enforce the use of tagging (prohibit creating untagged resources)

For more information, please refer to the following resources:

Cloud Landing Zone Lifecycle Explained!:

```
https://www.meshcloud.io/2020/06/08/cloud-landing-zone-
lifecycle-explained/
```

Governance in AWS

In this section, we will review the AWS services that allow governance at a large scale. The following diagram depicts AWS's multi-account hierarchy:

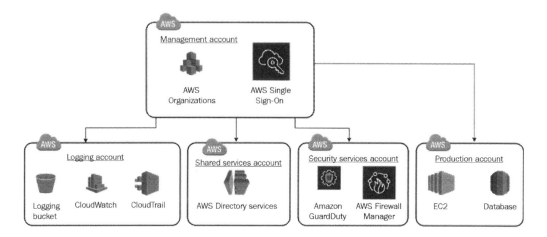

Figure 13.1 – AWS multi-account hierarchy

The preceding diagram shows the AWS Landing Zone concept. We will discuss this in the next section.

AWS Landing Zone

AWS Landing Zone is one of the AWS services that makes it easy for organizations to create multiple accounts as part of AWS organizations, in a secured and standard way.

While creating AWS landing zones, the following services are configured:

- **AWS CloudTrail**: This service creates an audit trail or API activities for each newly created AWS account. All logs are stored in a central S3 bucket in a log archive account.

- **AWS Config**: This service contains the configuration log files for each newly created AWS account and the AWS services inside that account. All logs are stored in a central S3 bucket in a log archive account.

- **AWS Config Rules**: This service provides rules for monitoring storage encryption (EBS, S3, and RDS), IAM password policy, root account MFA settings, public S3 buckets, and insecure security groups (such as allowing SSH access from any source).

- **AWS IAM**: This service is used to set an IAM password policy for the entire organization, SSO, and more.

- **Amazon VPC**: This service is used to remove the default VPC in all regions, configure network peering with the shared services' VPC, and more.

- **AWS Landing Zone Notifications**: This service provides notifications for items such as a root account login, failed console logins, and API authentication failures within an account.

- **Amazon GuardDuty**: This service is the central place to look for GuardDuty security findings (threats) for the entire organization.

For more information, please refer to the following resource:

AWS Landing Zone:

```
https://aws.amazon.com/solutions/implementations/aws-landing-
zone/
```

AWS Control Tower

AWS Control Tower is a service that allows organizations to create multi-accounts by following AWS best practices. Here are some of the best practices to follow:

- Set up a strong password for the AWS account root user and enable MFA.

- Select a region to be your home region for deploying landing zone settings and for storing S3 buckets for auditing and configurations.

- Configure AWS KMS keys to encrypt and decrypt resources within your AWS organization.

- Use AWS Service Catalog to configure which resources (such as VM images, servers, software, and databases) can be deployed by users in your AWS organization.

- Select service control policies to enforce policies and guardrails in your AWS organization.

- Configure AWS SSO to enforce the use of MFA and allow users to use a single login to gather resources across your AWS organization.

- Use AWS Security Hub to gather compliance and security alerts into a single console.

- Configure S3 life cycle policies to migrate less frequently used object storage data to the archive tier.

- Use AWS WAF to protect your entire AWS organization against application layer attacks.

For more information, please refer to the following resources:

AWS Control Tower FAQs:

`https://aws.amazon.com/controltower/faqs/`

Best Practices for AWS Control Tower Administrators:

`https://docs.aws.amazon.com/controltower/latest/userguide/`
`best-practices.html`

Migrating a Custom Landing Zone with RAM to AWS Control Tower:

`https://aws.amazon.com/blogs/mt/migrating-custom-landing-zone-`
`with-ram-to-aws-control-tower/`

AWS Organizations

AWS Organizations provides customers with a central way to provision AWS accounts according to various business needs (such as IT services, marketing, HR, and more), central configuration (using AWS Config), security mechanisms (such as CloudTrail and GuardDuty), and resource sharing (consolidated billing).

For more information, please refer to the following resource:

AWS Organizations FAQs:

`https://aws.amazon.com/organizations/faqs/`

Building Multi-Region and Multi-Account Tools with AWS Organizations:

`https://aws.amazon.com/blogs/architecture/field-notes-`
`building-multi-region-and-multi-account-tools-with-aws-`
`organizations/`

Security in AWS Organizations:

`https://docs.aws.amazon.com/organizations/latest/userguide/`
`security.html`

AWS Organizations – Checklist for 2021:

`https://www.chrisfarris.com/post/aws-organizations-in-2021/`

AWS service control policies (SCPs)

SCPs are organizational policies that allow customers to manage the maximum available permissions for all the accounts in the organization. These policies allow you to govern AWS root accounts.

The following are some examples of service control policies:

- Deny resource creation in regions outside Europe (due to GDPR).

- Require **multi-factor authentication** (**MFA**) to perform an API action (for example, stop or terminate an EC2 instance).

- Block service access for the root account (for example, block all actions related to the EC2 service using root account credentials).

- Prevents users from disabling CloudWatch and making changes to CloudWatch's configuration.

- Prevent users from disabling AWS config or making changes to its rules.

- Prevent users from disabling AWS GuardDuty or making changes to its configuration.

- Allow specific EC2 instance types to be created (to preserve cost).

- Require tags when creating new resources.

- Prevent users from deleting VPC flow logs.

For more information, please refer to the following resources:

AWS Service Control Policies (SCPs):

```
https://docs.aws.amazon.com/organizations/latest/userguide/
orgs_manage_policies_scps.html
```

Example Service Control Policies:

```
https://docs.aws.amazon.com/organizations/latest/userguide/
orgs_manage_policies_scps_examples.html
```

How to use Service Control Policies to Set Permission Guardrails Across Accounts in Your AWS Organization:

```
https://aws.amazon.com/blogs/security/how-to-use-service-
control-policies-to-set-permission-guardrails-across-accounts-
in-your-aws-organization/
```

AWS Resource Access Manager

AWS Resource Access Manager allows customers to share resources between AWS accounts, instead of having to create them in every AWS account.

The following are some examples of services that can be shared between accounts:

- Amazon EC2
- EC2 Image Builder
- AWS Network Firewall
- AWS License Manager
- AWS VPC
- AWS Systems Manager Incident Manager
- Amazon Aurora

For more information, please refer to the following resource:

AWS Resource Access Manager FAQs:

```
https://aws.amazon.com/ram/faqs/
```

Shareable AWS resources:

```
https://docs.aws.amazon.com/ram/latest/userguide/shareable.html
```

Security in AWS Resource Access Manager:

```
https://docs.aws.amazon.com/ram/latest/userguide/security.html
```

Summary

In this section, we reviewed the various alternatives that AWS offers customers to manage multi-account environments at a large scale.

Governance in Azure

In this section, we will review Azure services that allow governance at a large scale. The following diagram shows the Azure multiple subscription hierarchy:

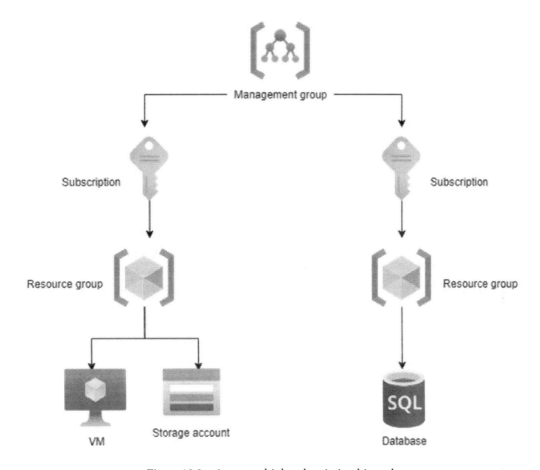

Figure 13.2 – Azure multiple subscription hierarchy

We'll discuss Azure landing zones in the next section.

Azure landing zones

Azure landing zones make it easy for organizations to create multiple subscriptions as part of an Azure tenant in a secured and standard way.

While Azure landing zones are being created, the following services are configured:

- Identity:

    - **Azure Active Directory**: Sets a password policy for the entire organization, MFA, and more.

- **Azure PIM**: Controls access to resources inside Azure AD and in Azure and enforces the use of MFA.

- Security:

  - **Azure Key Vault**: Encrypts/decrypts data, secrets, passwords, and more
  - **Microsoft Defender for Cloud**: Compliance and threat detection

- Networking:

  - **Azure DDoS**: A service that allows DDoS protection
  - **Azure DNS**: A managed DNS service
  - **Azure Firewall**: Provides a managed Layer 7 firewall, IDS/IPS, and URL filtering

- Monitoring:

  - **Azure Monitor**: A central repository for logs
  - **Azure Service Health**: Provides alerts about Azure services (worldwide) that may affect customers' services
  - **Azure Advisor**: Provides alerts based on best practices (reliability, security, performance, cost, and operational excellence)

- Cost:

  - **Azure Cost Management**: Configures budgets and budget alerts

For more information, please refer to the following resources:

What is an Azure Landing Zone?:

```
https://docs.microsoft.com/en-us/azure/cloud-adoption-
framework/ready/landing-zone/
```

Top 6 Tips for Configuring a New Microsoft Azure Environment:

```
https://techcommunity.microsoft.com/t5/itops-talk-blog/
top-6-tips-for-configuring-a-new-microsoft-azure-environment/
ba-p/2748637
```

Azure management groups

Azure management groups are a logical way to group multiple Azure subscriptions that have similar uses (such as all production subscriptions, all development subscriptions, and more). Once these subscriptions have been grouped, you can apply governance conditions to the management groups.

A common example of such a policy is to limit resource creation to a specific Azure region (prohibiting resource creation outside the EU due to GDPR).

Here are some of the best practices to follow:

- Use **role-based access control** (**RBAC**) to control users' access to subscriptions within a management group, according to business requirements and the least privilege principle.

- Use Azure Policy to centrally enforce settings over all the subscriptions inside a management group (as explained in the *Azure Policy* section).

- Configure a new management group (with Azure Policy) and set it as the default management group to avoid scenarios where newly created subscriptions are assigned to the root management group.

- Require authorization to create a new management group (change the default behavior where all users are allowed to create new management groups).

- Use Azure Activity Log to audit management groups.

For more information, please refer to the following resource:

What are Azure Management Groups?:

https://docs.microsoft.com/en-us/azure/governance/management-groups/overview

How to Protect Your Resource Hierarchy:

https://docs.microsoft.com/en-us/azure/governance/management-groups/how-to/protect-resource-hierarchy

Azure Policy

Azure policies are types of policies that allow customers to manage the maximum available permissions for all the subscriptions in the tenant (or in a management group).

The following are some examples of service control policies:

- Deny resource creation in regions outside Europe (due to GDPR).
- Enforce the use of MFA for all accounts with owner permissions on subscriptions
- Enable monitoring in Microsoft Defender for Cloud.
- Deploy Microsoft Defender for SQL servers.
- Enforce blob storage encryption using a customer-managed key during blob storage creation.
- Enforce an SSL connection for MySQL servers.
- Require a minimal TLS 1.2 on Azure SQL.
- Block internet access to VMs using RDP or SSH.
- Enforce an expiration date for the key vaults.

For more information, please refer to the following resource:

What is Azure Policy?:

```
https://docs.microsoft.com/en-us/azure/governance/policy/
overview
```

Azure Policy Built-In Policy Definitions:

```
https://docs.microsoft.com/en-us/azure/governance/policy/
samples/built-in-policies
```

Summary

In this section, we reviewed the various alternatives that Azure offers customers to manage multi-subscription environments at a large scale.

Governance in Google Cloud

In this section, we will review the GCP services that allow governance at a large scale.

Google Resource Manager

Managing large-scale environments based on Google Cloud means managing multiple GCP projects in a single Google organization.

Google Resource Manager allows customers to centrally create and manage multiple GCP projects. In some cases, projects are grouped by business needs into a logical grouping called folders (a folder for all production GCP projects, a folder for all development GCP projects, and more).

Using Google Resource Manager, you can enforce IAM policies on your entire Google organization (you can specify which user can take what actions – who can deploy VMs, who can create cloud storage, and more).

Here are some of the best practices to follow:

- **Plan**: Define your Google Cloud hierarchy according to your business or organizational needs (departments, teams, and GCP projects).

- Link your organization's accounts to Cloud Identity (such as Google Workspaces).

- Enforce the use of tags and labels during GCP project creation (for billing purposes and for identifying which resource or project belongs to the production, development, or test environments).

- Avoid creating labels that contain sensitive information in their label name or description.

- Set a project naming convention (allowing you to identify which project belongs to the production, development, or test environments).

- Create projects in an automated way (using Google Deployment Manager or HashiCorp Terraform).

- Set quotas and limits at the project level (avoiding scenarios where a single administrator can deploy a large amount of expensive VMs in a single project).

- Use Google Organization Policy Service to centrally enforce settings over your entire Google organization.

For more information, please refer to the following resources:

Resource Manager Documentation:

```
https://cloud.google.com/resource-manager/docs
```

Deployable Security Blueprints and Landing Zones:

`https://cloud.google.com/security/best-practices#section-2`

Manage Cloud Resources:

`https://cloud.google.com/architecture/framework/system-design/resource-management`

Resource Hierarchy:

`https://cloud.google.com/resource-manager/docs/cloud-platform-resource-hierarchy`

Google Organization Policy Service

Organization Policy Service allows you to configure restrictions on how resources can be used across your Google organization and define guardrails for your employees to stay compliant.

The following are some examples of organization policies:

- Deny resource creation in locations outside Europe (due to GDPR)
- **Cloud SQL**: Restrict public IP access on Cloud SQL instances
- **Cloud Storage**: Google Cloud Platform – Detailed Audit Logging Mode
- **Cloud Storage**: Enforce uniform bucket-level access
- **Compute Engine**: Enforce the use of shielded VMs
- **Compute Engine**: Restrict non-confidential computing
- **Compute Engine**: Define allowed external IPs for VM instances
- **Compute Engine**: Disable VM serial port access
- **Identity and Access Management**: Disable service account creation

For more information, please refer to the following resources:

Introduction to the Organization Policy Service:

`https://cloud.google.com/resource-manager/docs/organization-policy/overview`

Quickstart Enforcing Organization Policy:

```
https://cloud.google.com/resource-manager/docs/organization-
policy/quickstart-constraints
```

Organization Policy Constraints:

```
https://cloud.google.com/resource-manager/docs/organization-
policy/org-policy-constraints
```

Summary

In this section, we reviewed the various alternatives that Google offers customers to manage multi-GCP project environments at a large scale.

Automation using IaC

Managing large cloud environments requires a change in mindset. Manual deployment is prone to human mistakes, deviation from configuration standards, and is hard to maintain in the long run since it does not scale. The idea behind IaC is to switch from a manual to an automated way to deploy or make changes to resources in the cloud environment using code.

IaC helps bridge multiple organizations within a cloud service provider or even multiple cloud service providers. There are two ways to use IaC:

- **Declarative**: Define what the desired state is (for example, object storage must be encrypted at rest).

- **Imperative**: Define how the infrastructure needs to be changed to your requirements (for example, ordered steps to create networking configuration and then the compute resources within it).

The following are the benefits of using IaC:

- **Cost Reduction**: People can focus on tasks other than resource provisioning or resource change.

- **Fast Deployment**: Automation is always faster than manual work.

- **Reduce Risk**: Once the deployment has been tested, all future deployments will achieve the same results – no human errors.

- **Stable and Scalable Environments**: Once the deployment has been tested, it is simple to deploy new environments of any size (simply change the scale inside the configuration files).

- **Documentation**: Since every setting or change is written inside the code, you have full visibility of which configurations were implemented. You can store all the configurations in a central source repository and track configuration changes or drift detection from pre-configured policies.

- **Security Misconfigurations**: You can scan for non-compliance before provisioning.

Let's further discuss automation using infrastructure as code in AWS, Azure, and Google Cloud services.

AWS CloudFormation

AWS CloudFormation is the Amazon IaC service. CloudFormation allows you to deploy and update compute, database, storage, network, and many other AWS resources in a standard way.

Some of the best practices of AWS CloudFormation are as follows:

- Use AWS IAM to control access to deploy or update resources.

- Avoid embedding credentials inside AWS CloudFormation code – use AWS Secrets Manager to store credentials and secrets.

- Use AWS CloudTrail to audit CloudFormation API activity.

- Use an AWS Config rule to check for compliance against the pre-defined policy on resources stored inside CloudFormation Registry.

- Use AWS CloudFormation Guard to validate CloudFormation templates against rulesets (for example, all EBS volumes must be encrypted at rest).

- Use static code analysis to review your CloudFormation code for security vulnerabilities.

For more information, please refer to the following resources:

Security Best Practices for AWS CloudFormation:

```
https://docs.aws.amazon.com/AWSCloudFormation/latest/
UserGuide/security-best-practices.html
```

Introducing AWS CloudFormation Guard 2.0:

```
https://aws.amazon.com/blogs/mt/introducing-aws-cloudformation-
guard-2-0/
```

Azure Resource Manager (ARM) templates

ARM templates are an Azure IaC solution that allows you to create or update Azure resources.

Here are some of the best practices to follow:

- Use **Azure RBAC** to deploy or update resources.
- Avoid embedding credentials inside Azure ARM templates – use Azure Key Vault to store credentials and secrets.
- Use **securestring** for all passwords and secrets.
- Use **protectedSettings** to make sure your secrets are encrypted when they are passed as parameters to VMs.
- Use static code analysis to review your ARM template's code for security vulnerabilities.

For more information, please refer to the following resources:

What are ARM Templates?:

```
https://docs.microsoft.com/en-us/azure/azure-resource-manager/
templates/overview
```

Tutorial: Integrate Azure Key Vault in Your ARM template Deployment:

```
https://docs.microsoft.com/en-us/azure/azure-resource-manager/
templates/template-tutorial-use-key-vault
```

Google Cloud Deployment Manager

GCP Deployment Manager is the Google Cloud IaC solution that allows you to create or update GCP resources.

Here are some of the best practices to follow:

- Use **Cloud IAM** roles to control access to deploy or update resources using Deployment Manager.
- Avoid storing credentials in Deployment Manager code.
- Use version control to allow fallbacks to provide an audit trail for code changes.
- Use static code analysis to review your Deployment Manager code for security vulnerabilities.

For more information, please refer to the following resources:

Getting Started with Deployment Manager:

`https://cloud.google.com/deployment-manager/docs/quickstart`

Setting Access Control in a Configuration:

`https://cloud.google.com/deployment-manager/docs/configuration/set-access-control-resources`

HashiCorp Terraform

Terraform is considered the most used IaC solution. It works across cloud providers to deploy and update resources. Terraform should be considered as it provides standardized syntax across multiple cloud providers. It is an open source solution with a large community that provides support and has direct integration with cloud APIs.

The following are some of the best practices regarding Terraform:

- Enable logging for both troubleshooting and audit trails (check which user run the scripts and made changes to a specific environment or resource).
- When building from a build server, we will need to have good auditing on source control for who checked in or merged the code.
- Always deploy secured protocols (such as HTTPS/TLS 1.2).
- Store Terraform state remotely.
- Provision Terraform code using a build server.
- Maintain Terraform code in source control.
- Avoid storing credentials in code; instead, use solutions such as HashiCorp Vault to store all sensitive information (credentials, secrets, passwords, and more).
- Use static code analysis to review your Terraform code for security vulnerabilities.

The following code will block all S3 public access:

```
resource "aws_s3_bucket" "mytestbucket2021" {
    bucket = "mytestbucket2021"
}
resource "aws_s3_bucket_public_access_block" "mytestbucket2021"
{
    bucket = aws_s3_bucket.mytestbucket2021.id
    block_public_acls   = true
```

```
    block_public_policy = true
}
```

For more information, please refer to the following resource:

Introduction to Terraform:

https://www.terraform.io/intro/index.html

Summary

In this section, we reviewed common IaC solutions – both cloud vendor-oriented solutions and Terraform, which is open source and the most commonly used solution.

We have reviewed the security best practices for each of the alternatives.

Security in large-scale cloud environments

In the previous chapters, we reviewed services that allow us to protect our cloud environments – from patch management, configuration management, compliance, vulnerability management, and more.

Most of the services that are built in the cloud are regional (they function within the boundaries of a single region). Working in large-scale cloud environments requires us to have security controls while spreading across multiple accounts, in multiple regions.

Managing security at a large scale while working with AWS

In this section, we will review managed services, which can help us provide security controls in large AWS environments (containing multiple accounts, in multiple regions).

Patch management

To conduct patch management in AWS environments using cloud-native tools, follow these steps:

1. Use AWS Systems Manager Automation.

2. Deploy security patches based on your resource tags or group resources using AWS resource groups, based on the target account and region.

3. Create the **AWS-SystemsManager-AutomationExecutionRole** role in each of the target accounts to be able to deploy the necessary patches.

> **Note**
>
> AWS Systems Manager Automation is not a multi-cloud solution – third-party tools such as Ansible, Salt, and more are available to meet this requirement.

For more information, please refer to the following resources:

Running Automation in Multiple AWS Regions and Accounts:

```
https://docs.aws.amazon.com/systems-manager/latest/userguide/
systems-manager-automation-multiple-accounts-and-regions.html
```

Centralized Multi-Account and Multi-Region Patching with AWS Systems Manager Automation:

```
https://aws.amazon.com/blogs/mt/centralized-multi-account-and-
multi-region-patching-with-aws-systems-manager-automation/
```

Configuration management

If you wish to run configuration management in AWS environments, use the AWS Config service.

Use aggregator (an AWS Config resource) to collect resource configuration changes from multiple AWS accounts and multiple AWS regions – this will allow you to manage configuration changes at a large scale.

For multi-cloud or multiple AWS accounts, a third-party tool may be necessary to integrate with the AWS Config recorder.

For more information, please refer to the following resources:

Implementing a Cross-Account and Cross-Region AWS Config Status Dashboard:

```
https://aws.amazon.com/blogs/mt/implementing-a-cross-account-
and-cross-region-aws-config-status-dashboard/
```

Multi-Account Multi-Region Data Aggregation:

```
https://docs.aws.amazon.com/config/latest/developerguide/
aggregate-data.html
```

Security compliance

If you wish to run security compliance on AWS environments, use the Amazon Inspector service. Amazon Inspector allows you to scan EC2 instances, detect security vulnerabilities (due to missing security patches), find compliance against CIS benchmark (a well-known security standard), and misconfigurations (such as an open SSH port from the internet, also known as network reachability). Amazon Inspector allows you to check for security compliance through AWS Security Hub and integration with third-party CI/CD solutions.

For more information, please refer to the following resources:

How to Visualize Multi-Account Amazon Inspector Findings with Amazon Elasticsearch Service:

```
https://aws.amazon.com/blogs/security/how-to-visualize-multi-
account-amazon-inspector-findings-with-amazon-elasticsearch-
service/
```

Automate Security Scans for Cross-Account Workloads Using Amazon Inspector and AWS Security Hub:

```
https://docs.aws.amazon.com/prescriptive-guidance/latest/
patterns/automate-security-scans-for-cross-account-workloads-
using-amazon-inspector-and-aws-security-hub.html
```

Threat management

For threat management in AWS environments, use Amazon GuardDuty.

Amazon GuardDuty allows you to detect malicious activity based on Amazon CloudTrail (API audit trail), S3 data events, VPC flow logs (network), and Route53 DNS logs.

Choose one of your AWS accounts to administer Amazon GuardDuty on and connect accounts from your entire AWS organization as members, which allows Amazon GuardDuty to have a single view of threat management for your entire AWS organization.

It is recommended to integrate Amazon GuardDuty with AWS Security Hub or with third-party tools to support hybrid/multi-cloud environments.

For more information, please refer to the following resource:

Managing Multiple Accounts in Amazon GuardDuty:

```
https://docs.aws.amazon.com/guardduty/latest/ug/guardduty_
accounts.html
```

Summary

In this section, we reviewed some of the AWS security-related services that support patch management, configuration, compliance, and threat management over multiple accounts in the same AWS organization.

Managing security at a large scale while working with Azure

In this section, we will review managed services that can help provide security controls in large Azure environments (containing multiple subscriptions, in multiple regions).

Patch management

To conduct patch management in Azure environments, use Azure Automation Update Management. Update Management allows you to deploy security patches for machines in multiple Azure subscriptions that belong to the same Azure AD tenant. For a multi-cloud solution, it is recommended to look for a third-party patch management solution.

For more information, please refer to the following resource:

Update Management Overview:

```
https://docs.microsoft.com/en-us/azure/automation/update-
management/overview
```

Security compliance

If you wish to run security compliance on Azure environments, use Microsoft Defender for Cloud.

Microsoft Defender for Cloud allows you to collect and monitor security your compliance status from Azure VMs over multiple subscriptions, from a single console.

For more information, please refer to the following resources:

Protect Virtual Machines Across Different Subscriptions with Azure Security Center:

```
https://azure.microsoft.com/en-us/blog/protect-virtual-
machines-across-different-subscriptions-with-azure-security-
center/
```

Cross-Tenant Management in Security Center:

```
https://docs.microsoft.com/en-us/azure/security-center/
security-center-cross-tenant-management
```

Enable Security Center on all subscriptions in a management group:

```
https://docs.microsoft.com/en-us/azure/defender-for-cloud/
onboard-management-group
```

Threat management

For threat management in Azure environments, use Microsoft Defender for Cloud.

Microsoft Defender for Cloud supports multiple services – including endpoints, storage, databases (such as Azure SQL and managed databases for MySQL), and more.

Azure Defender allows you to detect threats (such as malicious activity on a VM, multiple upload/downloads from a storage account, potential breach attempts on managed databases, and more), all from the same console, and over multiple Azure subscriptions.

For more information, please refer to the following resource:

Enable Azure Defender on Multiple Subscriptions or Workspaces:

```
https://docs.microsoft.com/en-us/azure/security-center/enable-
azure-defender#to-enable-azure-defender-on-your-subscriptions-
and-workspaces
```

Summary

In this section, we reviewed some of Azure's security-related services that support patch management, compliance, and threat management over multiple subscriptions in the same Azure AD tenant.

Managing security at a large scale while working with Google Cloud

Google has a central service called that allows you to achieve the following goals in your Google organization (containing multiple GCP projects):

- **Compliance**: Check for compliance against industry standards (such as **Center for Internet Security (CIS)**) benchmarks, **Payment card standard (PCI-DDS)**, and more)

- **Vulnerability Management**: Detect well-known web application vulnerabilities on Google App Engine, Compute Engine, and GKE services

- **Container Vulnerability Management**: Detect suspicious binaries and libraries inside containers

For more information, please refer to the following resource:

Security Command Center Conceptual Overview:

```
https://cloud.google.com/security-command-center/docs/
concepts-security-command-center-overview
```

Summary

In this section, we have reviewed how Google Security Command Center helps you manage security while working with Google Cloud.

Summary

In this chapter, we focused on large-scale cloud environments that contain multiple accounts.

We discussed how to deploy a multi-account organizational structure and how to set policies to check and enforce compliance over our entire organization.

Then, we learned how to achieve automation in cloud environments using IaC – from built-in services from AWS, Azure, and GCP, to a more cloud-agnostic solution called Terraform.

Finally, we reviewed security-related services from AWS, Azure, and GCP that allow us to maintain patch management, compliance, and threat management over large organizations containing multiple accounts/subscriptions/projects from a central place.

The information in this chapter should have helped you learn how to manage security in large cloud environments.

What's next?

Now that you've reached the end of this book, we thought we would provide some recommendations regarding what you should do next.

Plan ahead

For each new project you review, from a cloud security point of view, thoroughly read through both the business and technological goals. Then, after understanding both of them, invest time into adding the relevant security controls.

Automate

This book covers many recommendations and best practices for using AWS, Azure, and GCP built-in services.

Invest some time into learning how to automate the recommended settings using IaC.

Consider learning about and using Terraform for IaC since it provides connectivity for all the major cloud providers and since it is becoming a standard that most organizations are using for automation.

Think big

Instead of looking at a specific cloud environment and how to secure it, think about highly scalable cloud environments that are spread across multiple data centers (or availability zones) and sometimes even across multiple regions.

Design environments that can serve thousands or even millions of concurrent customers, from day 1, to avoid having to re-architect at a later phase.

Continue learning

This book covers a lot of resources, but don't stop here.

Invest time into taking a deep dive into each service presented in this book, look at the references in this book, and continue learning about new products that are released each month to become a cloud security expert.

Index

J

K

L

W

Packt.com

Subscribe to our online digital library for full access to over 7,000 books and videos, as well as industry leading tools to help you plan your personal development and advance your career. For more information, please visit our website.

Why subscribe?

- Spend less time learning and more time coding with practical eBooks and Videos from over 4,000 industry professionals

- Improve your learning with Skill Plans built especially for you

- Get a free eBook or video every month

- Fully searchable for easy access to vital information

- Copy and paste, print, and bookmark content

Did you know that Packt offers eBook versions of every book published, with PDF and ePub files available? You can upgrade to the eBook version at packt.com and as a print book customer, you are entitled to a discount on the eBook copy. Get in touch with us at customercare@packtpub.com for more details.

At www.packt.com, you can also read a collection of free technical articles, sign up for a range of free newsletters, and receive exclusive discounts and offers on Packt books and eBooks.

Other Books You May Enjoy

If you enjoyed this book, you may be interested in these other books by Packt:

Mastering Microsoft Endpoint Manager

Christiaan Brinkhoff, Per Larsen

ISBN: 9781801078993

- Understand how Windows 365 Cloud PC makes the deployment of Windows in the cloud easy

- Configure advanced policy management within MEM

- Discover modern profile management and migration options for physical and cloud PCs

- Harden security with baseline settings and other security best practices

- Find troubleshooting tips and tricks for MEM, Windows 365 Cloud PC, and more

- Discover deployment best practices for physical and cloud-managed endpoints

- Keep up with the Microsoft community and discover a list of MVPs to follow

Mastering Azure Security

Mustafa Toroman, Tom Janetscheck

ISBN: 9781839218996

- Understand cloud security concepts
- Get to grips with managing cloud identities
- Adopt the Azure security cloud infrastructure
- Grasp Azure network security concepts
- Discover how to keep cloud resources secure
- Implement cloud governance with security policies and rules

Packt is searching for authors like you

If you're interested in becoming an author for Packt, please visit `authors.packtpub.com` and apply today. We have worked with thousands of developers and tech professionals, just like you, to help them share their insight with the global tech community. You can make a general application, apply for a specific hot topic that we are recruiting an author for, or submit your own idea.

Share your thoughts

Now you've finished *Cloud Security Handbook*, we'd love to hear your thoughts! Scan the QR code below to go straight to the Amazon review page for this book and share your feedback or leave a review on the site that you purchased it from.

https://packt.link/r/180056919X

Your review is important to us and the tech community and will help us make sure we're delivering excellent quality content.

Printed in Great Britain
by Amazon

85215031R00260